Writing on the Job

REVISED EDITION

Writing on the Job

Robert E. Mehaffy
American River College (CA)

Irene M. Mehaffy
Elk Grove School District (CA)

T. H. Peek, Publisher • P.O. Box 50123 • Palo Alto, California 94303

ISBN-0-917962-29-X

99 98 97 96 95
 8   7   6   5   4

Manufactured in the United States of America

Preface

At one time writing skills were not essential to success on the job. This is no longer the case. Today, employers consider writing skills one of the most important of all factors when hiring. *Writing on the Job* was designed for students who want to prepare themselves for the writing demands of the working world.

For those who need an introductory course prior to taking university level technical writing courses, this book presents the basic techniques and terminology needed to succeed in those rigorous courses. And for that group of students whose academic schedules allow only one college level writing course, this text is perfectly suited. It presents not only the basic techniques and terminology but also gives extensive examples of typical writing situations encountered in the working world.

Because the students in most introductory writing courses are too often alienated by traditional textbooks, *Writing on the Job* was developed in workbook format. Every concept presented in the text is followed by an example and an exercise. Where possible, the examples are student written to emphasize the fact that every student can write. In addition, the use of student written examples eliminates the confusion and demoralization that professionally written examples create for introductory students.

To enhance its flexibility, *Writing on the Job* is structured in such a way that it can be used in lecture-discussion or self-paced classes. The exercises, wherever possible, have answers in the appendix, thereby enabling students to check their own work. This design feature allows students to evaluate their understanding of the material immediately upon discovering a confusion, thus allowing for revision of the misunderstanding before it becomes firmly entrenched.

Contents

Sentences

Part One contains review material designed to help you become a better writer. You might be thinking that clauses, phrases, and sentences will not matter when you are on the job. But these elements are the foundation of all writing; they are vitally important to the quality of writing that you do, whether on or off the job.

As a job applicant you will be judged by your writing. An employer's first impression of you will probably be formed from your resume. Given two prospective employees with similar qualifications, the employer will be more interested in the person who has submitted a carefully written resume. After all, the applicant who wrote the better resume may also be a more productive employee.

Once you are on the job, improper punctuation and poorly written sentences in your reports and memos can lead to problems. When the reader cannot understand the message, expensive, time-consuming errors are inevitable. Clear, well-written sentences will ensure that the intended information is conveyed.

Part One is not designed to teach you everything about grammar; rather, it is designed to review what you have learned over the years. To help you become familiar and comfortable with the materials, Chapter 1 begins with the simplest concepts; by the end of Chapter 3 the concepts have gradually become more complex. Extensive exercises are included to help you review the material and practice your writing.

Be sure to work each item in every exercise carefully. If you encounter a question that you cannot answer, review the text. If you still are unable to answer the question, ask your instructor or a tutor for help. After completing all of the items in an exercise, turn to the Answer Key at the end of the book and check your answers. Avoid looking at the answers before you have completed the exercise, however.

As you check your answers with those given in the Answer Key, don't erase any incorrect answers. Simply draw a line through any incorrect answers so that you can easily see which ideas you already understand and which you still need to work on. Spend a few minutes evaluating the results before going on to the next exercise.

2   Writing on the Job

1

Recognizing Sentence Elements

When you have completed this chapter, you will be able to—

1. Distinguish between proper nouns and common nouns.
2. Label nouns and verbs in sentences.
3. Identify subjects and verbs.
4. Distinguish between action verbs and linking verbs.
5. Write sentences using auxiliary verbs to express time.
6. Write sentences using subject, object, and possessive pronouns.
7. Identify phrases and clauses.
8. Distinguish between independent clauses and dependent clauses.

Being able to recognize sentence elements is the first step in becoming an effective writer. Only by knowing the difference between phrases and clauses, for instance, will you develop a good understanding of punctuation. Furthermore, you will not begin to write well-constructed, interesting paragraphs until you can distinguish between the various types of sentences and learn to use them effectively. Studying parts of speech and diagraming sentences just to understand grammar may not be your goal; however, studying sentence parts and sentence types in an effort to improve your writing makes sense. No one will care whether you can distinguish between a gerund and a participle, but people will care whether you can write clearly and effectively.

Although there are eight parts of speech—nouns, verbs, pronouns, adverbs, adjectives, prepositions, conjunctions, and interjections—in your day-to-day writing, you will be concerned with identifying only three: nouns, pronouns, and verbs. You must be able to recognize these three parts of speech in order to identify sentence errors and recognize sentence types.

RECOGNIZING NOUNS

You have heard many times that *nouns* name persons, places, and things (concepts, actions, and qualities are also things). This definition is good even though it sounds somewhat simple. To make them easier to identify, nouns can be divided into two different categories: proper nouns and common nouns.

3

Proper nouns are those nouns that are always capitalized because they are the names of particular people, places, things, or events.

Particular people: Sandra Day O'Connor, King Juan Carlos, Tom Hanks

Particular places: the South, New York, Italy

Particular things: Bunker Hill Community College, General Motors

Particular events: Thanksgiving Day, Civil War, the Olympics

Common nouns are all other nouns. More specifically, common nouns are the general names for proper nouns. Compare this list of common nouns with the proper nouns you just looked at.

man	city	company
woman	country	holiday
area	college	war

There are three types of common nouns: **concrete, abstract,** and **collective** nouns. *Concrete nouns* describe things that can be seen or touched. *Abstract nouns* refer to some idea or quality that you cannot see or touch. *Collective nouns* refer to a group of people or things.

concrete nouns	abstract nouns	collective nouns
convertible	courage	jury
rooster	fear	council
dictionary	generosity	board
desk	selfishness	family
lawn	jealousy	flock

Exercise 1.1

The following list is a mixture of proper and common nouns. Identify each by writing **proper** or **common** in the appropriate blank. Then capitalize the proper nouns.

1. texas _____

2. vietnam war _____

3. memorial day _____

4. corporation _____

5. computer _____

6. johnson landscape company _____

7. highway _____

8. honda _____

9. photographer _____

10. new zealand _____

Check your answers with the Answer Key at the end of the book.

Exercise 1.2

Supply a noun that fits each description.

	person	place	event
proper noun	1. _____	2. _____	3. _____
	abstract	concrete	collective
common noun	4. _____	5. _____	6. _____

Have your work checked by your instructor or a tutor.

Simply recognizing that a noun is the name of a person, place, or thing is often not enough to identify a word as a noun. Many words that are used as nouns in one sentence may be used as verbs in the next sentence. Consider the following sentences.

NOUN	VERB
My **watch** stopped.	I **watch** the news on television at 6 p.m.
NOUN	VERB
She had a **fear** of heights.	Young children often **fear** barking dogs.

The way in which a word is used in a sentence determines its part of speech. In the examples *watch* and *fear* are first used as nouns and then as verbs. In these sentences the distinction between noun and verb is probably quite clear, but in others it will be more difficult. Whenever you are uncertain, you can use any of the following characteristics of nouns to identify them.

1. **Possessive Rule** Nouns can show possession by the addition of an apostrophe and an **s**. That is, a noun is a word that can show ownership.

The cat's fur is soft. [The fur belongs to the cat. Thus, the word *cat* is a noun.]

The speaker's voice excited the crowd. [The voice belongs to the speaker. Therefore, *speaker* is a noun.]

Anything that can be possessed—such as *fur* and *voice* in the above sentences—is also a noun. Observe the examples closely; notice that both the words with the apostrophes (cat, speaker) and the words which follow them (fur, voice) are nouns. It should be noted, however, that cat and speaker, while nouns, are actually being used as adjectives to describe fur and voice.

Pronouns can also show possession and function as adjectives, but unlike nouns, they do not use apostrophes:

Their supplier in Texas shipped the parts last week. [the pronoun *their* is used as an adjective describing the noun supplier.]

Larry misplaced his report. [the pronoun *his* is used as an adjective to describe the noun report.]

    2. Plural Rule   Common nouns can almost always be made plural as shown below.

book	books	tree	trees
student	students	disease	diseases
movie	movies	tragedy	tragedies

Since all these words can be made plural, they are all nouns.

    3. Article Rule   Many nouns have articles—*a, an,* or *the*—before them in sentences.

> **A storm** passed through the area last night.
> **The lawyer** glared at him.

Since both *storm* and *lawyer* have articles (*a* and *the*) before them, they are nouns. Frequently, an article will be separated from its noun by one or more adjectives, but the article still belongs to the noun.

> **The** battered old **truck** broke down on the highway.

Here, *truck* is still a noun and the article still belongs to it. The adjectives *battered* and *old* do not change the relationship.

    Most sentences you write will have more than one noun. You should, therefore, become accustomed to looking for more than one noun when you are asked to find them in sentences. All nouns are in boldface type in the following sentences. Notice that most of the nouns are preceded by articles.

> The new lighting **fixtures** will be installed in the dark **office**.
> A violent **quarrel** erupted as the department **managers** discussed the **budget**.
> The sales **representatives** wash their **cars** at least once a **week**.

Exercise 1.3

    Underline all nouns in the following sentences.

1. The alert secuity guard will report the incident.
2. A judge and jury decided his future in less than an hour.
3. Promptness, reliability, and dedication may result in a promotion.
4. During the hot, dry summer in California, a raging fire destroyed many families' homes.
5. The strange young man made both friends and enemies nervous.
6. Unable to complete the report, Elizabeth worked several additional hours last night.
7. Owning one's own business can be a tremendous burden.
8. When he typed the letter, Ben hoped it would help him get a job.
9. The telephone startled him when it rang.
10. The committee responded favorably to Joan's proposal.

Check your answers with Answer Key.

RECOGNIZING THE SUBJECT OF A SENTENCE

Subjects are usually either nouns or pronouns, so knowing how to recognize a noun will help you identify the subject. Because you will use more than one noun in most sentences, however, you must learn to distinguish the subject from the other nouns.

Simply stated, the *subject* of a sentence is who or what the sentence talks about. To find the subject, you merely ask, "Who or what is being talked about?" The answer to that question is the subject. Consider the following example:

The car was parked beside the road.

If you ask, "Who or what is being talked about?" you will come up with the *car* as the subject of the sentence. The example sentence has a second noun, of course, the word *road*. However, *road* could not be the subject because the sentence is not primarily about the road. The noun *road* simply tells where the car is.

The preceding example sentence illustrates the most basic sentence pattern: a subject followed by a verb near the beginning of the sentence. However, there are some sentence patterns in which identifying the subject is more difficult. Below are three such patterns.

1. **Understood you** (command sentence): When you tell another person to do something, you rarely include the subject. Rather than say, "You close the door," you say, "Close the door." Even though the subject *you* has been omitted in the second sentence, *you* is still understood to be the subject. When *you* has been omitted from a command sentence, it is referred to as the "understood you." When you are asked to identify the subject of a command sentence in the exercises, write *you* in as the subject. (Usually *you* is placed in brackets to show that it was omitted: "[*you*] Close the door.")

2. **Reverse Order:** In such a sentence, the subject is often placed near the end of the sentence rather than near the beginning. Reverse order sentences are used occasionally to emphasize a point.

I watched Bonita eat the fried rattlesnake. That delicacy **I could** never **eat**.

The subject of the second sentence above is not *that delicacy*, even though it is at the beginning of the sentence. The answer to the question, "Who or what is being talked about?" is *I*. Normally, such a sentence would be written "I could never eat that."

Another type of reverse order sentence is the one which begins with "There is/are . . ." or "Here is/are . . ." Such a sentence is called a *postponed subject* sentence.

There **are** seven *teams* **competing** in the tournament.
Here **is** your trip *itinerary*.

3. **Question:** When you ask a question, you usually change the order of the subject and verb. Your questions normally place the subject between the two parts of a verb.

When **are** *you* **leaving** for New Orleans?

The subject in the sentence above is *you*, and **are leaving** is the complete verb.

Exercise 1.4

Underline the subject of each of the following sentences. Write in any understood subjects.

1. The overworked dispatcher sent the delivery to the wrong address.
2. There were five people on the inspection team.
3. Buckle up or pay a fine.
4. Humpback whales do not normally swim into fresh water from the ocean.
5. Having transferred to Seattle recently, the insurance agent spent many days making new contacts.
6. The telephone poles and lines both needed to be replaced after the storm.
7. Did she clean his teeth last Monday?
8. Lacking confidence, he took his calculator everywhere with him.
9. They realized it was necessary to buy new equipment for the plant.
10. Embarrassed by his poor performance, the musician decided to quit the band.

Check your answers with the Answer Key.

Exercise 1.5

Write the type of sentence required. Underline the subject in each sentence.

1. Question _____

   _____

2. Reverse order _____

   _____

   _____

3. Understood *you* _____

   _____

   _____

Have your work checked by your instructor or a tutor.

RECOGNIZING VERBS

A *verb* expresses action or a state of being. A verb is a necessary part of a sentence. As a matter of fact, without a verb you cannot have a sentence. In some cases, you can leave out any other part of a sentence and still have a complete sentence. For example, a verb alone can be a complete sentence in a command such as ''Leave.'' If you omit the subject, it is still sometimes understood, but if you omit the verb, you have nothing.

Recognizing a verb can be easy if it is an *action verb*. All you have to do is look through a sentence until you find a word which shows some type of action.

The inspector found seven violations of the county building code.

The word *found* is the only word to describe an action; *found* then is the verb.

Unfortunately, finding the verb is not always so easy. Some of our most commonly used verbs—*linking verbs*—show no action at all. A *linking verb* connects the subject with an adjective that modifies it, or with a noun or pronoun that renames it. In the following sentences the linking verb *is* connects *he* to an adjective, a noun, and a pronoun.

He *is* tired. [adjective]
He *is* a CEO. [noun]
He *is* it. [pronoun]

In order to identify verbs in sentences, you should use the following verb recognition techniques.

Verb Recognition Technique 1: Memorizing

The first step in recognizing verbs is to memorize some of the linking verbs. The most common of these verbs are the various forms of the verb **be**. Learn these linking verbs immediately.

am, are, is, was, were, be, been, being

Verb Recognition Technique 2: Linking Verbs as Equal Signs

You can also learn to recognize linking verbs in sentences by thinking of them as equal signs (=). These verbs are called *linking verbs* because they connect two words that describe the same thing or person.

She was the committee's first choice. [she = choice]
Janis is excited. [Janis = excited]
I am tired. [I = tired]
It is I. [It = I]

Notice that you can replace the verb in each sentence with an equal sign. A linking verb is followed by a noun (choice), an adjective (excited, tired), or a pronoun (I).

A few other common linking verbs are the following:

seem, appear, feel, become, look, smell, sound, taste

Most of these linking verbs may also be used as action verbs. The meaning of the sentence will determine whether a verb is an action verb or a linking verb.

Action	Linking
The dog **smelled** the old shoe.	The breakfast **smelled** good.
Harriet **looked** out the window.	Harriet **looked** tired.

In the above examples, notice that the sentences in the left column describe an action, so each verb is an action verb. The sentences in the second column do not describe an action; therefore, each verb is a linking verb.

Exercise 1.6

After each sentence, write **action** or **linking** to describe the underlined verb.

1. Phil <u>is</u> an experienced pilot. _____

2. The investigator <u>installed</u> a hidden camera. _____

3. Charlie <u>enjoys</u> fishing. _____

4. The ghost <u>appeared</u> only for Hamlet. _____

5. The team <u>was</u> tired of losing. _____

6. The vacant house <u>smelled</u> musty. _____

7. The supervisor <u>feels</u> responsible for his crew. _____

8. The blind man <u>feels</u> his watch to tell the time. _____

9. Harry <u>retired</u> last month. _____

10. They <u>heard</u> the rocket engine an hour before dawn. _____

11. Sandy Vargas <u>was</u> sorry to dismiss her assistant. _____

12. When the caller asked to speak to Mrs. Carson, Judy replied, "This <u>is</u> she." _____

Check your answers with the Answer Key.

Verb Recognition Technique 3: Questioning

Whenever a sentence contains an action verb, you can identify that verb by asking the question, "What does the subject do?" The word that answers this question is an action verb.

The tree fell on the house.

In this short sentence, it is easy to see that the word *fell* answers the question, "What does the tree do?"

Verb Recognition Technique 4: Tense

Verbs are the only part of speech that can change form to show different time reference, traditionally called past, present, and future tenses. For this reason, many people merely use the tense technique to identify the verbs in a sentence. Any word in a sentence that can change to express future, present, or past tense is a verb. The following sentences illustrate how the verb changes to show different time references.

The copy machine **will need** repairs.	(future)
The copy machine **needs** repairs.	(present)
The copy machine **needed** repairs.	(past)
Marge **will be** tired after work.	(future)
Marge **is** tired.	(present)
Marge **was** tired.	(past)

If you are unsure which word in a sentence is a verb, simply apply the tense technique to it. If the word can be changed to different tenses, it is a verb; it cannot possibly be any other part of speech.

Exercise 1.7

In each sentence underline the subject with a single line and the verb with a double line. In the blank at the right, identify each underlined verb as *action* or *linking*.

Example: The <u>owner</u> of the company <u>flew</u> his own plane.   action

1. The tree looks healthy.   _____

2. Running to answer the telephone, Lisa demonstrated her enthusiasm.   _____

3. Carla Fuentes drove to the warehouse.   _____

4. Mrs. Mayfield offered him the job.   _____

5. The forms in the file are obsolete.   _____

6. The committee members debated the issues for hours.   _____

7. Completed just last week, the new office complex has only a few vacancies left.   _____

8. The mail arrives every morning at the same time.   _____

9. Several problems developed in the heating system.   _____

10. His briefcase was almost new.   _____

Check your answers with the Answer Key.

Helping Verbs (Auxiliary Verbs)

Changing the tense of a verb to show different time references is not always as easy as changing the form of just one word. Sometimes two, three, or even four verbs work together to indicate the exact time you wish to express in your sentence. When this happens, the verbs which help show the proper time (referred to as tense) are called *helping verbs*. The following list presents the most commonly used helping verbs.

is	being	does	might
am	been	did	must
are	have	can	could
was	has	shall	should
were	had	will	would
be	do	may	

The following sentences show how these helping verbs are used to show time change.

I **work** for IBM.	(present)
I **worked** for IBM last summer.	(past)
I **will work** for IBM next winter.	(future)
I **have worked** for IBM for twenty years.	(present perfect)
I **had worked** many years for IBM when I quit.	(past perfect)
I **will have worked** for IBM for twenty-seven years when I retire.	(future perfect)

Notice that the *present perfect* tense refers to an action that began in the past and is continuing at the present time. *Past perfect* refers to an action that was begun and stopped in the past. *Future perfect* refers to an action that will be completed in the future. The helping verbs *have, has,* and *had* always accompany the perfect tenses.

Exercise 1.8

For each item, write a sentence using a verb in the tense indicated. Use the same basic verb in each sentence.

1. Present _____

_____

2. Past_____

_____

_____

3. Future_____

_____

_____

4. Present perfect _____

_____

_____

5. Past perfect _____

_____

_____

6. Future perfect _____

_____

_____

Have your work checked by your instructor or a tutor.

RECOGNIZING PRONOUNS

Pronouns are merely substitutes for nouns. By using them in place of nouns, you can avoid repeating the same noun again and again. Compare the following short paragraphs; the first paragraph uses only nouns while the second uses both nouns and pronouns.

> *Peter and Nancy* bought a *house* in *Santa Barbara* seven years ago. Although the *house* was expensive, *Peter and Nancy* loved the *house* and *Santa Barbara*. Unfortunately, the *house* payment and the high utility bills made living in *Santa Barbara* very difficult. Finally, *Peter and Nancy* had to sell the *house* so *Peter and Nancy* could avoid bankruptcy.

> *Peter and Nancy* bought a *house* in *Santa Barbara* seven years ago. Although *it* was expensive, *they* loved *it* and the town. Unfortunately, the *house* payment and the high utility bills made living *there* very difficult. Finally, *they* had to sell the *house* so *they* could avoid bankruptcy.

Although the first paragraph communicates the message, it is awkward because *Peter and Nancy, house,* and *Santa Barbara* are repeated too many times. By contrast, the second paragraph sounds more pleasing and natural to the reader.

Because you use pronouns constantly in conversations, you should have few problems using them in your writing. However, if you do have a problem with pronouns, it will most likely be in choosing whether to use a *subject pronoun* or an *object pronoun*. When deciding whether you should use a subject or object pronoun, it will be necessary to determine the pronoun's function.

Subject Pronouns

Subject pronouns are most often placed *before* the verb. Anytime you want to replace a noun that functions as the subject of a sentence, you must use one of these *subject pronouns*.

> I, you, he, she, it, we, they, who

Make sure you select the subject pronoun that properly identifies the noun you are replacing, as in the following examples:

> **Margaret** submitted an excellent resume.
> **She** submitted an excellent resume.
>
> With deepening despair, **the workers** voted to go on strike.
> With deepening despair, **they** voted to go on strike.

Subject pronouns are also used after linking verbs, as in the following examples:

> The winners of the lottery were Tony and **I**.
> It is **I**.
> The person with whom you must speak is **she**.

Object Pronouns

Just as subject pronouns are most often found before the verb, object pronouns are usually found *after* the verb. If the pronoun receives the action of the verb, you must use one of these *object pronouns*:

> me, you, him, her, it, us, them, whom

> Mrs. Gonzales gave **John** a promotion.
> Mrs. Gonzales gave **him** a promotion.

In the preceding example, you would use the object pronoun *him* because John received the promotion. In studying the following examples, notice that object pronouns can be direct objects, indirect objects, or objects of the preposition.

> The new computer is for **you**. [object of preposition]
> Betty gave **him** the tickets for the trip to Bermuda. [indirect object]
> The receiver caught the ball and then fumbled **it**. [direct object]
> The electricians can't complete the job for **us** today. [object of preposition]
> Under the tree, the searchers found **them** huddled together. [direct object]
> John gave **me** a raise. [indirect object]
> The customer glared at **her** across the counter. [object of prepostion]

The best method of identifying an object pronoun is to put the prepositions *of, to, for* or *with* before any pronoun you think is objective, if it doesn't already have a preposition there. Many of the example sentences above either have or could have one of these prepositions.

Possessive Pronouns

Unlike both subject and object pronouns, *possessive pronouns* show ownership.

---
my, mine, your, yours, his, her, hers, its, our, ours, their, theirs
---

Possessive pronouns can be used at any point in the sentence, as in the following examples:

> **Her** ear was sore from talking on the telephone for so long.
> A tree fell on **their** car during the storm.
> The dog held up **its** injured foot.

Possessive pronouns replace possessive nouns in sentences.

Noun	*Pronoun*
The **woman's** ear...	**Her** ear...
Bill and Shari's car...	**Their** car...
The **dog's** foot...	**Its** foot...

Notice that personal possessive pronouns do not require apostrophes to show ownership, but nouns do. Even possessive pronouns that end with an **s** in the examples above do not require apostrophes. [Be particularly cautious when using *its*. *Its* is easily confused with *it's*, a contraction of the words *it is*. Anytime you use *it's* in a sentence, determine if you can replace it with *it is*. Only if you mean to say *it is* will you use an apostrophe before the *s* ending.]

When the possessive pronouns *my, your, her, our,* and *their* come just before the nouns that they modify, they do not take a final **s**. However, when these pronouns come after the nouns they modify, they require a final **s**. Note the following examples.

My car...	**Our** car...
That car is **mine**.	That car is **ours**.
Your car...	**Their** car...
That car is **yours**.	That car is **theirs**.
Her car...	**Whose** car...
That car is **hers**.	That car is **whose**?
His car...	
That car is **his**.	

Observe that *her* is used both as an object pronoun and a possessive pronoun.

> **Sue's** parents gave **her** the car. [object pronoun]
> **Her** car was wrecked. [possessive pronoun]

Exercise 1.9

In the blank on the right, write the correct pronoun that would be used to replace the underlined nouns.

1. Sal and Mary attended <u>Mary's</u> reunion. _____
2. Harold sent the report to <u>Anita and her super-visor</u>. _____
3. The winners of the sales competition were <u>Joe and April</u>. _____
4. My <u>sister</u> was recently employed there. _____
5. Mrs. Chang asked <u>Scott</u> to revise the report. _____
6. Alex returned the <u>estimate</u> to the contractor. _____
7. <u>Ruth's</u> sickness caused us all to worry. _____
8. Without concern for the consequences, <u>Susan and Harry</u> recommended cuts in personnel. _____
9. The inspector on the project team is <u>John Dunbar</u>. _____
10. The auctioneer said <u>Carol and Marty's</u> bid was lowest. _____

Check your answers with the Answer Key.

Exercise 1.10

Write a sentence using each of the following pronouns.

1. him _____

_____

2. they _____

_____

3. hers _____

_____

4. mine _____

_____

5. us _____

_____

6. me _____

_____

7. she _____

_____

Have your work checked by your instructor or a tutor.

Exercise 1.11

Write *subject, object,* or *possessive* in the blank on the left to identify each underlined pronoun in the paragraph below.

1. _____ Sandra and Carlos were both hired by the sales

2. _____ department six months ago, but (1)their records are

3. _____ quite different. Carlos immediately enrolled in night

4. _____ classes and studied hard for (2)them. He also used

5. _____ many of (3)his evenings to call on clients. As a result,

6. _____ (4)his sales increased, and (5)he will probably be pro-

7. _____ moted soon. Sandra, on the other hand, has not done

8. _____ as well. A bad case of flu forced (6)her to miss two

9. _____ weeks of work. Shortly thereafter, (7)her car lost (8)its

10. _____ brakes; (9)it has been repaired, but (10)she was unable

11. _____ to call on (11)her clients for several days. Sandra is now

12. _____ working very hard to improve (12) her performance.

Check your answers with the Answer Key.

RECOGNIZING CLAUSES AND PHRASES

Just as subjects and verbs are the basic words in sentences, clauses and phrases are the basic *word groups* found in sentences. Without clauses and phrases, sentences simply wouldn't exist. A complete understanding of clauses and phrases will help you write and punctuate sentences correctly.

Clauses

A *clause* is a meaningful group of words that contains a subject and a verb. You may include more than one clause in a sentence, but you cannot write a complete sentence that does not have at least one clause. You will use two types of clauses as you write: independent clauses and dependent clauses.

Independent Clauses—An *independent clause* is any group of words that contains a subject and a verb and expresses a complete thought. That same definition describes a simple sentence, so an independent clause and a simple sentence are the same. The following independent clauses are also simple sentences.

> **Companies fail.**
> Many **companies** quickly **fail.**
> Many poorly managed **companies** quickly **fail** each year.

Although the first example sentence has only two words, it is an independent clause; it has a subject and verb, and it expresses a complete thought. Notice that all three sentences are built around the same subject-verb combination.

Dependent Clauses—A dependent clause contains a subject and a verb, but it does *not* express a complete thought. Therefore, it cannot stand alone as a complete sentence. As the name *dependent clause* suggests, it needs something to hang on to. Because it is not a complete thought, you must always connect such a clause to an independent clause to have a complete sentence.

Dependent clauses, like independent clauses, are built around a subject-verb combination. Unlike independent clauses, though, dependent clauses have a signal word before the subject and verb. The *signal word* alerts your reader to the dependent clause and makes the dependent clause less important than the independent clause to which it is attached. The following are commonly used signal words:

after	once	when
although	provided	whether
as	since	where
because	though	who
before	unless	which
if	until	while

Notice what happens when a signal word is placed before each of the independent clauses used as examples earlier.

> **After** companies fail
> **Although** many companies quickly fail
> **Because** many poorly managed companies fail each year

Placing signal words in front of these sentences changed each from an independent clause to a dependent clause. A signal word makes the clause an incomplete thought because it suggests that some other idea will be presented. (What happens "*After* companies fail"?) Therefore, a dependent clause that stands alone is a sentence fragment. Signal words—technically called subordinators—can warn you of potential sentence errors.

To avoid writing a sentence fragment, usually considered a serious writing error, attach every clause containing a signal word (any dependent clause) to an independent clause. The preceding fragments have been attached to independent clauses to make complete sentences.

> After companies fail, others take their places.
> Although many companies quickly fail, others are successful.
> Because many poorly managed companies quickly fail each year, good management could be our key to success.

Phrases

In contrast to the clause, a *phrase* is a group of words that does not have a subject and verb combination. Phrases are usually short groups of words ending with a noun, such as:

on the desk	walking to the store
under his feet	to the end zone
over her head	his favorite jacket
across the field by the tree	the large white house

Occasionally, phrases will seem longer when two or more are joined together as in the last example in the left column. No matter how many are connected together, however, phrases can never be sentences because they have no subject-verb combination.

Exercise 1.12

Identify clauses with a **C** and phrases with a **P**.

1. the motor sputtered and died _____

2. when she lost her job last week _____

3. the extra copies on the desk _____

4. running beside the highway _____

5. while operating machinery _____

6. who attended the conference _____

7. as the computer screen faded to black _____

8. pencils break _____

9. the truck with a diesel motor _____

10. the lightning hit the tree _____

Check your answers with the Answer Key.

Exercise 1.13

Identify the underlined portions of the following sentences; use **C** for clauses and **P** for phrases.

1. <u>The three clerks returned</u> from lunch early.   _____

2. <u>When their team won</u>, the celebration lasted for days.   _____

3. The plant dumped chemicals in the river, <u>polluting it.</u>   _____

4. The copy machine, <u>without a sound</u>, quit working.   _____

5. Lemon trees, <u>according to the horticulturist</u>, cannot stand freezing weather.   _____

6. The travel agent, <u>although his office was busy</u>, took the trip to Hong Kong.   _____

7. The desk lamp refused to work <u>after it fell over.</u> _____

8. <u>On the wall near the coffee machine</u>, she posted the notice.   _____

9. You can see, <u>for instance</u>, why the spotlight is needed.   _____

10. We'll choose the employee <u>who can relocate to another city</u>.   _____

Check your answers with the Answer Key.

Exercise 1.14

Complete each of the following.

1. Define the word *clause*. _____

_____

_____

2. Define the word *phrase*. _____

_____

_____

3. Describe how a dependent clause differs from an independent clause. _____

_____

_____

4. Write three independent clauses. _____

_____

_____

5. Write three dependent clauses. _____

_____

_____

6. Write three phrases. _____

_____

_____

Have your work checked by your instructor or a tutor.

CHAPTER

2

Using Sentence Types

When you have completed this unit, you will be able to—

1. Identify simple, compound, and complex sentences.
2. Write simple, compound, and complex sentences.
3. Use compound subjects and compound verbs in the sentences you write.
4. Correctly use two methods of building compound sentences.
5. Correctly use three methods of ordering complex sentences.
6. Write sentences that use a series.
7. Use sentence variety to achieve more interesting writing.

Writing good sentences is the art of joining clauses and phrases correctly and effectively. If you become good at this process, sentences will become surprisingly easy to write. More importantly, when you thoroughly understand how to develop clauses and phrases into sentences, errors such as sentence fragments and run-on sentences will no longer be a problem.

The reason for writing good sentences is to get your ideas across to other people easily and effectively. Sentences that communicate your message precisely will involve the reader in what is being said, but poorly written, wordy sentences will be confusing and distracting. The more complete your understanding of sentence structure, the better your sentences and paragraphs will be. If you can effectively use simple, compound, and complex sentences as you write memos, letters, resumes, research papers, and reports, you will have no difficulty making the reader understand what you want to say.

SIMPLE SENTENCES

A simple sentence is nothing more than an independent clause. That is, it is a group of words that contains a subject, a verb, and a complete thought. To identify a simple sentence, then, you only have to make sure it has these three elements: a subject, a verb, and a complete thought. Beginning writers sometimes confuse simple sentences with fragments. A fragment is any group of words punctuated as a complete sentence that does not have a subject, a verb, and a complete thought.

A phrase cannot stand alone because it fulfills none of the three requirements of a complete sentence.

23

   inside the building
   driving on the freeway

Neither of these word groups has a subject-verb combination; therefore, both are phrases. The following word group fails the sentence test, too.

   when she was being followed

Even though this group of words has a subject and a verb, it is **not** a sentence because it does not contain a complete thought. Actually, this group of words is a dependent clause, identified by the signal word "when." Dependent clauses, when punctuated as complete sentences, are always fragments.

Exercise 2.1

  Identify each complete sentence in the following list by writing **S** in the appropriate blank. Use **F** to identify any item that is a fragment (not a sentence).

1. beside the clanking copier   _____

2. waiting patiently for the memo   _____

3. he broke the seal on the letter   _____

4. with the help of the foreman   _____

5. as if she had all the answers   _____

6. they wanted to leave immediately   _____

7. the proposal was rejected yesterday   _____

8. sale prices on all merchandise in the store   _____

9. it worked   _____

10. secretaries in the renovated building   _____

Check your answers with the Answer Key.

Basic Simple Sentences

  The basic pattern of the simple sentence is one subject followed by one verb.

      S   V
   The new copier arrived this morning.
    S   V
   Harold installed the new software.
   S V
   We wanted to complete the project.

This basic pattern is effective when used sparingly, but it produces boring paragraphs when used excessively. A short simple sentence in a paragraph creates power because it emphasizes an idea. Too many short simple sentences in a paragraph, however, will make it rough and choppy.

Simple Sentences with Compound Subjects and Compound Verbs

To avoid a rough, boring quality and still use simple sentences, you can develop sentences that have two or more subjects and two or more verbs. A sentence that has two or more subjects has a *compound subject*. A sentence with two or more verbs has a *compound verb*. Consider the following simple sentence.

Lou and Betty have hepatitis.

In this sentence, the complete subject contains two simple subjects, *Lou* and *Betty*, so it is called a compound subject. It has only a simple verb, however, because *have* is the only verb.

Lou and Betty have hepatitis but want to keep working.

The sentence now has a compound subject and a compound verb. Two people, *Lou* and *Betty*, do two things, *have* and *want*.

When you are using compound subjects, be aware that interrupting phrases will often make it difficult to identify the second subject. The following examples show this difficult construction.

Firemen from the local station and several **volunteers** were sent to the fire.

The **desks** in the office and the **chairs** in the reception area have been replaced.

Each of these example sentences has two subjects separated by a phrase. If you know how to look for these interrupting phrases, you should have no difficulty identifying a compound subject. To find both subjects in the first example, ask, "Who was sent to the fire?" The answer is the *firemen* and the *volunteers*. In the second example, you can identify the complete subject by asking, "What has been replaced?" The answer is *desks* and *chairs*.

Interrupting phrases may also make it difficult to identify compound verbs. The following sentence, for instance, shows how difficult it can be to iden-tify a compound verb when an interrupting phrase separates the two verbs.

We **arrived** at the conference late yesterday and **missed** an important seminar.

Notice that the first verb, *arrived*, is close to the subject and easy to identify, but the second verb, *missed*, is so far from the subject that it could be overlooked easily.

Exercise 2.2

In the following sentences, underline the subjects once and the verbs twice. In the first column of blanks on the right, write *simple* or *compound* to identify the subject of each sentence. And in the second column, identify the verb as *simple* or *compound*.

	Subject	Verb
1. The truck has new tires and brakes.	_____	_____
2. Bay trees have deep color but grow slowly.	_____	_____
3. The warehouse manager requested new wiring and lights.	_____	_____
4. Three linemen and a supervisor solved the problem.	_____	_____
5. They missed the turn and became lost.	_____	_____
6. John and Les attended the seminar in the morning.	_____	_____
7. He typed letters and answered the phones each afternoon.	_____	_____
8. Don and Sharon wrote and edited the report.	_____	_____
9. The garage door spring broke.	_____	_____
10. Joan cancelled the meeting and later rescheduled it.	_____	_____

Check your answers with the Answer Key.

Simple Sentences with Linking Verbs

A variation of the basic simple sentence pattern is the simple sentence with a linking verb. Writers frequently have problems with this verb. The following are simple sentences using the linking verbs that you learned in Chapter 1 (*am, are, is, was, were, be, been, being*). The following linking verbs are in boldface type to help you identify them.

The new employee **is** also a student.

I **am** unemployed.

Their building **was** huge.

Her mother and father **were** excited.

That mysterious person on the radio **is** she.

Remember that linking verbs connect the subject with another part of the sentence that tells more about the subject. If you think of the linking verb as an equal sign, you will rarely forget that the words after the linking verb belong to the same independent clause.

The new house **was** large and beautiful and expensive.

In the example above, the linking verb connects the subject, *house*, to three adjectives that describe the house—*large* and *beautiful* and *expensive*. The independent clause ends after the word *expensive*, not after *large*.

You will also use words other than "be" verbs as linking verbs; the other common linking verbs listed in Chapter 1 are *seem, appear, feel, become, look, smell, sound,* and *taste.* Since you will use linking verbs often in your writing, you should become familiar with them.

The same *be* verbs that are used as linking verbs will also be used as helping verbs to show a particular time reference (*am, is, are, was, were, be, been, being*).

Debbie **is working** for an insurance company.

Debbie **was working** for an insurance company.

In the example above, the *be* verb helps the main verb, *working,* express time and is, therefore, called a helping verb. In the first example the verb *is* expresses an action that is currently happening. In the second example, *was* makes it clear that the action described happened in the past.

Exercise 2.3

Write a sentence using the type of subject, verb, and other elements indicated in each of the following.

1. Simple subject and simple verb (action verb) _____

_____

2. Simple subject and compound verb (action verb) _____

_____

_____

3. Compound subject and simple verb (action verb) _____

_____

_____

4. Compound subject and compound verb (action verbs)_____

_____

_____

5. Compound subject and simple verb (linking verb) _____

_____

_____

6. Subject, linking verb, and noun _____

_____

_____

7. Subject, linking verb, and adjective _____

_____

_____

8. Subject, linking verb, and pronoun_____

_____

_____

9. Subject and *be* verb used as a helper _____

_____

_____

10. Simple subject, linking verb, and adjective _____

_____

_____

11. Compound subject, linking verb, and pronoun_____

_____

_____

12. Compound subject and *be* verb as helper _____

_____

_____

Have your work checked by your instructor or a tutor.

Inverted Simple Sentences

To give your simple sentences more variety and power, you will occasionally need to change the pattern of the sentences you write. The variations you studied in the exercise above will make your writing more interesting. You should occasionally use one other variation, however: the inverted sentence. The inverted sentence attracts your reader's attention because it is unusual. To write an inverted sentence, you could write it as a conventional sentence first and then change the word order to emphasize your point. The following sentences demonstrate inverted word order.

We rarely see such loyalty. [normal order]
becomes
Such loyalty we rarely see. [inverted order]

We are Americans. [normal order]
becomes
Americans we are. [inverted order]

Exercise 2.4

Write simple sentences following the directions in each item.

1. Change the following sentence into an inverted sentence.

True love stands like a statue of liberty on a far shore.

_____

_____

2. Change the following inverted sentence into normal word order.

More of the endless rain I can't stand.

_____

_____

3. Write an inverted sentence with a simple subject.

_____

_____

4. Write an inverted sentence with a compound subject.

_____

_____

Have your work checked by your instructor or a tutor.

COMPOUND SENTENCES

Although using compound subjects and verbs will help you avoid choppy sentences, too many simple sentences of any kind will still create a monotonous paragraph. This is especially true when those sentences contain closely related ideas. The following paragraph has an excessive number of simple sentences; notice the rough, elementary sound of the paragraph.

> Cross country skiing offers many rewards for winter sports enthusiasts. First, it gives skiers an opportunity to be alone with nature. No crowds are found on the trails. There can be great opportunities for a couple or small group to share. Cross country skiers hear birds. They hear the swishing of skis. Second, cross country skiing is very inexpensive. Skiers do not have to buy lift tickets or fancy clothing. Cross country skis, bindings, and shoes cost only a fraction as much as comparable downhill equipment. Finally, cross country skiers spend all of their time skiing. They don't spend their time waiting in lift lines. They don't have to wait for the crowds to thin out to ski. They don't have to stop skiing to help pick up fallen skiers. The rapid growth of the sport suggests many skiers have discovered its beauties.

Even though the paragraph above sounds acceptable, the roughness in it can be removed by combining some of the short simple sentences. Observe the improvement in the paragraph when some of the simple sentences are joined into compound sentences.

> Cross country skiing offers many rewards for winter sports enthusiasts. First, it gives skiers an opportunity to be alone with nature. No crowds are found on the trails, **but** there can be great opportunities for a couple or small group to share. Cross country skiers hear birds, **and** they hear the swishing of skis. Second, cross country skiing is very inexpensive, **for** skiers do not have to buy lift tickets or fancy clothing. Cross country skis, bindings, and shoes cost only a fraction as much as comparable downhill equipment. Finally, cross country skiers spend all their time skiing. They don't spend their time waiting in lift lines, they don't have to wait for the crowds to thin out to ski, **and** they don't have to stop to help pick up fallen skiers. The rapid growth of this sport suggests many skiers have discovered its beauties.

A **compound sentence** is two or more simple sentences joined together. Suppose that you want to join the following two simple sentences into a compound sentence.

> s   v   s   v
> The dog barked ferociously. The child screamed in terror.

You can use a comma and a conjunction to join the two simple sentences.

> s   v   s   v
> The dog barked ferociously, **and** the child screamed in terror.

Or you can simply use a semicolon to join the two sentences.

> s   v   s   v
> The dog barked ferociously; the child screamed in terror.

The most natural method of joining simple sentences into compounds is to use conjunctions. However, this requires more than the ability to spell each conjunction correctly. Each of the most common conjunctions has a specific meaning. Unless the correct conjunction is used to join the two simple sentences, the resulting compound will seem awkward. The following words are called *coordinating conjunctions* because they are commonly used to join two equal, closely related sentences into compound sentences.

and, but, or, nor, yet, for

Notice that each conjunction expresses a particular relationship between the two sentences it joins. *And* explains that *in addition to* what is explained in the first sentence, the situation in the second sentence is also true.

The team won the world championship, **and** the party went on for days.

But shows a *contrast* between what was described in the first sentence and what you would expect to be described in the second sentence.

She went to work on Monday, **but** her mind was still on the glorious weekend.

Or connects two sentences that describe *alternate* possibilities.

The company will have to offer better salaries, **or** all the employees will quit.

Yet, like *but*, is used to show a *contrast*. Use *yet* when you wish to show a greater contrast.

The California condor is a gigantic bird with no natural enemies, **yet** humans have almost driven it to extinction.

For can be used to show a *cause* relationship between two simple sentences.

The contractor was embarrassed, **for** he forgot to put a closet in one of the bedrooms.

In the last example, the first sentence is a result of the second sentence. Be careful when you use *for* as a conjunction, however, because this word is often used in other ways. You have used it correctly, if you can replace the *for* with *because*.

Exercise 2.5

In the blank after each item, write the conjunction that most clearly shows the relationship between the two sentences being joined. Use *and, but, or, nor, yet,* or *for* in each.

1. The new copier has arrived, _____ it is slower than the old one.   _____
2. The frozen pipes in the basement burst, _____ the phone lines were flooded.   _____
3. The flight arrived late, _____ the airport had been fogged in.   _____
4. A fire swept through the warehouse complex, _____ no one was killed.   _____
5. They must qualify for the loan, _____ they will not be able to buy the building.   _____
6. The trucks are kept in good repair, _____ the company doesn't have the capital to buy new ones.   _____
7. The crew that widened the road worked hard, _____ they couldn't finish the job before dark.   _____
8. Flo must buy a new car this week, _____ she will be forced to drive the company car.   _____
9. The hurricane hit Florida, _____ many homes were destroyed.   _____
10. The electrical company must pay a fine to the IRS, _____ they missed the filing deadline.   _____

Check your answers with the Answer Key.

Recognizing Compound Sentences

In order to write and recognize compound sentences easily, it is necessary to be able to distinguish compound sentences from simple sentences with compound subjects and verbs. The simple sentence with a compound subject and verb names one or more subjects that do the same thing. For instance:

Simple sentence: The children and dogs ran and played all morning.

Here, both children and dogs did the same things: ran and played. Compare that simple sentence above with the compound sentence below.

Compound sentence: The children played, and the dogs ran all morning.

Notice that in the compound sentence, the children and dogs did different things. The first half explains that the children played; the second half explains that the dogs ran. Both halves of the sentence are complete sentences if separated. "The children played" has a subject and a verb and makes a complete statement, so it is a simple sentence. The same is true of "dogs ran." Since the whole sentence has two sentences properly combined with a comma and a conjunction, it qualifies as a compound sentence.

Exercise 2.6

Write *SS* for all simple sentences and *CD* for all compound sentences.

1. The computer was easy to use; it made writing letters quite simple.   _____

2. Edmundo writes several memos a day, but John prefers the telephone.   _____

3. The memos require more time but do provide a written record of communications.   _____

4. She had better learn to speak more intelligently, or she will never get the job.   _____

5. The blue jay jumped into the fountain and splashed water everywhere.   _____

6. The repair work must be started immediately, or the contract will be cancelled.   _____

7. Her office was on the fifth floor, yet she usually used the stairs.   _____

8. Maria received the sales award and displayed it on her office wall.   _____

9. The students were angry, for their opinions were not considered.   _____

10. According to Lana, movies are too expensive and not worth watching.   _____

Check your answers with the Answer Key.

Exercise 2.7

Write a compound sentence using each of the following conjunctions.

1. *but* _____

_____

2. *or* _____

_____

3. *for* _____

_____

4. *and* _____

_____

5. *yet* _____

_____

Have your work checked by your instructor or a tutor.

Relationship Between Clauses

As you write compound sentences, you must also be sure the ideas you join are closely related, or the reader will become confused. The word *coordination* describes joining two sentences that are equal in importance into a single compound sentence; hence, writing compound sentences is often referred to as coordinating ideas. As a writer you must know when two sentences should not be joined because they are not closely related. The ideas in the following sentences are not closely related, so they should not be joined into one sentence.

> **Not related:** Three members of the committee resigned. The secretary took perfect notes.

Since the ideas in these two sentences are not clearly related, the two sentences cannot be joined into a compound sentence.

> **Related:** Three members of the committee resigned, and they blamed the secretary for creating the problems.

These two simple sentences produce an acceptable compound sentence because an obvious relationship exists between them.

Exercise 2.8

Look carefully at each of the following pairs of sentences. If the two sentences should not be joined because they are not closely related, write **N R** in the space. If, however, the sentences can be properly joined into a compound sentence, write **C D** in the space.

1. _____   Peterson Electronics will not open on that corner. Other businesses in that location have had few customers.

2. _____   Hank's favorite sport is ice hockey. Hank is a journeyman plumber.

3. _____   They attended the meeting this morning. They skipped the afternoon seminar.

4. _____   The manager has not yet read the report. It was delivered just an hour ago.

5. _____   The warehouse accepts deliveries twenty-four hours a day. It contains office equipment.

6. _____   The telephone rang repeatedly. He refused to answer it.

7. _____   The instructor gave the student a failing grade. The student had not passed one test.

Check your answers with the Answer Key.

COMPLEX SENTENCES

The complex sentence is very similar to the compound sentence: both are made up of two or more clauses. There is one important difference, however: while the compound sentence is made up of two or more independent clauses, *the complex sentence is made up of one independent clause and one or more dependent clauses.* The following sentences illustrate the difference.

> **Compound sentence:** Joggers were out running around the track, *but* they were freezing cold.

> **Complex sentence:** Joggers were out running around the track *although* they were freezing cold.

The first sentence is *compound* because it has two independent clauses joined by a comma and a conjunction (*but*). The second sentence is *complex* because it contains a dependent clause beginning with a signal word (*although*).

The compound sentence was changed into a complex sentence by performing two steps: (1) dropping the coordinating conjunction *but* and (2) adding the signal word *although*. Many compound sentences can be converted into complex sentences as easily.

The reason for changing compound sentences to complex sentences is to achieve variety. By changing your sentence patterns frequently, your writing will be far more interesting to read and thus more effective. Complex sentences help achieve this variety because there are three different complex sentence patterns you can use.

Complex sentence pattern 1

s v v   s v v
When he was hit by the falling limb, the tree trimmer was knocked out of the tree.
[dependent clause at beginning of sentence]

Complex sentence pattern 2

s v v   s v v
The tree trimmer was knocked out of the tree **when** he was hit by the falling limb.
[dependent clause at the end of sentence]

Complex sentence pattern 3

s   s v v   v v
The tree trimmer, **when** he was hit by the falling limb, was knocked out of the tree.
[dependent clause interrupting the independent clause]

These examples contain almost exactly the same words, but putting the dependent clause in different places in the sentences makes them appear quite different.

In addition to the variety you achieve by using complex sentences, you can also make one part of a sentence more important than the other. Put the more important idea in the *independent* clause; place the less important idea in a *dependent* clause. In the example sentences above, the most significant idea is that the tree trimmer was knocked out of the tree. The fact that he was hit by the falling limb is made less important by placing that idea in a dependent clause.

You should write complex sentences when one idea is more important than another. Use a compound sentence when the ideas are approximately equal in importance.

Exercise 2.9

Complete the following sentences by supplying the missing clauses.

1. (complex) The workers celebrated all night *after* _____

_____

2. (compound) Highway paving crews often work long hours, *and*_____

_____

3. (complex) Although the cheerleaders missed the bus, _____

_____

4. (compound) Many of the workers were sick on Monday, *but* _____

_____

5. (complex) Marie, *because*_____

_____, quit attending college.

6. (complex) If you get there before I do, _____

_____

7. (complex) We should plan to visit Ireland next summer *since* _____

_____

8. (complex) After the boss gave her a generous bonus, _____

_____

9. (complex) Whenever you are ready to leave, _____

_____

10. (complex) The six new employees are to attend orientation sessions *until* _____

_____

Have your answers checked by your instructor or a tutor.

Dependent Clauses

The exercise you have just completed includes complex sentences that use the most common signal words. You encountered many of these in Chapter 1. You should become familiar with this expanded list, which includes the words from Chapter 1. (There are additional signal words that are not listed here.)

Signal Words

after	before	since	when	whether
although	even though	though	whenever	while
as	if	unless	where	
because	provided	until	wherever	

When you use a signal word to form a dependent clause in a complex sentence, the signal word must always be followed by a subject and a verb. Signal words are often called *danger words* because they warn the writer that the clause being written is a dependent clause. The alert writer immediately makes certain that the clause is attached to an independent clause before going on to the next sentence. For the reader, a signal word is an indication that the following clause is dependent on the other part of the sentence.

The punctuation of complex sentences differs noticeably from the punctuation of compound sentences. In a compound sentence, the two independent clauses are separated by a comma followed by a coordinating conjunction. By contrast, notice how the complex sentences below are punctuated.

When the dependent clause comes *before* the independent clause, one comma is required after the dependent clause. This comma tells the reader to pause before reading the independent clause.

>   S   V   S   V
> **Because** she loved its softness, Marlene bought the cashmere sweater.

The following sentence requires no comma because the dependent clause, the least important clause, appears *after* the independent clause.

>   S   V   S   V
> Marlene bought the cashmere sweater **because** she loved its softness.

Commas are used before and after the dependent clause when it is placed between the subject and verb of the independent clause.

>   S   S   V   V
> Marlene, **because** she loved its softness, bought the cashmere sweater.

Be careful to punctuate your complex sentences like these examples, or they will be considered incorrect.

Exercise 2.10

Write complex sentences in the following blanks using the signal words given. Be sure you use the pattern requested and punctuate them correctly.

1. *when* (dependent clause first) _____

    _____

    _____

2. *after* (dependent clause last) _____

    _____

    _____

3. *because* (dependent clause interrupting the independent clause) _____

    _____

    _____

4. *since* (dependent clause first) _____

    _____

    _____

5. *although* (dependent clause last) _____

    _____

    _____

Have your work checked by your instructor or a tutor.

Special Signal Words: Relative Pronouns

Another commonly encountered group of signal words, technically called relative pronouns, is used to begin dependent clauses. These special signal words are easy to recognize because they almost always begin dependent clauses that have been inserted between the subject and verb of an independent clause. The following example shows a dependent clause using *who,* one of these special words.

$$\text{S} \quad \text{S} \quad \text{V} \qquad\qquad\qquad \text{V}$$
Mary, **who** has strawberry blond hair, works in the library.

Notice that a subject does not immediately follow this special signal word. The signal word *who* is the subject of the dependent clause. The words in this group serve two functions: (1) as the signal word and (2) as the subject of the dependent clause. A list of the most common of these special words follows:

that	which	whoever
what	who	whom

Punctuating sentences which use relative pronouns should be easy if you recognize them as you write. There are two ways of punctuating clauses with relative pronouns.

The first situation requires the same punctuation as any other complex sentence in which the dependent clause interrupts the independent clause.

> Dick McCall, **who** is the foreman in the shipping department, drives the classic Corvette.
>
> Mount Lam Lam, **which** is the highest point on the island of Guam, provides a challenging hike.

In these two sentences, commas must be placed before and after the dependent clause because the information contained in it is not essential to understanding the independent clause. By setting the dependent clause off with commas, you signal the reader that the clause can be omitted without changing the meaning of the sentence.

On the other hand, when the dependent clause is essential to the sentence, it is not set off with commas. The following sentences do not have commas because the dependent clause is essential to the meaning of the sentence.

> All voters **who seriously care about their country** will be at the polls next Tuesday. [The dependent clause tells which voters.]
>
> The cars **which pollute the air** should be taken off the road. [The dependent clause tells which cars.]

In the first sentence, the dependent clause "who seriously care about their country" tells which voters will be at the polls. It is not set off with commas because that dependent clause is essential to the meaning of the sentence. If that clause were omitted, the sentence would have a different meaning. The writer did not mean to say that all voters will vote. The same is true in the second sentence. The writer does not mean that all cars should be taken off the road—only those cars "which pollute the air." Since the meaning of the sentence would change if the dependent clause were omitted, no commas should be placed around it.

Exercise 2.11

Complete the dependent clauses in the following sentences. Then decide if the clause you have written is essential to the meaning of the sentence. Place commas around the dependent clause where necessary.

1. Mr. Bradley *who* _____

plans to retire this year.

2. The woman *who* _____

designed the clothes worn by the blond model.

3. German shepherd dogs *which* _____

_____ are often trained to be guard dogs.

4. The man *who* _____

plans to build a two-story Spanish-style house.

5. The car *that* _____

barely runs.

Have your work checked by your instructor or a tutor.

SENTENCE VARIETY

You have already learned the advantage of using sentence variety. The result of using too many sentences of the same type and length is boring, lifeless writing that no one enjoys reading. You might write the most informative report of your life, but if you use too many similar sentences, the report will lose its impact. Overcoming this problem in your writing does not require a special gift, only a knowledge of sentence variety and a determination to use it.

Varying Sentence Length

Using sentences of different lengths is a basic technique for achieving sentence variety. Too many short sentences are bad; too many long sentences are even worse. Writing a paragraph containing sentences that are all the same length creates a choppy effect if the sentences are all short. If the sentences are all long, it creates a heavy effect that will put your reader to sleep. Although you may have to deliberately write paragraphs having sentences of various lengths at first, you will automatically mix sentence lengths as you gain experience. The following paragraph illustrates an interesting variety of sentence lengths.

As the manager of Hazel's, a women's clothing store, I have three primary responsibilities. First, I must make sure my employees are treating the customers properly, as well as making sure they are keeping the store clean and presentable. Second, I must also be the "housekeeper." If the store runs out of any supplies, I am responsible for replacing them. I will buy anything from toilet paper to decorations, even a Christmas tree. The third and most difficult part of managing is the hiring and firing of employees. I must be able to choose the right person for Hazel's. To be able to make the right choice, I must ask the proper questions while interviewing and get the interviewees to talk a little about themselves. I carefully check the applications for neatness, job experience, and legitimacy of past jobs listed. I also call past employers to check references. The people I hire do not always work out, and that requires calling them into the office, telling them why they didn't work out, and letting them go. Nevertheless, I love my job. I love the challenge and the many responsibilities connected with my job.

The twelve sentences in the paragraph above range in length from five to twenty-eight words. Sentences you write may very well range from four to fifty words, depending on your writing style and on the complexity of the subject.

Varying Sentence Types

Varying sentence types works together with varying sentence lengths. Generally, you can most easily achieve a variety in your paragraphs by deliberately making each sentence pattern different from the one before it. To say there are three sentence types is an oversimplification. In reality, each of the three basic sentences—simple, compound, and complex—has several variations. It is these variations that can make two sentences of the same type seem quite different.

Simple Sentence Variations   The simple sentence has far more potential variety than most writers ever realize. Consider the following sentences:

> *Simple subject and simple verb:*
> The new copier performed flawlessly.

> *Compound subject and compound verb:*
> The new copier and the new computer performed flawlessly and saved the company tremendous time and money.

By adding more subjects and verbs you can completely change the appearance of a sentence.

> *Verb series:* The aging sewing machine **broke needles, knotted thread,** and **clattered noisily**.
> *Adjective series:* The typist was **fast, neat,** and **knowledgeable**.
> *Repetition verb series:*   The frightened deer **ran** and **ran** and **ran**.
> *Subject series:* The **concrete**, the **roofing**, and the **insulation** all arrived at the job at quitting time.

These four simple sentences illustrate how different series can look. The first example has a series of verbs making up a compound verb. This sentence pattern is extremely effective when you are describing a number of actions performed by the subject. The second example sentence uses a series of adjectives to describe the subject of the sentence. Series of this type are easy to write provided that you recognize the linking verb, in this case *was*. The third example sentence shows the most unique kind of series. Although you won't have an opportunity to use this pattern often, the repetition series produces an excellent effect when you wish to emphasize a seemingly endless action, such as raining, talking, barking, crying, or yelling. The final example sentence works well when you wish to show that a number of people or objects are doing the same thing.

Punctuating the series properly is important. The basic rule for punctuating any series is to use one comma fewer than items in the series. That is, you should use *two* commas in a series of *three* items. However, the third example sentence illustrates an exception to the rule. Whenever you use the repetition series, you use no commas because all items in the series are separated by conjunctions.

Compound Sentence Variations   When you join two simple sentences into a compound, you can use either of two techniques. You may use a comma and a coordinating conjunction, or you may use just a semicolon.

> The jury debated for three days, **and** it surprised everyone by finding the accused guilty.

> The jury debated for three days; it surprised everyone by finding the accused guilty.

Either of these patterns is perfectly acceptable provided that your sentences flow smoothly. You will often discover, however, that one pattern makes the sentence sound better than the other.

To decide whether to use a semicolon or a coordinating conjunction, think about the relationship you want to show between the two ideas you are joining.

1. Use a *semicolon* when you simply want to connect the ideas together. A semicolon serves the same purpose as the conjunction *and*.

2. Use a *coordinating conjunction* when you want to show a particular relationship between the ideas (*but* or *yet* to show contrast; *or* to show alternate possibilities; *for* to show cause).

Notice in the following examples that the first sentence sounds decidedly better than the second.

> The truck was obviously overloaded, *but* it never faltered.
> The truck was obviously overloaded; it never faltered.

The sentence containing the semicolon fails to communicate the message clearly because the relationship between the two independent clauses is not clear without *but*. Although the semicolon may not be familiar to you, you should learn to use it; the semicolon is an excellent method of connecting two halves of some compound sentences.

You may also join three simple sentences into a compound sentence by punctuating the sentence just as you would any series.

> Merchants use computers to record inventory flow, buyers use them to record expenses, **and** consumers use them to balance checkbooks.

When joining sentences in a series, be sure to include a conjunction. If you leave the conjunction out, you will have a run-on sentence.

Complex Sentence Variations   Of the three types of sentences, the complex sentence offers the most potential variety. The danger with complex sentences is that you will become overly dependent upon one pattern and thus neglect the other two. Remember that you can vary the order of a complex sentence by placing the dependent clause before, after, or in the middle of the independent clause. The following examples illustrate the three complex sentence types.

> The horse, **after it knocked me off on a low limb**, ran back to the barn.
>
> **After it knocked me off on a low limb**, the horse ran back to the barn.
>
> The horse ran back to the barn **after it knocked me off on a low limb**.

Although the first order shown is the most rarely used, it offers the best variety because it separates the subject from the verb in the independent clause.

Exercise 2.12

Identify the following sentences, using **SS** for simple, **CD** for compound, and **CX** for complex.

1. The report, which is not yet completed, is already twenty pages long.   _____

2. Four roads led out of town, but all were flooded.   _____

3. Only a few applicants are qualified for the job; it requires a college degree.   _____

4. After the trees were removed, the road was widened.   _____

5. Charles emptied the cash box, counted the money, and drove to the bank.   _____

Check your answers with the Answer Key.

Exercise 2.13

Write the sentences indicated.

1. Complex sentence with interrupting dependent clause

    _____

    _____

2. Compound sentence with semicolon

    _____

    _____

3. Simple sentence with repetition verb series

    _____

    _____

4. Simple sentence with verb series

    _____

    _____

5. Complex sentence with dependent clause first

    _____

    _____

6. Simple sentence with inverted order

    _____

    _____

Have your work checked by your instructor or a tutor.

Varying Sentence Order

By now it should be clear that excessive use of any sentence length or type weakens the overall impact of your writing. Overuse of the basic sentence order can be equally bad. The basic order has a subject followed by a verb at the beginning of the sentence. Constant use of that order should be avoided. The following student paragraph demonstrates the effect of beginning each sentence with a subject-verb combination.

> The *crew* of the doomed *Titanic was* unfamiliar with the ship. *Most* of them *were brought* aboard the ship for the first time on the day the ship sailed. The *men were obtained* from other ships in the area. The *White Star Line owned* the *Titanic*. The *company* desperately *needed* the crewmen to compensate for a massive rush of passengers due to a local coal strike. The coal *strike had hit* England in January of 1912, causing coal to be very scarce. Because of this, the shipping *line had* to buy coal from other ships just to have enough to get the *Titanic* to New York. *It took* the equivalent of 300 boxcars of coal to power the ship across the Atlantic. Many other *ships* scheduled to leave *were forced* to cancel their voyages for lack of coal. *This left* hundreds of people rushing to the only ship departing: the *Titanic*. *Most* of the sailors brought aboard for the trip *had* only a few hours to become familiar with the ship. *Few understood* their jobs or how to get around the ship when it departed for the United States.

Although this paragraph is readable as it stands, it loses some of its effectiveness because of the excessive use of the same sentence order. To make the paragraph read more smoothly, you simply combine sentences, change some from compound to complex, and add or subtract a few words. The following paragraph illustrates just five of the possible changes.

> The crewmen of the doomed *Titanic* were very unfamiliar with the ship. Most of them were brought aboard the ship for the first time on the day the ship sailed; the men were obtained from other ships in the area. The White Star Line, which owned the *Titanic*, desperately needed crewmen to compensate for a massive rush of passengers due to a local coal strike. The coal strike had hit England in January of 1912, causing coal to be very scarce. Because of this, the shipping line had to buy coal from other ships just to have enough to get the *Titanic* to New York; it took the equivalent of 300 boxcars of coal to power the ship across the Atlantic. Many other ships scheduled to leave were forced to cancel their voyages for lack of coal, which left hundreds of people rushing to the only ship departing: the *Titanic*. Because most of the sailors brought aboard for the trip had only a few hours to become familiar with the ship, few understood their jobs or how to get around the ship when it departed for the United States.

Exercise 2.14

Revise the following paragraph to add a variety of sentence lengths, types, and orders.

> I was almost thirty years old. I decided to change the direction of my life. I wanted to make some positive life and career changes. The world of studying, homework, professors, and running for classes had always been a foreign world to me. The mystique of the college classroom was a definite challenge in the back of my mind. I decided to take the big step. With some trepidation, I picked the college of my choice and registered for my first semester. My expectations for college were a jumble of contradictions. I was excited. I would finally find some positive direction in my life. I was also uncertain. I had been a housewife for ten years. I did not know what to expect. Above all, I was terrified. I thought I might not measure up to my expectations. I put my negative feelings in the back of my mind. I strove forward to create my own destiny.

_____

_____

_____

_____

_____

_____

_____

_____

_____

_____

_____

_____

_____

_____

_____

_____

_____

Have your work checked by your instructor or a tutor.

3

Improving Sentence Structure

When you have completed this unit, you will be able to—

1. Identify appositives in sentences.
2. Create sentences using appositives.
3. Use conjunctive adverbs to show the correct relationship between two clauses in compound sentences.
4. Distinguish between conjunctive adverbs and transitions.
5. Properly punctuate sentences using conjunctive adverbs and transitions.
6. Revise sentences with faulty parallel construction.
7. Write sentences using correct parallel construction.
8. Write sentences using verbals.

Using polished, precise sentences is like putting paint on a house. Although paint isn't necessary to make the house livable, it does make it much more pleasant to look at. Similarly, rough, wordy sentences might communicate a message, but polished, well-written sentences will make your writing much more pleasant to read. And just as the painted house suggests good things about its owner, so good writing suggests a careful person who takes the time to do a job correctly.

At this point, you know how to write the various sentence types and how to achieve variety. You are now ready for the final step before you begin writing real-world assignments. That final step is to polish your sentences until they are clear enough to communicate your message with everyone who reads them. In this chapter, you will study techniques that will help you get smoothly from one part of a sentence to the next, and from one sentence to the next. This will require you to use transitional words, phrases, and devices. You will also develop techniques of combining sentences so that you can write one precise sentence rather than two wordy ones. All of this will be very important to you as you write resumes, memos, reports, and research papers because people in the real world don't have time to waste on wordy, confusing writing.

APPOSITIVES

Appositives are words or word groups that provide additional but nonessential information about nouns or pronouns. They are usually located immediately after the noun they explain. Using appositives helps you more fully describe a person, place, or thing without adding another sentence. Although they may be quite long on occasion, appositives are usually only a word, or a short phrase. The appositives are in bold type in the following sentences.

Bill Walsh, **the coach,** stood nervously on the sidelines.

They traveled to Yosemite National Park, **the most famous park in California.**

His chosen profession, **selling computers,** provided him with a good income.

All donations—**cash, checks, money orders, IOU's**—were readily accepted.

Appositives are usually set off from the remainder of the sentence by commas because they are not actually part of the basic message. Using commas before and after the appositive signals the reader that this material can be omitted without changing the meaning of the sentence. As shown in the last example, when an appositive contains commas, you may set off the appositive with dashes to avoid confusion.

Although most appositives are set off with commas, you will occasionally write sentences containing appositives that need no commas. The rule is simple: whenever the appositive is needed to help identify the noun it renames, you should omit the commas. Consider the following sentences in which the appositives are in bold type.

Commas needed	No commas needed
Stephen King, **a best selling author,** writes fiction.	Stephen King's novel **Skeleton Crew** is exciting.
Milt Jackson, **the quarterback,** was injured.	The quarterback **Milt Jackson** was injured.
Jack, **Marge's son,** graduated last semester.	Marge's son **Jack** graduated last semester.

Since the subject of each sentence in the left column is clearly identified by name, the appositive is unnecessary. It is, therefore, set off with commas. By contrast, the appositive in each sentence in the right column is needed to clearly identify the subject; thus, no commas are used to set off the appositive.

Appositives are used to supply additional information about a noun. That is how they can be most valuable to you. But they can also be very helpful when you need to smooth out a number of short sentences in a row. Rather than using a short simple sentence to give additional information about a person, place, or thing, you can use an appositive. By doing so, you easily eliminate short sentences and wordiness. The examples below illustrate how two sentences can be combined into one more precise sentence.

Ms. Fineburg works in Sarasota. She is a stock broker.

Using an appositive, this becomes

Ms. Fineburg, **a stock broker,** works in Sarasota.

The ceremony will be held at Alumni Grove. The grove was the site of many similar ceremonies in the past.

Using an appositive, this becomes

The ceremony will be held at Alumni Grove, **the site of many similar ceremonies in the past**.

Notice that using an appositive instead of another sentence omits many unnecessary words. Thus appositives help you communicate the same message in fewer words.

Exercise 3.1

Underline all appositive words and phrases in the following sentences.

1. The raise, the first one in years, made the workers very happy.
2. Harry, Lee, and Elaine work for Mitchell and Sukimoto, an accounting firm in San Francisco.
3. The new copier, an automated wonder, intimidates many of the office employees.
4. The bid process has begun for Highway 119, a new state bypass planned for next year.
5. Juan Ruiz, the lawyer on our staff, addressed the city council last week.
6. The corn farmers had only two problems last year: hungry grasshoppers and high interest rates.
7. The author Alice Walker wrote *The Color Purple*, a novel about African Americans.
8. The music teacher and three students—Gina, Charles, and Steve—were in the building when the earthquake struck.
9. One of the company's vice presidents, Vernon Winton, argued for the expansion plan.
10. Jerry Beck, an architect, and Ron Murphy, a real estate broker, worked together to market the new house.

Check your answers with the Answer Key.

Exercise 3.2

Using appositives, combine the following sentence pairs.

1. Audiences filled the theater each night to see the play by Mamet. He is a very popular playwright.

_____

_____

_____

2. Many tourists from other countries visit the Grand Canyon. It is a spectacular natural wonder.

_____

_____

_____

3. Ms. Spaulding wrote a flawless progress report last week. She is a new employee.

_____

_____

Check your answers with the Answer Key.

CONJUNCTIVE ADVERBS

Like appositives, conjunctive adverbs allow you to avoid an excessive number of simple sentences. Although the term _conjunctive adverb_ might be unfamiliar, you almost certainly use these words every day, some repeatedly.

Chapter 2 examined the coordinating conjunction and semicolon techniques of creating compound sentences. A conjunctive adverb is another way of combining two simple sentences into a compound sentence. Placed between the two sentences, it is always preceded by a semicolon and followed by a comma. These words are very easy to use once you have learned them. The conjunctive adverbs are in bold type in the following examples.

The permit has been issued; **therefore**, construction will begin this week.

Low interest rate loans are available; **however**, very few borrowers have applied for them.

The recent growth of Tucson, Arizona, has caused problems for residents; **indeed**, housing costs have increased at an alarming rate.

None of the conjunctive adverbs above should be unfamiliar to you; indeed, they are all used frequently. Learning to use the conjunctive adverbs correctly as you write, however, may be challenging because you probably rarely use them in your own writing.

Sometimes conjunctive adverbs can show the exact relationship and emphasis you intend in compound sentences better than a semicolon or a coordinating conjunction. The advantage of using conjunctive adverbs should be clear when you study these example sentences.

> The temperature fell below freezing, **and** the citrus crop was destroyed.
>
> The temperature fell below freezing; **therefore**, the citrus crop was destroyed.
>
> He was in the right place at the right time, **and** he became the first man to walk on the moon.
>
> He was in the right place at the right time; **thus**, he became the first man to walk on the moon.

In these examples, the second sentence in each pair has more power because of the emphasis created. Not every compound sentence sounds better when joined by a conjunctive adverb; however, when you wish to emphasize or clarify a particular relationship between two independent clauses, the simple conjunction is often not as effective.

To use conjunctive adverbs effectively, you must first decide what relationship you wish to emphasize. You then select the word that will best show the relationship. The following words are commonly used as conjunctive adverbs. You should begin by learning all of the words on the list and the relationships they emphasize. Although many other words could be added, the words in the list below will fit most situations.

Relationship to be shown	Conjunctive adverb to use
adding to	moreover, furthermore
conceding	of course
contrasting	however, nevertheless
emphasizing	indeed, in fact
illustrating	for example
restating or summing up	in other words
resulting or concluding	therefore, thus

To decide which conjunctive adverb to use, read the first independent clause carefully. Then read the second sentence and ask yourself how it is related to the first.

> On Pete's desk were piles of papers, numerous files, outdated calendars, and dirty coffee cups; _____, his workspace was a mess.

Given these two independent clauses, you can see that the second clause is merely summing up the first. Looking at the list of conjunctive adverbs, you find that *in other words* expresses that relationship, so you would insert it in the proper space and read the sentence. Since the resulting sentence reads smoothly, you can assume that your choice is correct.

More than one conjunctive adverb will occasionally work equally well between two clauses, so you should think about how others would sound. In the preceding example, if you wanted to emphasize the second clause even more, you could use an emphasizing adverb: *indeed* or *in fact*.

> On Pete's desk were piles of papers, numerous files, outdated calendars, and dirty coffee cups; **in fact**, his workspace was a mess.

Exercise 3.3

In each sentence, supply a conjunctive adverb that clearly shows the relationship between the two clauses. Work thoughtfully and slowly.

1. Her inability to read well was a handicap; _____, she did not advance in the company because of it.

2. Many employees complained about the telephone system; _____, a new system is being installed next month.

3. The technician said he could no longer work for a company that did not appreciate its employees; _____, he quit his job.

4. Kathy sold three houses last month; _____, she has listed several more this month.

5. Joe has decided to return to college; _____, applications will soon be taken for his job.

6. Vacations serve an important function; _____, they are time for relaxation and renewal.

7. The shipping department has been commended for its safety practices; _____, the custodial department has had several accidents already this month.

Check your answers with the Answer Key.

Exercise 3.4

Add an independent clause to each conjunctive adverb in the following sentences.

1. Her old electric typewriter still works well; *however*, _____

_____.

2. Sharon was promoted to office manager last week; *of course*, _____

_____.

3. Their company has a very good retirement plan; *furthermore*, _____

_____.

4. The drapes at the south window have been damaged by the sun; *in fact,* _____

_____.

5. Many employees favor staggered work hours; *nevertheless,* _____

_____.

6. The student has not attended class or done the homework; *in other words,* _____

_____.

7. Many people don't know how to reduce stress in their lives; *thus,* _____

_____.

Have your sentences checked by your instructor or a tutor.

Exercise 3.5

Write a compound sentence using each conjunctive adverb given. Be sure to use the correct punctuation with the conjunctive adverb.

1. moreover

_____

_____

_____

2. of course

_____

_____

_____

3. however

_____

_____

_____

4. indeed

_____

_____

_____

5. for example

_____

_____

_____

6. in other words

_____

_____

_____

7. therefore

_____

_____

_____

Have your sentences checked by your instructor or a tutor.

TRANSITIONS

Transitions are words, phrases, or sentences that connect sentences or paragraphs together. By using these transitions properly, you can eliminate many confusions and make your writing far easier to follow.

Using Connecting Words

The *connecting word* transitions will be the easiest for you to use at this point because they include the same words you learned to use as conjunctive adverbs. In fact, exactly the same relationships are shown by these words whether they are used as connecting words for separate sentences or as conjunctive adverbs in compound sentences. In the following example, the second sentence begins with a transition word that connects it to the previous sentence.

> The surveyor criticized the new level, insisting that it was ugly. **Nevertheless,** he always looked for it when he gathered up equipment for a day's work in the field.

The transition word *nevertheless* effectively connects the two sentences because they have contrasting ideas. One sentence comments that the new level was ugly; the next states that the surveyor always looked for it when he gathered his equipment. The two sentences are obviously not in agreement, so a connecting word that shows contrast is used.

The following list of commonly used transitions includes many of the conjunctive adverbs you learned earlier in this chapter.

as a matter of fact	nevertheless	third
for example	of course	on the other hand
furthermore	therefore	in addition
however	as a result	also
indeed	thus	consequently
unfortunately	first	then
in other words	second	in fact
moreover		

Although the following paragraph uses more connecting words than you should ordinarily use, the paragraph clearly shows how transitions work.

> The Molokai mule ride appeals to those people who don't mind discomfort. The discomfort begins, **in fact**, with a very early departure. Mules, it would seem, are early risers. **Moreover**, there is the long ride down the face of the cliff to the leper colony to consider. As the mules slip and almost fall on the rocky trail, the rider is tossed around like a rag doll in a puppy's mouth. **As a matter of fact**, the riders do so much slipping and sliding around in the saddle that saddle sores on tender bottoms are not uncommon. After the long ride down the cliff and the tour through the leper colony, there is, **unfortunately**, one more agony remaining: the long ride back up the mountain to the mule barns. In spite of all the discomforts, **however**, the adventurous souls who take the mule ride put fun before discomfort and never seriously complain.

This paragraph uses a variety of transition words in different places in the sentences. Two of the transition words are placed at the beginning of the sentence. For most writers, the first word position is the easiest to master. But placing the transition in other positions in sentences gives your writing variety and more properly placed emphasis. Closely examine the other three transitions in the paragraph. Because they appear at various places in the sentences, good variety is achieved.

Punctuating transitions is particularly challenging. Anytime a transition appears as the first word in a sentence, it must be followed by a comma. That much is easy. When a transition is used anywhere else in a sentence, it must have punctuation before and after it. Consider the punctuation of the transition word in the following sentences.

> **However**, the tree was infested with aphids.
> The tree, **however**, was infested with aphids.
> The tree was, **however**, infested with aphids.
> The tree was infested, **however**, with aphids.
> The tree was infested with aphids, **however**.

Since transitions are adverbs, they can be correctly placed almost anywhere in a sentence to achieve the desired effect. The important thing to remember is that the punctuation of these sentences is very different from the punctuation of conjunctive adverbs in compound sentences. Conjunctive adverbs must be preceded by a semicolon and followed by a comma unless the conjunctive adverb is in the middle of the second independent clause, as in the third example below. Compare the following sentences.

Transition: The firemen, **in fact**, did not get a raise.

Conjunctive adverb: The firemen did not get a raise; **in fact**, they were asked to work longer hours for the same pay.

Conjunctive adverb: The firemen did not get a raise; they were, **in fact**, asked to work longer hours for the same pay.

The first example requires a comma before and after the transition. By contrast, the second example requires a semicolon before the conjunctive adverb because it separates two complete sentences. (A semicolon can only be placed between two complete sentences.) In the third example, the phrase *in fact* serves as a conjunctive adverb. The two sentences are still joined with a semicolon, and the conjunctive adverb is preceded and followed by a comma.

Exercise 3.6

Identify and correctly punctuate the eight transitions and conjunctive adverbs in the following paragraph.

The most obvious of all problems that face working students is of course the lack of sufficient study time. For instance if students averaged six hours at work, four hours at school, and the usual eight hours of sleep, there would be only six hours remaining for homework. Out of that six hours however all necessary functions such as traveling to work and school, preparing and eating meals, and cleaning living quarters and clothes would have to be done. When the time required for these functions is subtracted from that six hours of study time, very little time remains for actual studying. Indeed this dilemma of not having enough hours in the day frequently plagues those students who hold jobs as a result they often wonder if they can continue to hold up under the strain. Confronted with this problem on a daily basis however successful working students eventually learn unique methods of time management. Procrastination and the like are eliminated as new, faster methods of solving problems are developed. Nevertheless only small amounts of time are available thus many students sacrifice the luxury of social interaction and become educational hermits.

Check your answer with the Answer Key.

Exercise 3.7

Write each sentence called for, using the word given. Be sure to correctly punctuate your sentences.

1. compound sentence (use *however* as a conjunctive adverb)

   _____

   _____

   _____

2. simple sentence (use *in other words* as a transition at the beginning)

   _____

   _____

   _____

3. simple sentence (use *therefore* as a transition between the subject and verb)

   _____

   _____

   _____

4. complex sentence (use *in fact* as a transition at the beginning)

   _____

   _____

   _____

5. compound sentence (use *also* as a conjunctive adverb)

   _____

   _____

   _____

6. compound sentence (use *unfortunately* as a transition between the subject and verb of one clause)

   _____

   _____

   _____

Have your work checked by your instructor or a tutor.

PARALLELISM

As you learn to use more carefully developed and varied sentences, you will find that writing becomes less difficult. You must, however, avoid errors that come with more sophisticated writing. For instance, parallel construction in your sentences can easily become a problem as you write sentences using a pair or a series. Parallel construction refers to writing your sentences in such a way that *all similar parts agree*. This type of construction is used to make transitions clear and to make the thoughts in sentences connect smoothly.

> **Not parallel:** I want a job as **a computer operator, a marine biologist,** or **running my own business.**
>
> **Parallel:** I want a job **operating a computer, working as a marine biologist,** or **running my own business.**
>
> **or**
>
> **Parallel:** I want a job as **a computer operator, a marine biologist,** or **a self-employed businessman.**

Although you will normally find more than one way of correcting each sentence structure problem, one method of correcting faulty parallelism will usually produce a better sounding sentence than all others.

Essentially, all errors in parallelism involve the same problem. Because they appear in different places from sentence to sentence, however, they can be very difficult to see. The following are the most commonly encountered types of faulty parallel construction; some possible methods for correcting each are suggested.

Parallelism in Pairs

Although a sentence with noun or verb pairs should be the easiest to write, some writers have endless problems making pairs parallel. Whenever joining two words together with a conjunction like *and*, both parts of the pair must agree in form. For example, if you place an *-ing* word before the conjunction, you must also place one after it. Examine the faulty parallel construction in the following sentences and study the revisions.

> **Not parallel:** She enjoyed **painting** and **the river** most of all.
>
> **Parallel:** She enjoyed **painting** and **sitting** by the river most of all.
>
> **Not parallel:** The dog liked **to jump** on people and **running** in the park.
>
> **Parallel:** The dog liked **jumping** on people and **running** in the park.
>
> **or**
>
> **Parallel:** The dog liked **to jump** on people and **to run** in the park.
>
> **Not parallel: Filling** orders and **to ship** them each day are her responsibilities.
>
> **Parallel: Filling** orders and **shipping** them each day are her responsibilities.

Parallelism in a Series

When you use a series of subjects, verbs, or other sentence parts, you should make them all parallel in form. The following sentences use a series of three subjects. Notice how the sentence is improved when all three subjects are made parallel in form.

> **Not parallel: Driving** all night, **stopping** only for fuel, and **to haul** large loads are the goals of many truckers.
>
> **Parallel: Driving** all night, **stopping** only for fuel, and **hauling** large loads are the goals of many truckers.
>
> **or**
>
> **Parallel: To drive** all night, **to stop** only for fuel, and **to haul** large loads are the goals of many truckers.

To overcome problems in a series, merely ignore the rest of the sentence until you identify the series and make the items parallel. Underlining the parts of the series as you examine your rough draft is a good technique.

In addition to the subject series, verb series are commonly used. The majority of parallel construction problems will involve the second or last verb in the series rather than the first one because the first verb is close to the subject and thus easy to identify when faulty. In a series of verbs, all the verbs must be in the same tense. In the following sentence, the verb series is made parallel by putting all three verbs in the past tense.

> **Not parallel:** The painter **slipped** off the scaffold, **fell** into the bushes below, and **breaking** his arm.
>
> **Parallel:** The painter **slipped** off the scaffold, **fell** into the bushes below, and **broke** his arm.

Again, underlining the verbs in a series can help you identify any faulty parallelism and correct it.

Parallelism in Phrases

Many times you will use a series of phrases in the sentences you write. If one phrase is incomplete or different from the others, the entire series will appear awkward.

> **Not parallel:** She evaluated people she met **on their speech, on their shoe shines, their cars,** and **on their friends.**
>
> **Parallel:** She evaluated people she met **on** their speech, **on** their shoe shines, **on** their cars, and **on** their friends.
>
> **Not parallel: By insulting close friends, by giving new acquaintances the cold shoulder,** and **ignoring invitations to parties,** some people become social hermits.
>
> **Parallel: By** insulting close friends, **by** giving new acquaintances the cold shoulder, and **by** ignoring invitations to parties, some people become social hermits.

Parallelism in Coordinators

Using proper parallelism in pairs, as discussed at the beginning of this section, is important. It is also important to use the appropriate pairs of coordinators to avoid confusing your reader. The most common of these coordinator pairs are *either. . .or, neither. . .nor, not. . .but, not only. . .but also*. A sentence that omits part of the coordinator pair will almost certainly be weaker than the sentence with both parts.

> **Weak:** Joe's actions suggest that he is careless **or** stupid.
> **Stronger:** Joe's actions suggest that he is **either** careless **or** stupid.
> **Weak:** She finds her job **not only** unrewarding **but** unchallenging.
> **Stronger:** She finds her job **not only** unrewarding **but also** unchallenging.

The coordinator pair must also be placed properly in the sentence. If you put the first part of the pair in the wrong place, you will often completely change the meaning of the sentence. Whenever possible, you should place the first half of the coordinator after the sentence's subject and verb.

> **Weak: Either** the compressor has a broken crankshaft **or** a broken piston.
> **Stronger:** The compressor has **either** a broken crankshaft **or** a broken piston.
> **Weak:** That company **not only** sells computers **but also** fax machines.
> **Stronger:** That company sells **not only** computers **but also** fax machines.
> **Weak:** The house was **not** attractive because of its unique architecture, **but** because of its perfectly trimmed yard.
> **Stronger:** The house was attractive **not** because of its unique architecture, **but** because of its perfectly trimmed yard.

If you place the first coordinator too early in the sentence, you will confuse the reader. The coordinators should be placed just before the items you are to compare or contrast.

The objective with all writing, of course, is to be consistent whenever possible. Consistency will allow you to avoid problems with parallelism. Just as you wouldn't design a car with three black doors and one red door because they would create a peculiar contrast, so you shouldn't use dissimilar sentence parts.

Exercise 3.8

Revise the faulty parallel construction in the following sentences.

1. The instructor told the students that their grades would be based on attendance, on homework, attitude, and on test scores.

_____

_____

_____

2. Underwater photography means buying good equipment, having patience, and knowledge of light refraction.

_____

_____

_____

3. The doctor neither understood the patient nor the disease.

_____

_____

_____

4. Walking through old castles, talking with people, and to eat in pubs makes a visit to England a memorable experience.

_____

_____

_____

5. Until the plans are complete, until the bids are in, and the weather has improved, construction cannot begin.

_____

_____

_____

6. Maria dislikes being late and long meetings.

_____

_____

7. Swimming not only is good exercise but also a clean hobby.

_____

_____

8. By using a helicopter in their logging operation, the Siller Company avoids destroying young trees and creation of erosion-causing skid trails.

_____

_____

_____

_____

9. The objectives of writing are to be brief, to communicate clearly, and creating sentences that will not offend your reader.

_____

_____

_____

10. Ms. Conrad told me to take the blueprints to the job site and that I should hurry back.

_____

_____

_____

Check your answers with the Answer Key.

Exercise 3.9

Write the sentences required, being careful to use correct parallel constructions.

1. A sentence using *either...or*

_____

_____

2. A sentence using *not only...but also*

_____

_____

3. A sentence using a series of phrases beginning with *by*

_____

_____

_____

4. A sentence using a series of phrases beginning with *for*

_____

_____

_____

5. A sentence using a series of *-ing* words [driving, stopping,...] as the subject

_____

_____

_____

6. A sentence using a pair joined by *and*

_____

_____

Have your work checked by your instructor or a tutor.

VERBALS

Improving sentences is a matter of knowing how to correct a faulty sentence, how to punctuate sentences correctly, and how to use transitions. All of that is important. Equally important, however, is knowing how to avoid wordiness. Wordiness, an error that seriously damages too much professional writing, often results when a writer communicates the desired message in two sentences when one would do. The solution to this weakness is to combine ideas in sentences. You have already learned some techniques for combining ideas in sentences—appositives, compound sentences, and complex sentences.

Another excellent technique for combining ideas is to use verbal phrases. Commonly called verbals, *verbal phrases* are those phrases which begin with an *-ed* or *-ing* verb. The verbs used to begin verbals are the same as those used with auxiliary verbs.

-ing verb with auxiliary: She **was helping** with the inventory.

-ing verbal phrase: Helping with the inventory, Mary worked overtime every night last week.

Verbal phrases can be used at the beginning of a sentence, between the subject and verb, or at the end of the sentence. Consider the verbals (in bold type) in the following sentences.

> The children, **waiting for the school bus**, began throwing snowballs.
>
> **Connecting the jumper cables**, the mechanic started the car.
>
> The nurse walked through the ward, **checking every patient's chart.**
>
> **Shocked by the kitchen's condition**, the new cook quit.
>
> The money bag, **dropped by a careless employee**, was lying in the middle of the road.

These example sentences, containing at least two ideas each, all use typical verbals. In addition to eliminating wordiness, verbals can make your writing more sophisticated. Consider, too, the variety you achieve by using verbals occasionally.

It is easy to create sentences using verbals. Anytime you have two or three very closely related ideas about a single subject, you can use a verbal to join them.

> The tractor was plowing the orange grove. It became hopelessly stuck in the mud.

Using a verbal, these two sentences become

> **Plowing the orange grove**, the tractor became hopelessly stuck in the mud.
>   **or**
> The tractor, **plowing the orange grove**, became hopelessly stuck in the mud.

> The warehouse is considered unsafe. It has been abandoned by Lancaster Pool Supply.

Using a verbal, these two sentences become

> **Considered unsafe**, the warehouse has been abandoned by Lancaster Pool Supply.
>   **or**
> The warehouse, **considered unsafe**, has been abandoned by Lancaster Pool Supply.

Although these sentences were correct when written as two simple sentences, they offer more variety and demonstrate more writing skill when combined into a single sentence.

You can also use -*ing* verbs as the subjects of sentences, as shown in the following sentences.

> **Running down the stairs** is a good way to break your neck.
>
> **Singing** makes some people happy.

Although the idea that a verb can be used as the subject of a sentence might be confusing at first, -*ing* verbs can function like nouns. Since nouns serve as subjects, -*ing* verbs may also be used as subjects. Such verbs cannot, however, stand alone as main verbs in clauses. You can't say, for instance, "Henry *running* down the stairs." You could say, "Henry *is running* down the stairs," but in such a case you are using the *-ing* verb with the helping verb *is*. The rule is that *-ing* verbs can never stand alone as verbs but may stand alone as subjects or modifiers. The following examples show the various uses of the *-ing* verb.

> **-ing verbal: Singing for his customers,** the waiter earned huge tips.
>
> **-ing verb as subject: Singing** makes some people happy.
>
> **-ing verb as modifier:** The **singing** waiter was always popular.

Exercise 3.10

Combine the following pairs into single sentences using *-ing* or *-ed* verbals.

1. The electrician received a tremendous electrical shock. He fell off the ladder. (*-ing* verbal at beginning of sentence)

   _____

   _____

2. The plan was rejected by the planning commission. It will be resubmitted next week. (*-ed* verbal at beginning of sentence)

   _____

   _____

3. He knew the answer to every question the MC asked. Henry Gordon made winning the prize look easy. (*-ing* verbal at beginning of sentence)

   _____

   _____

4. Farmers in the area have abandoned their farms. They were ruined by high interest rates and low crop prices. (*-ed* verbal at beginning of sentence)

   _____

   _____

   _____

5. John was inspired by Mel's example. John completed the report in record time. (*-ed* verbal between subject and verb)

   _____

   _____

   _____

Check your answers with the Answer Key.

Exercise 3.11

Write sentences using the -*ed* or -*ing* verbal called for.

1. -*ing* verbal at the beginning

_____

_____

2. -*ing* verbal at the end

_____

_____

3. -*ed* verbal between the subject and verb

_____

_____

4. -*ing* verbal between the subject and verb

_____

_____

5. -*ed* verbal at the beginning

_____

_____

Have your work checked by your instructor or a tutor.

SUBJECT-VERB AGREEMENT

An *agreement* error merely means that the subject and verb of a sentence do not refer to the same number of people or things. You should always use a singular verb with a singular subject and a plural verb with a plural subject. Making the subject and verb agree is easy when you write a simple sentence and the subject and verb appear close together. The following examples would rarely cause you any difficulty.

> **Singular:** The **heat exchanger has** a crack in it.
>
> **Plural:** The **heat exchangers have** cracks in them.

When a *compound verb* is used, it is slightly more difficult to make the subject and verb agree. But you should not have difficulty if you consciously search for a second verb. In the following examples, notice how it becomes increasingly difficult to identify the second verb as additional words separate the two verbs.

> The **nurseryman watered** and **pruned** the bushes.

The **nurseryman watered** the bushes beside the house and **pruned** those beside the driveway.

The **nurseryman watered** the bushes beside the house in the morning and **pruned** them in the afternoon.

Sentences with compound verbs are very common in our speech, so it is logical for you to use them when writing. To avoid agreement problems in such sentences, remember to check for a second verb following a conjunction. The following examples show an error of this type and how to cure it.

Incorrect: She once **sold** houses to out-of-town buyers but now **manage** rental properties.

The verb **manage** must agree with its subject **she.**

Correct: She once **sold** houses to out-of-town buyers but now **manages** rental properties.

A *compound subject* can also cause agreement problems. You will rarely have a problem when the subjects appear together.

Tractors and **cows were** all he cared about.

Tracey and **Lori agree** to work in the harvest.

As with the compound verb, the more words that appear between the two subjects, the more difficult it is to achieve proper agreement.

The **boy** with the curly blond hair and the **cocker spaniel play** together every day.

But the most troublesome compound subject situation arises when the pairs *neither. . . nor* and *either. . . or* are used to join two subjects. In a sentence using either of these pairs, the verb is always singular when the subjects are *both* singular.

Neither **Jack** nor **Jennifer wants** the governor to be reelected.

Either the **singer** or the **conductor has** the music.

The verb is always plural when the subjects are *both* plural.

Neither the **Republicans** nor the **Democrats want** the governor to be reelected.

Either the **sopranos** or the **altos have** the melody.

Problems can arise, however, when one of the subjects is singular and one is plural. In this case, you make the verb agree with the subject closer to the verb. When the subject closer to the verb is plural, the verb must be plural. But if the subject closer to the verb is singular, the verb must be singular.

Neither **Jack** nor the **ladies want** the governor to be reelected.

Either the **singers** or the **conductor has** the music.

In the first example, the second subject *ladies* is plural; therefore, a plural verb *want* must be used. In the second example, the second subject *conductor* is singular, so the verb *has* must be used.

In addition to these common agreement problems, a number of special situations can create agreement problems.

1. **Singular indefinite pronouns** cause more agreement errors than any of the other problems. The following words are the most common singular indefinite pronouns.

anybody	everybody	no one
anyone	everyone	one
each	neither	somebody
either	nobody	someone

When these words are used at the beginning of a sentence, you must be alert because they usually function as the subject. Since these pronouns are singular, they take singular verbs.

> **Anyone is** eligible to win.
>
> **No one left** the party early.

Frequently, a prepositional phrase appears between the singular indefinite pronoun and the verb, and that causes errors.

> **Each** of the boys **is** eligible to win.
>
> **Neither** of the women **was** at the party.

Even though each of the sentences has a prepositional phrase inserted between the subject and the verb, that phrase does not change the verb. The verb must be singular because the subject of each sentence is a singular indefinite pronoun.

2. **Group nouns** are words that refer to a group of people or things. When they refer to that *group as a whole*, they are considered singular and take a singular verb. When group nouns refer to the *individuals* in the group, they are plural and require plural verbs.

> The **jury has deliberated** for three days. [group action]
>
> The **jury have cast** their ballots. [individual action]

3. **The subject followed by a phrase** beginning with "together with," "as well as," or "in additon to" is normally singular.

> The **fireman**, together with the truck, **was** engulfed by flames.
>
> The **chief**, in additon to the widow, **is crying** openly.

Both example sentences need a singular verb because each sentence is concerned primarily with the first noun, which is the subject. The nouns *truck* and *widow* appear in the above phrases, but they are not the subjects. It is possible, however, for the noun in the phrase to be considered part of the compound subject if it is intended to be read in that way.

> The new **camera, together with the lenses, cost** a staggering amount of money.

Here, the plural verb *cost* is used because the writer intends the subject to be the same as *camera and lenses*, which is plural.

Obviously, it is hard to tell in such a case whether the writer meant the subject to be singular or plural. When you encounter this problem, you can overcome it by using a conjunction to connect the two parts of the compound subject.

> The new **camera and lenses cost** a staggering amount of money.

4. **Quantities** that appear as the subject of a sentence take a single verb whenever that quantity is considered a unit.

> **Twenty dollars is** nothing.
>
> **Sixteen pounds** of walnuts **is** given to each staff member at Christmas.

Although a quantity will usually be singular, you will occasionally write sentences using quantities as individual units. When you want the reader to interpret a group as individual items, you must use a plural verb.

> **Two teaspoons** of salt **are added** to the sauce.
>
> **Six dollar bills are** all I have in the register.

5. **"There is"** and **"there are"** also cause problems because few writers realize that *there* is not a subject. The subject of a sentence that begins with *there* will almost always be found *after* the verb.

> There **is** a **winner**.
>
> There **are rules** that we should all live by.

Exercise 3.12

Underline the subjects once and verbs twice in the following sentences. In the blank on the left, write the word that would be needed to correct the agreement problem in each sentence. Write **C** before any sentences that are correct as they stand.

_____ 1. The engine stalls on cold days but run fine during the summer.

_____ 2. Neither the two orange trees nor the olive tree has ripe fruit.

_____ 3. There is a lounge and a pharmacy on the first floor.

_____ 4. The welder with the scarred face and the secretary goes out on dates regularly.

_____ 5. Each of the telephone operators complain about working over-time.

_____ 6. Either the two newsmen or Jackie know the answer.

_____ 7. The heater and the two air conditioners arrive tomorrow.

_____ 8. Anyone with the answers earn a passing grade.

_____ 9. The orchestra have played its first engagement.

_____ 10. Three-fifths of our supplies were used last month.

_____ 11. Everyone on the committee was present at the meeting.

_____ 12. Kathy's pickup, along with her coat, was stolen.

_____ 13. The mob was fighting among themselves.

_____ 14. Two quarts of hot coffee were all that remained in the giant pot.

_____ 15. Either Sharon or Linda have taken the test.

Check your answers with the Answer Key.

Exercise 3.13

Complete the following sentences, making certain the subjects and verbs agree.

1. Neither Bill nor Eileen_____

_____

2. The foreman and the two drillers _____

_____

3. The roof together with the windows _____

_____

4. None of the football players _____

_____

5. The girl in the red sweater and her friend _____

_____

6. Three dollars _____

_____

7. Either the soldiers or their sergeant _____

_____

Have your work checked by your instructor or a tutor.

AWKWARD

Awkward sentences are among the hardest to identify in your own writing. They are far easier to see in someone else's writing. Any number of things might produce an awkward sentence: an unclear meaning, an incorrectly used word, a word out of place, even an omitted word. Often an instructor will merely mark a sentence "Awk" when it contains a vague reference or a poorly worded message, thereby forcing you to closely reexamine what you have written. By marking a sentence "Awk," your instructor is asking you to look again at the faulty sentence.

If you can easily identify a misplaced word or a confused thought in the awkward sentence, the revision is fast and simple. If the problem is not a single word, however, you should immediately rewrite the entire sentence. Too often writers make the revision of an awkward sentence unnecessarily difficult by refusing to rewrite it. In reality, rewriting is normally the fastest way to correct an "Awk." Consider the following awkward sentences and the suggested revisions.

Awkward: It does seem irrational to deprive a relatively harmless substance from the terminally ill.

Revision: It does seem irrational to deprive the terminally ill of a relatively harmless substance.

Awkward: By pointing to one's faults is one sign of jealousy.

Revision: Repeatedly pointing out another person's faults is one obvious sign of jealousy.

The person reading the two original sentences would be confused by the illogical constructions. When you revise awkward sentences, you should begin by deciding what the basic message should have been. As in the second example, the revision might require many additional words.

Exercise 3.14

The following sentences were taken from a student paper about eagles. Revise each so that the message is clear.

1. Poisons were used to kill other birds of prey, thus killed the eagle.

   _____

   _____

2. Today, the eagle faces the same problem of survival, if not more than years ago when the settlers arrived.

   _____

   _____

   _____

3. Sheepmen hire planes to shoot eagles out of the sky.

   _____

   _____

Check your answers with Answer Key.

PRONOUN AGREEMENT

Pronoun agreement errors occur when a pronoun refers to a different number of people or things than its antecedent.

> **Incorrect:** This article tells a **beginning jogger** everything **they** need to know.

This example contains a pronoun, *they*, which refers to more than one jogger; but its antecedent, *beginning jogger*, refers to a single jogger. To correct this type of error, you can change either the pronoun or the antecedent. Both of the following revised sentences are correct.

> **Correct:** This article tells **beginning joggers** everything **they** need to know.
> **or**
> **Correct:** This article tells a **beginning jogger** everything **he** or **she** needs to know.

Pronouns must also agree with their antecedents when they are in separate sentences.

> **Incorrect:** Jackie's **arm** was badly mangled by the bullet from the attacker's gun. **She** has healed very slowly.

Here, the antecedent of *she* is *arm*, but *she* can only refer to a person.

Correct: Jackie's **arm** was badly mangled by the bullet from the attacker's gun. **It** has healed very slowly.

The pronoun and its antecedent agree because *it* properly refers to *arm*.

Pronouns must also agree in number when the antecedent is an indefinite pronoun that functions as the subject of the sentence.

> **Singular: Each** of the workers has brought **his** lunch.
>
> **Plural: All** of the drivers have fueled **their** trucks.

Exercise 3.15

Correct the pronoun agreement errors in the following sentences. First circle the error; then write the correct pronoun in the blank. Correct the verb, too, if necessary.

_____ 1. None of the bargaining units negotiated their own contract.

_____ 2. The typical mechanic works on friends' cars during off hours. They have unique skills that are in demand.

_____ 3. Every saleswoman in the department complained that they were not given enough consideration.

_____ 4. The Actors Guild presented their demands to the producers.

_____ 5. Every young person who makes retired people suffer should think of their own future.

_____ 6. Cashiers in the department store come in contact with many different types of people; therefore, one must be polite and courteous at all times.

Check your answers with the Answer Key.

SHIFTS IN PERSON OR TENSE

Shifting a person or tense is a sure way to confuse the reader. A *shift in person* is a change from the person in which you begin writing a paragraph to another person.

> **An employee** who works hard every hour on the job will undoubtedly be considered for promotion one day. Such **a worker's** habits will attract the employer's attention. **You** would do well, therefore, to be serious about working on every job.

The first two sentences in the example are written in *third person*, but the last sentence is in *second person*. To be consistent, you will need to change that third sentence to make it agree with the third person. The following revised example illustrates one possible method of revision.

An employee who works hard every hour on the job will undoubtedly be considered for promotion one day. Such **a worker's** habits will attract the employer's attention. **Anyone** wanting to advance, therefore, should be serious about working on every job.

When you correct a shift in person, you will often change the wording of an entire sentence or two to achieve smoothness, as in the revised example. When you realize that you have made an error by shifting person, you may discover that you began the paragraph in the wrong person and have to go back to revise the beginning. The important consideration is consistency.

Consistency of verb tense is also important in writing. If you move from present tense to past or future tense, your reader will not be able to follow your thinking.

As a child, Karintha's life **was planned** by the old and young men in her community. Old men **rode** her hobbyhorse upon their knees, hoping she would remember them when she grew up. Young men **danced** with her at frolics when they should have been dancing with girls their own ages. This **is leading** to no good for Karintha. The men **are** only **thinking** of their own desires.

Look closely at the verbs in this five-sentence paragraph. Notice that all verbs in the first three sentences are in *past tense.* To correct the error, you must change the last two sentences to past tense or the first three to present tense.

Exercise 3.16

Correct the shift problems in the following student paragraphs. Convert the first paragraph into past tense and the second one into present tense. Remove all shifting of person as you work. Submit your final copy on notebook paper. Your work must be neatly written in ink or typewritten.

1. The article in question was about flight attendants who were striving for a new image. It is a special report that describes the typical sex exploitation you find in the airline business. The authors said that the skies are not so friendly because people thought of them as sex symbols. They want you to view attendants as professionals in the future.

2. No matter what it is, if you can buy it, you can also find out how good it is, or if something else is better. Many buyers work for private research groups, and testing things is their job. This expert testing can be a big help to you or anyone else who wanted to buy something. Reports of tests done by these experts are published in magazines and in special customer guides. You'll find them in your library and on newsstands. The two best known monthly consumer magazines are *Consumer Reports* and *Consumer's Research Magazine.* There's no reason for anyone to buy "blind." There was much expert help written every year.

4

Punctuation

No highway engineer would consider a new road complete until all lines had been painted and all signs installed. Without these guides, roadways would be chaotic. At intersections, drivers would not know when to start or stop; as a result, confusion would take over. There would be many accidents and much frustration. Drivers would be miserable every time they had to travel on such a road.

The same confusion and frustration occur every time a person has to read unpunctuated writing. Without signs to warn of a pause, a stop, or a change in direction, the reader must guess what the writer has in mind. In such a situation, mistakes are inevitable. The placement of a single comma can completely change the meaning of a sentence. Properly used, a mark of punctuation will make your writing a pleasure to read. Improperly used, punctuation will make your writing almost impossible to read. Fortunately, punctuating effectively is no more complicated than following a set of rules for using each type of punctuation.

RULES FOR THE COMMA

Rule 1—Items in a series are separated by commas. When you are describing someone or something, you will often use three or more words that are equal in importance.

She was **dirty**, **tired**, and **hungry**.

Because the three words used to describe the person are equal, commas are used to separate them. The basic rule for punctuating items in a series is to use one comma less than the number of items in the series. Because the example contains three items, it should have two commas. Many people consider the comma appearing just before the conjunction to be optional in a series. That comma is, in fact, technically unnecessary in the example because it is a short, simple sentence. However, in a more complicated series the "series" comma is necessary for clarity. For that reason, you should become accustomed to using it in all series.

A series may appear in many different places in the sentence. Consider the following possibilities.

A series of subjects:

The **heat**, the **dryness**, and the **sand** make walking in a desert very difficult.
Carol, **Marg**, and **Flo** suffered terrible losses last month.
Running the copy machine, **distributing the mail**, and **answering the telephone** are Mary's duties each morning.

A series of verbs:

He **raked** the leaves, **cleaned** the fountain, and **mowed** the lawn.
The dog **yelped**, **fell** down, **got** up, and **ran** after being hit by the car.

A series of objects:

We gave him **gardening gloves**, **shears**, and **three rose bushes** from the nursery.
The car needed new **tires**, a **tune-up**, and a **muffler**.

A series of modifiers (may be only two items):

The **tired**, **dirty**, and **frightened** miners finally reached the surface.
The people of the area are **friendly**, **industrious**, and **interesting**.
The **cold**, **clear** water was perfect for drinking.

A series of phrases:

The speeding car went **down the road**, **around the corner**, and **out of sight**.
The clothes were scattered **over the dresser**, **on the floor**, and **under the bed**.

A series of clauses:

He cleaned his gun, **he sharpened his knife**, and **he bought new ammunition** before hunting season opened.

Note: Do *not* place a comma between the series and the remainder of the sentence.

Exercise 4.1

Correctly punctuate each of the series in the following sentences.

1. The basketball fans were clapping shouting and cheering.
2. Carla John Ellen and Ray flew to Denver attended the seminar and returned home in one day.
3. Playing in the band singing in the choir and writing music take up all Justin's spare time.
4. While driving through Arizona, they ate ribs they toured a cactus garden and they visited an Indian reservation.
5. A regular jack-of-all-trades, he built his own house repaired his own car and grew his own vegetables.
6. The new delivery van has tinted windows air conditioning an automatic transmission and carpeting.

Check your answers with the Answer Key.

Rule 1 Continued

As you can see, there are many ways a series can be used in a sentence. There are, however, two instances when you will not use commas in a series.

(1) Do *not* use commas when the items in a series are all separated by conjunctions.

> The dog **barked** and **barked** and **barked** until the neighbors complained.
> When the winter finally arrived, it **snowed** and **snowed** and **snowed**.

Such a series would be used when you wish to create emphasis.

(2) Do *not* use commas if there are only two items joined by a conjunction.

> The book was **tattered** and **torn**.

Exercise 4.2

Correctly punctuate each of the series in the following sentences. Write **C** in front of any sentence that is already punctuated correctly.

1. On his day off the overworked repairman sleeps and sleeps and sleeps.
2. The foamy dirty frigid water poured over the spillway and into the river.
3. They're waiting for a calm sunny day before they start painting.
4. An eager courteous salesperson will invariably sell more than one who is pushy or overbearing or threatening.
5. On Jason's desk were three pens a stack of paper and a dictionary, but he continued to work at the efficient computer.
6. Before April 15, he organized his records he reviewed his expenditures and he visited his accountant.

Check your answers with the Answer Key.

Rule 2—Transitions and interrupters are used to connect an idea used in one sentence or paragraph to an idea in the following sentence or paragraph. Commonly called "bridges," these words and phrases help the reader follow your thinking from one sentence or paragraph to the next. Although they are easy to use, you must remember that transitions and interrupters only serve as bridges when they are punctuated properly.

Transitional words or phrases at the beginning of sentences are usually followed by commas.

> **However,** the audience didn't think the jokes were funny. [transitional word]

> **As a matter of fact,** only the comedian's wife laughed. [transitional phrase]

There are many standard transitional words and phrases. Only the most common transitions are listed here.

also,	for instance,	moreover,
as a matter of fact,	furthermore,	nevertheless,
consequently,	however,	therefore,
for example,	in addition,	though,

Interrupters, which are merely transitions that appear in the middle of a sentence, are always preceded and followed by commas.

> The hardware business, **however,** did not challenge him.
>
> His hobby, **therefore,** received more and more of his time.

Often interrupters are most effective if they are placed between the subject and verb. In some instances, though, you may find it more effective to place the interrupters elsewhere in your sentence. Only by trying them in various places in the sentence will you be able to discover the best location.

> The children, **however,** did not know right from wrong.
>
> The children did not, **however,** know right from wrong.
>
> The children did not know, **however,** right from wrong.
>
> The children did not know right from wrong, **however.**

The correct placement of interrupters depends on the intended meaning. However, the punctuation always remains the same; a comma is used before and after the interrupter (even in the case of the last example, where a comma is used before and a period after).

Exercise 4.3

Correctly punctuate the following sentences.

1. We will therefore hold another meeting next week.
2. The sales staff did reach their goal however.
3. Unfortunately the tournament was cancelled due to rain.
4. Nevertheless the gardeners continued to overwater.
5. That lawsuit for instance was settled out of court.

Check your answers with the Answer Key.

Exercise 4.4

Place commas wherever necessary in the following paragraph. Note that some items require you to practice Rule 1, the punctuation of a series. Other items require you to use Rule 2 for punctuating transitions and interrupters. Not all sentences in the paragraph will need additional punctuation.

John Larry and Pete had talked about their camping trip for months. In fact all their friends were tired of hearing about their plans to go swimming to catch fish and to take long hikes. The three did not take the time however to make a list of what to take or to plan their meals. As a result they arrived at the campground with a large tent three sleeping bags ten cans of vegetables and a bottle of hot spicy barbecue sauce. Stakes for the tent matches a frying pan and meat had all been left behind. Fortunately the men were able to solve the problem when Pete drove to a nearby store for supplies John made tent stakes out of kindling and Larry borrowed a frying pan from some nearby campers. The trip would have been a great success, but that night it rained and rained and rained. Therefore the river rose the tent leaked and the hiking trails were washed out. The three wet unhappy campers decided to go home early the next day.

Check your answers with the Answer Key.

Rule 3—Appositives are normally punctuated in the same way as interrupters, with a comma before and either a comma or a period after.

Sam Powell, **a realtor,** helped them find the ranch.

Norman Schwarzkopf, **the Gulf War general,** has now retired.

Skin Diver, **a magazine popular with divers,** encourages safety.

Notice that each of these sentences would make perfect sense without the appositive. Because most appositives only offer extra comments about the noun they follow, they are considered *nonessential.* By placing commas before and after the appositives, you indicate to your reader that the phrase is nonessential.

But in some instances, your appositives will be *essential.* That is, without the appositive, the meaning of the sentence would be different. When you use an appositive that is essential, do *not* set it off with commas.

The magazine **Yachting** is one of the finest publications for sailors.

The huge lineman **Davidson** cultivated a ferocious look designed to intimidate his opponents.

She really likes her friend **Lee.**

Exercise 4.5

Correctly punctuate the appositives in the following sentences. Write **C** if the punctuation is already correct.

1. The restaurant Jake's Place is a popular hangout for college students.
2. The writer John Steinbeck lived in California.
3. The tools belonging to the plumber Martin Sachs were stolen.
4. Many fans still visit the home of the singer Elvis Presley.
5. The movie *Gone with the Wind* has been seen by millions.
6. His cousin Anita has taken a position with an electronics firm.

Exercise 4.6

Use appositives to combine the sentences below. Punctuate them correctly.

Example: Joyce Martin planted annuals in the border. She is the gardener.
Joyce Martin, the gardener, planted annuals in the border.

1. They vacationed in Hawaii. It is the Aloha State.

   _____

   _____

2. Kevin and Cory are graduates of the local university. They are my nephews.

   _____

   _____

3. Hanging in baskets in the shade were her favorite flowers. She liked begonias and fuchsia.

   _____

   _____

4. The new paint made the office seem darker. It was an unusual shade of green.

   _____

   _____

Exercise 4.7

Correctly punctuate the appositives in the following sentences. Write **C** if the punctuation is already correct.

1. The new supervisor Janet Henderson changed their assigned duties.
2. The deadline for the order April 30 is quickly approaching.
3. Copies of the painting *Water Lilies* can be found in many poster shops.
4. For lunch he ordered trout his favorite fish.
5. The lawyer Sam Silva will represent the company.

Check your answers with the Answer Key.

Rule 4—Independent clauses may be joined with a comma and a conjunction (*and, or, but, for, yet*). The most common error when joining two independent clauses is omitting either the comma or the conjunction. Both the comma and the conjunction *must* be included to avoid punctuation errors.

> The giant octopus crawled upon the anchor, **and** no one wanted to be the one to make it get off.
>
> Butch and Marietta dove in together, **but** they went different directions after they were underwater.

The two example sentences above are compound sentences, of course, because they are made up of two simple sentences that have been properly connected. But this creates confusion for some beginning writers who cannot distinguish between compound sentences and simple sentences with compound verbs or compound subjects.

> The plywood **might get** wet and **delaminate**. [Simple sentence with compound verb]
>
> The **truck** with the camper shell and the brown **car** both need a tune-up. [Simple sentence with compound subject]

These two example sentences need no comma before the conjunction because they are simple sentences. To know whether you need to place a comma before the conjunction, you need to be certain you are joining two complete sentences. Simply make sure you can identify a complete sentence before the conjunction and another complete sentence after the conjunction. If you apply this test to your sentences when you use a conjunction, you will rarely have trouble with commas in compound sentences.

Exercise 4.8

Punctuate the following sentences. Rules 1-4 are covered by this exercise. Write **C** before any sentence that is already punctuated correctly.

1. The ship was heading for the dock but the fog rolled in.
2. The sailors were eager to go ashore and their families were waiting impatiently.
3. They went sledding in the morning and skiing in the afternoon.
4. Home ownership requires one to paint to care for a yard and to make repairs.
5. Therefore the Silvas put their house up for sale and waited for someone to buy it.
6. All the real estate agents liked the house and were eager to sell it.
7. John Hansen Phillip Andrews and Susan Alvarez brought prospective buyers to see it.
8. One couple walked into the living room saw the large back yard and rushed out the front door.
9. An agent wanted to buy the house herself but she decided it was too large.
10. Furthermore she did not like yard work.
11. One agent Evelyn Morgan was certain the house would sell quickly.
12. She showed the home to the Petersons, who had looked and looked and looked for a place that would suit them.
13. They liked the house immediately because of its neat uncluttered appearance.
14. They also appreciated the obvious care the owners gave to the hardwood floors to the yard and to the appliances.
15. The Petersons therefore decided to buy the house.
16. They were concerned that they would not qualify for a loan however.
17. John Matthews the loan officer told them the loan would be approved.
18. The Silvas sellers of the house were as happy as the buyers.
19. They packed their belongings and moved out quickly.
20. The Petersons now have a new home and the Silvas live in a townhouse.

Check your answers with the Answer Key.

Rule 5—Punctuating introductory material requires you to know the various types of structures commonly used at the beginning of sentences.

Introductory words: In addition to the transitions presented in Rule 2, you will occasionally use other introductory words to add emphasis to your writing. The most common of these words are *yes, no, oh, well, true,* and *granted*. Using a comma after an introductory word signals your reader to pause briefly after reading the word, thereby placing emphasis on that word.

Yes, you will have to take a test.

No, you can't go on to the next chapter yet.

Oh, I don't know about that.

Well, the game was not very exciting.

True, the teams both have enough experience.

Granted, weather can dampen a ball player's enthusiasm.

Each example uses a comma after the introductory word to create a pause.

Short introductory phrases: In short introductory phrases where a pause is desirable for emphasis, a comma may also be used.

> **In short,** he acts like an absolute beginner. [Emphasis helps strengthen the point being made]
>
> **On Monday,** you had better be on time. [Emphasis increases power of the threat]

Usually, however, a single short prepositional phrase at the beginning of a sentence is not followed by a comma. Most prepositional phrases should be blended into the sentence smoothly.

> **On Monday** I will meet you outside of the office.
>
> **On the wall** he wrote the phone number.
>
> **Under the bed** she found her son's shoes and socks.

All of these introductory phrases sound better without being set off by commas because no emphasis is intended.

Long introductory phrases: Longer introductory prepositional phrases are set off by commas to avoid confusion. Any time you use two or more prepositional phrases at the beginning of the sentence, you should place a comma after the last one.

> **On the floor by the bed,** they found the cigarette butt that started the fire.
>
> **With her heart in her throat,** the swimmer watched the shark.

Introductory dependent clauses: Always place a comma after an introductory dependent clause.

> **After we had been jogging for twenty minutes,** we were too tired to eat.
>
> **When the job was done,** the field crew drove happily back to the office.

Introductory verbals: Many introductory verbals must also be set off with commas. A *verbal* is a verb form used as a modifier or as a noun. If the introductory verbal is a *modifier*, place a comma after the verbal.

> **Running along the beach,** the joggers got sand in their shoes. [modifies joggers]
>
> **To work for a large corporation,** one must be willing to accept impersonality. [modifies one]

If the verbal functions as a *noun*, do not use a comma. In the following example, the verbal is the subject of the sentence, so it cannot be separated by a comma.

> **Working toward a goal** kept her interested.

To punctuate a sentence using an introductory verbal, check to see if a comma is required by covering up the verbal. If you still have a complete sentence after the verbal is covered, a comma is needed. By contrast, if only part of a sentence remains when the verbal is covered, no comma is needed.

> **No comma needed: Filling out the accident form** was a terrible experience.
>
> **Comma needed: Filling out the accident form,** Jamie felt terrible.

Exercise 4.9

Correctly punctuate the following sentences. Write **C** before any sentence that is already punctuated correctly.

1. Preparing for the harvest the sugar cane workers spent long hours in the fields.
2. For weeks before they burned the fields the workers did not water the cane.
3. When the leaves had been burned off the stalks the cane was ready to be harvested.
4. On Friday the field crews always sang and laughed as they worked.
5. In town on weekends the field crews forgot about the dirty jobs in the cane fields.
6. To enjoy life fully the field crews got up early and stayed up late.
7. True not all of the workers enjoyed the weekends but they all were glad to quit on Friday night.
8. Although cane was once harvested with a cane knife it is harvested today with machinery.
9. Tractors clamshells and diesel trucks have replaced the large crews and horse-drawn wagons.
10. Escaping from work in a cane field is still not possible however.

Check your answers with the Answer Key.

Exercise 4.10

Write and correctly punctuate the sentences indicated.

1. Compound sentence with conjunction

_____

_____

_____

2. Complex sentence using introductory dependent clause

_____

_____

_____

3. Sentence using introductory verbal as a modifier

_____

_____

_____

4. Simple sentence using two or more introductory prepositional phrases

_____

_____

_____

5. Simple sentence with introductory transition

_____

_____

_____

6. Simple sentence with interrupter

_____

_____

_____

7. Simple sentence beginning with short prepositional phrase emphasized

_____

_____

_____

8. Simple sentence with compound verb

_____

_____

_____

9. Sentence with a series of independent clauses

_____

_____

_____

Have your work checked by your instructor or a tutor.

Rule 6—Nonessential dependent clauses that interrupt must also be set off with commas. Essential dependent clauses, however, are never set off with commas. The only way to know whether or not to place commas around an interrupting dependent clause is to determine if it is essential to the meaning of the sentence. If the clause is needed to help the reader make sense of the sentence, no commas are used. If the clause is not needed, commas are placed around it.

As a rule, dependent clauses that interrupt are set off with commas because they are usually not essential.

> The forest fire, **after it burned for five days,** was finally brought under control.

> The car, **although it served us well for years,** caused us endless problems this year.

Both of these sentences make perfect sense without the dependent clauses, so commas are needed.

Although most interrupting dependent clauses are set off with commas, a special group of dependent clauses are frequently essential and, therefore, are not set off by commas. These clauses begin with the relative pronouns you memorized in Chapter 2—*that, what, which, who, whoever, whom.*

> A house **that is built of logs** is hard to heat.

You will usually put commas around an interrupting dependent clause that refers to a subject who is identified by name.

Nonessential:	Mary, **who has no formal medical training,** knows much about medicine. [Mary is identified by name, so the clause is nonessential.]
Essential:	The salesman **who has no previous experience with the product** is not very effective. [The dependent clause is needed to help identify the salesman.]
Nonessential:	The punctuation rules, **which most people forget if they don't use them,** work very well.
Essential:	The airplane **that we took to Chicago** was new.

When a dependent clause comes *after* the independent clause, you will rarely place a comma before it unless you wish to emphasize the dependent clause.

No comma:	He was disappointed **because he didn't get the job.**
No comma:	The security guard closed the gate **after the trucks entered.**
Comma:	He wants to finish the project, **although the weather will make that difficult.**
Comma:	She plans to apply for the job, **even though she is not qualified.**

When a comma is placed before a dependent clause, the reader is signaled to pause before reading that clause, thereby giving emphasis to it.

Interrrupting nonessential phrases are punctuated exactly like nonessential clauses.

Nonessential:	Romans, **having to fight terrible traffic,** are frequently late for appointments. [The phrase here is not necessary to the meaning of the sentence, so commas are used.]
Essential:	The townspeople **having to fight terrible traffic** are frequently late for appointments. [This phrase is essential because it explains which townspeople.]

Exercise 4.11

Correctly punctuate the following sentences. Write **C** before any sentence that is already punctuated correctly.

1. The girl who loved to read wished she could live in the library.
2. Patty's cat running from the dog was glad to see the tree.
3. Bill Morgan who has long worked for the district office has been appointed principal of the high school.
4. The team that wins the game Saturday goes to the Rose Bowl.
5. Bob who was sweeping the walk cut his hand on a rose bush.
6. In spite of public concern the slaughter of harp seals continues.
7. Having confidence in the "healers" many people travel to the Philippine Islands to have their ills cured.
8. Because the "healers" have no formal medical schooling other people insist that allowing them to operate is foolish.
9. Nevertheless the "healers" do have a remarkable following although they do not advertise their skills.
10. After work the drilling crew took a shower and ate before going home.
11. On the way to the theater the couple was involved in an accident but they both escaped injury.
12. As a matter of fact the accident was more exciting than the movie.
13. The movie however was far less expensive than the accident.
14. Bertha Morrison who loved hang gliding quit the sport after her friend's injury.
15. The trip to the snow and the party at the lodge made the vacation worthwhile.

Check your answers with the Answer Key.

Rule 7—Names used with direct quotations are set off with commas or periods. If the name interrupts a sentence, commas are placed before and after the name. If the name comes at the end of a sentence, however, a comma is placed before and a period after the name.

"I refuse," **said Henry,** "to give up the throne."
"I refuse to love an outlaw," **said Marian.** "I am above that."

When a person is quoted indirectly, that person's exact words are not used. In such a case, the name is not set off with commas.

Manuel said that he would meet you at the theater.

Rule 8—Addresses and dates must include commas. Basically, the rule is to place a comma after each part of the address or date if two or more parts are given.

The meeting took place at **128 Market Street, Denver, Colorado,** the weekend before Easter.

They were married on **October 14, 1969,** in **Minden, Nevada.**

Exercise 4.12

Punctuate the following sentences. Write **C** before any sentence that is already punctuated correctly.

1. "I will send you a check" said Jane "as soon as I can."
2. "I hate working in the movie industry" said Skip "It is too false."
3. Pete said that he would help us move.
4. Our new address will be 1284 North K Street Tacoma Washington.
5. She was born on July 19 1946 in Carmel California.
6. The teacher told the class "Anyone can take good pictures."
7. She added that she would teach them the principles of photography.
8. "You must also realize" she said "that even expert photographers occasionally take bad pictures."

Check your answers with the Answer Key.

COMMA FAULTS

Comma faults may be either fused sentences (often called run-ons) or comma splices. *Fused sentences* are two or more sentences joined without any punctuation. *Comma splices* are two or more sentences that are joined with only a comma.

Fused sentence: The sun went down the farmers continued working.

Comma splice: The sun went down, the farmers continued working.

Comma splices and fused sentences are easily corrected by using any of the following methods:

1. Correct by using a *comma* and a *conjunction*:

   The sun went down, **but** the farmers continued working.

2. Correct by using a *semicolon*:

   The sun went down; the farmers continued working.

3. Correct by using a *semicolon* and a *conjunctive adverb*:

   The sun went down; **however,** the farmers continued working.

4. Correct by using *two separate sentences*:

The sun went down. **The** farmers continued working.

5. Correct by using a *dependent clause* to create a complex sentence:

After the sun went down, the farmers continued working.

Each of the five methods shown for correcting comma faults is acceptable. One will often be more effective than all others in a particular situation. When you are revising your sentences, consider each method before deciding which is best. Be cautious not to divide long sentences into two short sentences too often because you may create a choppy paragraph.

Exercise 4.13

Correct the following comma faults by using the method indicated.

1. Gary fell from the top of the eighty-foot tower he survived. (Use a comma and a conjunction.)

_____

_____

2. The wind was very strong it broke a limb off the tree. (Use a dependent clause to form a complex sentence.)

_____

_____

3. The report indicated that older women are the best employees they seldom miss a day's work. (Use a semicolon.)

_____

_____

_____

4. The snow was packed and powdery the skiers moved rapidly. (Use a semicolon and a conjunctive adverb.)

_____

_____

5. At dusk all the people in the campground took binoculars and walked to the meadow they wanted to see the elk that came out to feed on the grass. (Use two complete sentences.)

_____

_____

_____

_____

6. The beautiful beach is less than a mile from their house Marian and Jerry swim almost every day. (Use a dependent clause to form a complex sentence.)

_____

_____

_____

7. The gopher came up out of the hole without looking the cat was waiting. (Use a semicolon.)

_____

_____

8. The elephant seals are only slightly bothered by humans they must know that the law protects them. (Use two complete sentences.)

_____

_____

_____

9. Stacy killed a deer the first day she went hunting she has never gone hunting since. (Use a semicolon.)

_____

_____

_____

10. The shortage of petroleum is threatening our way of life but optional power sources can be found. (Use a conjunctive adverb to replace the conjunction.)

_____

_____

_____

Have your work checked by your instructor or a tutor.

RULES FOR THE SEMICOLON

Semicolons are usually used in only two instances: (1) *to join two independent clauses into a compound sentence* and (2) *to separate phrases that already contain commas*. When joining two independent clauses, the semicolon takes the place of a comma and a conjunction.

> The plywood is rough on both sides; it was never intended for use in cabinet making.

You will sometimes use a conjunctive adverb to emphasize the relationship between two clauses in a compound sentence. The conjunctive adverb is preceded by a semicolon and followed by a comma.

> Money was no object to her; **therefore,** she spent it all on clothes.
>
> He loved to go jogging; **however,** he seldom had enough time to jog regularly.

The semicolon is also used *to separate phrases that already contain commas*. This is helpful in sentences that contain many groups, such as names and titles.

> The company's top executives are John Stevens, president; Susan Klein, director; Wayne Fong, senior vice president; and Robert Osborne, vice president.

To avoid confusion in such a sentence, the semicolons are used instead of commas to separate the groups in series. Without the semicolon after *president*, it would be hard to be sure who was president, John Stevens or Susan Klein.

Semicolons are an effective mark of punctuation if they are not overused. Therefore, you should use them sparingly.

RULES FOR THE COLON

Because the names are so similar, many people confuse the colon and semicolon, but such a confusion is easily overcome. Basically, the semicolon is almost always used between two complete sentences, and the colon is rarely used between two complete sentences. The colon is most effectively used between a complete sentence and *a series*. It tells the reader to note what follows. It often comes after "as follows" and "the following."

> The sumptuous meal we had on the island of Burano included the following: wine, soup, fish, squid, octopus, pasta, and pastry.
>
> She had only two problems in life: men and money.

The colon here emphasizes the series. It stops your reader for a second, thus emphasizing the point that follows. The colon can be used to achieve some measure of humor, as in the last example above.

The colon is also used to introduce *a quote or a formal question*.

> King Richard brought tears to his friends' eyes when he said: "I was not made a horse; And yet I bear a burden like an ass..."
>
> The real question we must ask is: "Are men only animals?"

A colon should **not** be used after "such as," "namely," or "for example." In addition, a colon never follows a verb.

> Classes such as literature, history, and philosophy require a great deal of reading.
>
> The members staff are John Simmons, Dorothy Gould, and Melissa Delgado.

Like the semicolon, the colon is most effective when used sparingly.

Exercise 4.14

Write the sentences called for and correctly punctuate them.

1. Compound sentence using semicolon but no conjunctive adverb

2. Compound sentence using conjunctive adverb

3. Sentence using semicolons to separate a series of names and titles

4. Sentence using colon

5. Sentence using city and state

_____

_____

_____

6. Sentence using date and year

_____

_____

_____

7. Sentence using indirect quote

_____

_____

_____

8. Sentence using direct quote

_____

_____

_____

9. Sentence using interrupting nonessential dependent clause

_____

_____

_____

10. Sentence using interrupting essential dependent clause

_____

_____

_____

Have your work checked by your instructor or a tutor.

RULES FOR THE DASH

Dashes are used to create emphasis and to indicate a dramatic pause. You should avoid overusing the dash, of course. But using an occasional dash creates excellent variety in your writing.

> The three big "S" sports in my life—sailing, scuba, and skiing—all involve the outdoors.
>
> The couple discovered—much too late to stop construction of their new swimming pool—that a new family member was on the way.

When typing, use two hyphens to indicate a dash. In handwriting, the dash is as long as the width of two letters.

RULES FOR THE HYPHEN

The hyphen, which is really a short dash, is most commonly used in two ways: in compound words and in numbers.

> Their two **mothers-in-law** came to visit on the same day.
>
> Harriet once lived on **Seventy-seventh** Street.
>
> **Two-thirds** of the audience left before the play was over.

You will also use the hyphen with certain prefixes.

> The remark was attributed to **ex-President** Nixon.
>
> She is very good at **self-criticism**.

Since most prefixes do not use a hyphen, you should check a dictionary to see if a hyphen is used in a word containing a prefix.

RULES FOR THE APOSTROPHE

The apostrophe is used to show *possession*. For most singular nouns you only have to add an apostrophe and an **s**.

> Jan's chair is adjustable. [The chair belongs to Jan.]
>
> He will use his assistant's computer. [The computer belongs to his assistant.]

There are, however, some problems associated with using the apostrophe. The first problem is plurals. When a plural noun ends with **s**, add only an apostrophe after the **s**.

> The secretaries' chairs are adjustable. [The chairs belong to more than one secretary.]

When a plural noun does not end with **s**, add an apostrophe and an **s**.

> The children's rooms were freshly painted. [The rooms belong to the children.]

The word *children* is plural without an **s**, so an apostrophe precedes the **s**. Other everyday words that are plural without an **s** are *women* and *men*.

Another problem in using the apostrophe occurs when you have to use one with a singular noun ending in **s**. If an apostrophe **s** results in a word that is difficult to pronounce, it is acceptable to use the apostrophe only.

> the class's assignment
>
> Lois's paper
>
> the Jones's house
>
> Yeats' poetry
>
> Jesus' followers
>
> for goodness' sake

The apostrophe also helps you express the *plurals of numbers, letters,* and *words*.

> The gambler hoped to see no **7's** or **11's**.
>
> Her speech was good except that she used too many **and's** and **uh's**.

In this case, the apostrophe does not show ownership; it merely indicates that the word is plural.

The other use of the apostrophe is *contractions*. Whenever you join two words into one, leaving part of one out as you do so, you will use an apostrophe to indicate the omitted portion. The most common contractions are the following:

do + not = don't   let + us = let's
will + not = won't   we + have = we've
has + not = hasn't   they + had = they'd
have + not = haven't   you + are = you're
were + not = weren't   I + am = I'm
we + are = we're   it + is = it's

Be particularly careful with *it's*, which is used only when you intend to say *it is* in a sentence. Do not confuse *it's* with *its*. *Its* is a possessive pronoun that shows ownership.

> **It's** almost summer.
>
> The horse licked **its** injured ankle.

Any time you use *it's* or *its* in a sentence, check to see if you can substitute *it is* for the contraction. If you can, you must use *it's* (with the apostrophe).

RULES FOR QUOTATION MARKS

Use quotation marks to show the words of another person.

Shakespeare said, "All the world's a stage...."

Using quotation marks in your writing is extremely important because you must not take credit for someone else's words. Using someone else's writing as if it were your own is a form of stealing, and it is subject to severe criticism. To indicate that a group of words, a sentence, or a paragraph has been borrowed from someone else, simply place the borrowed part in quotation marks like the quote in the example. The dots at the end of that quote indicate that it is only part of the sentence written by Shakespeare. (The dots are called ellipses.)

The **titles** of songs, poems, magazine articles, essays, and short stories are also placed within quotation marks.

Crane's short story **"Maggie"** was considered scandalous.
Elvis Presley's **"Blue Suede Shoes"** was an instant success.

However, the names of books, magazines, newspapers, and movies are underlined (or italicized in printed material).

Exercise 4.15

Punctuate the following sentences. Place **C** before any sentences that are already punctuated correctly.

1. Send the letter to James Haskell at 2301 Sixty fifth Street Portland Oregon.
2. Many people hope the movie *Citizen Kane* is never colorized.
3. Although Hals request for supplies was submitted some time ago he hasnt received anything yet.
4. They were talking about their friends as they always did when Jerry walked in.
5. Only three things mattered to him money position and power.
6. Californias grain is harvested in May by contrast Northern Irelands grain is harvested in August.
7. Awards for outstanding service were presented to John Bishop engineer Phil Gonzales technician and Suzanne Friedman mechanic.
8. You have put too many ls in *parallel* and not enough ss in *misspell*.
9. They gave him wouldnt you know it a watch for his retirement.
10. The plane was late it had run into strong headwinds.
11. They drove to the active volcano although it was raining too hard to see anything.
12. After they ate lunch the surveyors climbed back up the steep muddy hillside.
13. Running for office was a waste of money.

14. The mechanics who join the union must pay monthly union dues of twenty two dollars.

15. Bill will drop by at noon tomorrow and he will have a contract with him.

16. He and Craig will design and build the gazebo for the back yard.

17. Liz Castro who usually takes notes was unable to attend the meeting.

18. Marge McElroy the companys attorney just returned from a vacation in the tropics.

19. You wouldnt believe she said how beautiful the weather was.

20. Yes I know its important to arrive on time.

21. At that instant in time her actions were controlled by just two things fear and hunger.

22. At first we thought the airplane might crash.

23. The students cars were parked behind the buses.

Check your answers with the Answer Key.

FRAGMENTS

A *fragment* is part of a sentence punctuated as a complete sentence. If you remember that a sentence is a group of words with a subject, a verb, and a complete thought, you will quickly identify fragments. If any of these three qualities is missing in something you have written, you have created a fragment rather than a sentence.

Most fragments result from one of three problems: (1) omitting the subject; (2) omitting the verb; or (3) punctuating a dependent clause as a complete sentence.

Omission of the subject often occurs when you are writing a number of sentences about the same person, object, or event, and you neglect to remind the reader of the subject being discussed. A typical phrase fragment follows:

The forest fire destroyed everything in its path. Burned two buildings, many trees, some brush, and a tractor.

The second part of the example is a phrase fragment because it does not have a subject. To correct such a fragment, place a subject before the verb, as in the following example.

The forest fire destroyed everything in its path. *It* burned two buildings, many trees, some brush, and a tractor.

Omission of the verb is a more common cause of fragments than the omission of the subject. Often beginning writers omit a portion of the verb, leaving only an incomplete predicate. The following examples are phrase fragments because all or part of the verb is missing.

The woman who lived in the old Victorian house.

Reggie making a commercial at the time.

To correct the problem of an omitted verb or verb part, you need to isolate the subject and verb. In the first example sentence, the subject is obviously *woman*, but the verb is completely missing. You could correct the problem in either of the following ways:

> The **woman lived** in the old Victorian house. [omit the relative pronoun *who*]
>
> The **woman** who lived in the old Victorian house **was** sick. [place a verb and any other necessary words after the dependent clause]

Occasionally, a part of the verb will be omitted as in the fragment, "Reggie making a commercial at the time." This type of error occurs when an *-ing* verb is left to stand alone. Such *-ing* words function as verbs only if they are accompanied by helping verbs.

> **Reggie was making** a commercial at the time.

Omission of both the subject and the verb results in a phrase fragment, one that completely interrupts the flow of ideas in your paragraph.

> The little girl was hiding from the dog. Behind the door.

In this example, the phrase fragment "behind the door" is separated from the clause it was intended to modify. Typically, a phrase fragment should be attached to the independent clause immediately before it. However, if you were to join the clause and phrase in the example, the resulting sentence would be unlikely to make sense.

> The little girl was hiding from the dog behind the door.

In this sentence it is unclear whether the girl or the dog is behind the door. The only practical method of solving the problem is to move one of the phrases or to develop the second phrase into a sentence.

> The little girl was hiding behind the door from the dog.
>
> The little girl was hiding from the dog. She was behind the door.

Dependent clause fragments are different from the other fragments because they always have subjects and verbs. The problem is that these fragments also contain a signal word at the beginning of the clause.

> **Because** senior **citizens have had** a variety of experiences.
>
> **Although** many **people consider** them inferior.

The two clause fragments above would be complete sentences without the signal words attached to the beginning. To correct clause fragments, you can use any of a number of procedures.

1. The simplest technique is to omit the signal word. The first example would then read:

> Senior **citizens have had** a wide variety of experiences.

Although this technique sounds attractive at the outset, it has the serious drawback of producing another short simple sentence.

2. The more practical technique of correcting a clause fragment is to attach it to an independent clause that comes before or after the fragment.

> Even though senior citizens have had a wide variety of experiences, many people still consider them inferior.

Connecting the clause fragment to the following independent clause, as in the example, provides more power, smoothness, and variety. A dependent clause fragment could be just as easily connected to an independent clause that precedes it.

> Senior citizens are often the most valuable employees on the job, although many people consider them inferior.

Exercise 4.16

Identify the following fragments as phrase or clause fragments by writing **P** or **C** in the blanks.

_____ 1. While on the beach in the tropics.

_____ 2. On top of the desk beside the phone.

_____ 3. Until we received the message.

_____ 4. When Rick gave Ann the news.

_____ 5. After she came to work Tuesday morning.

_____ 6. The girl who won the beauty contest.

_____ 7. Smiled sweetly at the judges throughout the competition.

_____ 8. With a strong back and a weak mind.

_____ 9. Beside the road where it fell.

_____ 10. Because the electricians were on vacation.

Check your answers with the Answer Key.

Exercise 4.17

The following items contain clause and phrase fragments. Underline the fragments; then rewrite the items to eliminate the fragments.

1. They knew they would get to see all the family members again. In the course of the party.

_____

_____

_____

2. Without the help of the Department of Agriculture advisor. The farmer would have made an expensive mistake.

_____

_____

_____

3. In too many modern houses, fireplaces are designed for looks. They only produce a minimum of heat. No matter how much wood is burned.

_____

_____

_____

_____

4. Because of faulty wiring. The building caught fire and burned to the ground.

_____

_____

_____

5. The wind howled across the valley for days. Blew leaves and dust into houses and barns everywhere. It also destroyed crops.

_____

_____

_____

_____

6. The roads were impassable. Although road crews worked day and night for a week.

_____

_____

_____

7. The plant polluting the river. As a result, the company will be fined by the government.

_____

_____

_____

8. The ranch had many fruit trees. Such as pear, apple, peach, prune, and quince.

_____

_____

_____

9. In the September issue of the magazine *Machines.* You advertised an interesting machine. It was called a Dynamite Z2800.

_____

_____

_____

_____

10. John who has worked as a service manager for one of the largest auto dealers in the area. Everyone is impressed with his work.

_____

_____

_____

_____

Check your answers with the Answer Key.

PART TWO

Short Forms:
Everyday Communication on the Job

In most organizations, every employee must be able to write. Although entry-level personnel may not be expected to write much, you can be certain that everyone else will. Even managers find themselves writing more and more every day. At one time many managers had secretaries who did most of their writing for them. The computer age changed that. Now managers and other supervisory personnel frequently find their secretaries have been replaced by computer terminals. As an employee in a large company, you will often be known to most other employees through the memos and reports you write. Your coworkers may form an opinion of your abilities before meeting you in person because they will have already read your memos, letters, and reports.

But your writing will also be important before you ever go to work for a company. The fact is that many companies will carefully assess your writing ability when you apply for a job. More and more companies are asking prospective employees to include a resume with their job application forms. The content of that resume may not be as important as the fact that you know how to write one. Most employers believe that clear writing shows orderly thinking. What this means, of course, is that you will need to write a resume even to get an interview for the job you want.

This section of the book covers four separate writing situations you may face in the business world. Writing the memorandum is an everyday on-the-job task for most employees in the business world. Therefore, you will almost certainly need memo writing skills. As a general rule, you will write memorandums only to people within your own company. The second type of writing you will practice in this section is the business letter. The business letter is used for all communication with people outside your company. The third type of writing is the resume, which you will use to get a job. The final type of writing in this unit is the standardized form, which you will encounter frequently no matter where you are employed.

Regardless of the type of writing you do on the job, you can be certain you will encounter the most significant recent innovation: the computer. In most work environments, all other writing instruments are becoming as uncommon as a horse and buggy on a freeway. You may not have keyboard skills now or your keyboard skills may be minimal, but the reality is that you will be a much more valuable employee if you have keyboard skills and at least a basic working knowledge of computers. What you should do is obvious: you should enroll in at least an introductory computer course. Since you obviously want to improve yourself professionally, you should enroll in such a course next semester if you haven't already done so.

5

Writing Memorandums

When you have completed this chapter, you will be able to—

1. Describe the advantages of writing memorandums.
2. Follow standard conventions in writing memos.
3. Write formal, informal, and very informal memos when appropriate.
4. Write memo headings that are complete and consistent.
5. Use memos to confirm telephone conversations.
6. Stop yourself from sending a memo written in anger.
7. Avoid writing memos that are not useful.

The memorandum is the most common form of written communication in the business world today. Commonly referred to as a memo, the memorandum is a vital part of the office of every business, school, government, and service organization. Often written somewhat hastily and about a matter requiring the immediate attention of the person to whom it is addressed, the memo is the accepted method of getting ideas and requests from one person to another within a business.

WHEN TO WRITE A MEMO

The basic philosophy behind the memo is simple: people forget. If you call someone on the telephone and communicate a message, your message may be forgotten, especially if the person to whom you speak is busy at the time. For this reason, many companies automatically distribute memo pads to all employees. The heading of one common memo pad shown here clearly expresses the attitude of employers regarding messages:

INTEROFFICE MEMORANDUM
Don't Say It, Write It!

There are many situations that call for writing a memo; the following are some of the most common.

• Use a memo to confirm a telephone call. The telephone remains important in the business world; don't ever doubt that. There is no better way to get information instantly. If you need a fact, a name, or a time when someone can meet with other staff members, you should use the telephone; but avoid using the telephone to communicate important ideas to your fellow workers. If you must use the phone to ask someone to do something or to supply you with something other than a simple fact or name, follow up your call with a memo and keep a copy.

Using the memo in this way cuts down on communication mistakes. If you call someone with a request and that person is busy, you would almost certainly not know it, but that person might forget your request a short time later. If you follow up your call with a memo, however, you can effectively remind the person to whom you spoke of your request. By keeping a copy of your memo, you can easily document your telephone conversation in case of a subsequent conflict about your original request. For just such reasons as these, many large corporations recommend that you immediately confirm a telephone conversation about an important matter by writing a memo. If there has been any misunderstanding, the person you spoke with will instantly recognize the problem when your memo arrives and will call to clear up the confusion.

• A second reason to use the memo is to save time. When you must ask everyone in your organization or department to attend a meeting, you will find it far faster to write one memo and send a copy to everyone you want to attend than to try to call them all. Your memo will also save time because you won't have to answer a dozen "When/where was the meeting?" questions if the people who are to attend have a memo on their desks to remind them of the time and location.

• A third important advantage you gain by writing a memo is self-protection. When mistakes are made, some people will deny the responsibility for their mistakes. In such a case, you may be accused of saying or ordering something you didn't. If you used the telephone to communicate a message, you have no proof of what you said. However, a memo provides written proof of what you said, provided you remembered to keep your copy of the memo. Both the sender and the receiver should keep a copy of a memo until the issue is closed.

• A fourth good reason to write memorandums is to put your "best foot forward" in a verbal sense. When you speak, you speak quickly and without carefully considering what you say. But when you write a memo, you have time to go back and edit your message before you send it out. This is important in the corporate world because people in the company will often make lasting judgments about your ability based on what you first say or write. Even a few minutes spent organizing your message will make it sound far more convincing and make you appear a more informed and valuable employee.

WHEN NOT TO WRITE A MEMO

Employees in large companies often complain that their world seems buried in paper. Don't add to the problem. If you don't need to write a memo, use the telephone or speak with the other people individually. Consider the following instances when writing a memo is not a good idea.

• When the information you want can be gotten in a conversation with a single individual, you should probably avoid writing a memo. For instance, if you need to find out more about some new product the company is going to carry, you can save time for yourself and others by going directly to the person or persons who have the information you need. You will not only save the time it would take you to write a memo, but you will also save the time you would have to wait to get an answer.

• Write a memo only when you don't have more pressing work to get done. Many employees find that writing memos earns them a degree of recognition they could not achieve any other way, so they repeatedly send out memos about insignificant issues. Granted, they are able to keep their names before everyone else in the company by doing so, but they also run the risk of making every other employee groan at the sight of another of their memos. Eventually, the recognition they once earned by writing memos turns to a negative force.

Avoid flooding your workpeople with unnecessary memos by evaluating each one before it is written. Many short, insignificant memos can be combined into a single, larger publication. One employee made himself popular among fellow employees recently when he began publishing a department newsletter that appeared only once a month; his newsletter included items of interest that didn't require anyone's immediate attention. Bill asked other members of the department to forward general interest items to him by the end of the fourth week of the month. Items such as the projects committees were working on, the new equipment being purchased that would benefit everyone, the special achievements and awards of employees, and minutes of meetings were all presented in the newsletter. Everyone appreciated Bill's creativeness, of course. But more important to everyone in the department was that their desks were no longer flooded with dozens of short memos every day. Perhaps the most significant advantage was that everyone took time out each month to read the newsletter, even those who never read their memos normally. And still another advantage of combining memos is that it saves paper, which means that it helps to save our environment.

• Using memos to criticize is a mistake to be avoided. When there is an employee or group of employees doing something that is detrimental to the company, don't write a memo about it. One supervisor lost the respect of many employees when she wrote a memo criticizing department members for using the copy machine excessively. In fact, the supervisor knew who the offending employees were but didn't want to confront them directly. And the employees not guilty knew who the offending employees were, too. When the memo appeared, it immediately became obvious that the supervisor was unwilling to confront the problem directly. As a result of the memo, the copy machine use increased because the employees who had previously controlled their machine usage felt that their supervisor suspected them. As an act of rebellion, they almost all increased their usage, and the supervisor had a much larger problem than she had set out to solve.

All problems between management and employees or between one employee and another employee must be solved directly, not by a memo. Writing a memo about employee performance is never a good idea, unless the purpose is to document a problem that has previously been discussed with that individual.

• Don't write a memo when you are angry. Even if you are convinced you are correct, never write a memo and mail it before you have had time to cool off and reconsider the issue. Sending someone a written message saying how angry you are will lose you far more friends than it will win, and in the business world you will need all the friends you can get. In the long run telling someone how displeased you are is much better done in person anyway, if you must talk about it. It will be much easier for the person with whom you are displeased to forget about a conversation the two of you had than to forget about an angry memo that sits on the desk and reminds him or her of your anger.

Exercise 5.1

Briefly answer each of the following questions.

1. What is the basic reason for using a memo?

_____

_____

2. What are the four good reasons to write memos on the job?

(1) _____

(2) _____

(3) _____

(4) _____

3. Why would you use a confirming memo when someone calls you?

_____

_____

4. Give three instances when you should not send a memo.

(1) _____

(2) _____

(3) _____

Check your answers with the Answer Key.

WHAT DOES A MEMO LOOK LIKE?

Memos are very different in appearance. Some companies provide employees with standard form memo pads, which are usually printed on a $5\frac{1}{2}'' \times 8\frac{1}{2}''$ inexpensive white or light-colored paper. These vary markedly depending on company policy and needs. When large organizations wish to make it easy to identify the sender's area, they occasionally supply each department with a different color memo paper. In this way the person who receives a memo can instantly identify its source, even if the sender's name is not familiar. But size and color are only two of many variations.

Many companies now use a multiple-copy memo form. This modern form usually consists of three pages of self-carbonizing paper. When the person who originates the communication writes a message, he or she makes three copies automatically. The third copy is detached immediately and filed. The other two copies are sent to the addressee, who responds by writing a return message on the memo and detaching the second copy for his or her files. The remaining copy is returned to the person who originated the memo, to be filed as written proof of the correspondence.

Perhaps even more common in the business community currently is the memo that is generated on the computer at one's desk. Such memos use the same heading as a handwritten memo, and many of them are just as short as any of the hand-written memos. The computer generated memos, however, look much better than the hand-written ones, which means that most employees generally favor them. At first, writing a memo on a computer takes a little longer, but as your keyboard skills and writing skills improve, you will find that writing your memos on a computer is almost as fast as on the memo pad.

You can expect to see all three of these types of memos in the business world. Some professionals, in fact, use all three. They use the memo pad on their desks for their shorter communication needs, use the multiple form memo paper when they need to force a response, and use their computers for longer, more involved memos.

One other type of business communication should be mentioned here. Electronic mail, also known as E-Mail, is frequently used between companies or within a company or business. With E-Mail, an individual composes a message on the computer and posts it electronically to another person or persons. Used within a company, the message can function as a memo, but it can be sent instantaneously, with the possibility of an immediate reply. This type of memo can be stored indefinitely on a floppy disc, or a hard copy can be printed as a permanent record of the communication.

Heading the Memo

The vast majority of memorandum forms begin with a letterhead. Although the word *letterhead* may suggest a company name, address, and telephone number, memo forms are rarely this complete. In fact, on many memo forms nothing more than the word *MEMORANDUM* appears at the top. Such a heading perfectly fits the memo's basic concept of informality. The following are typical memo letterheads.

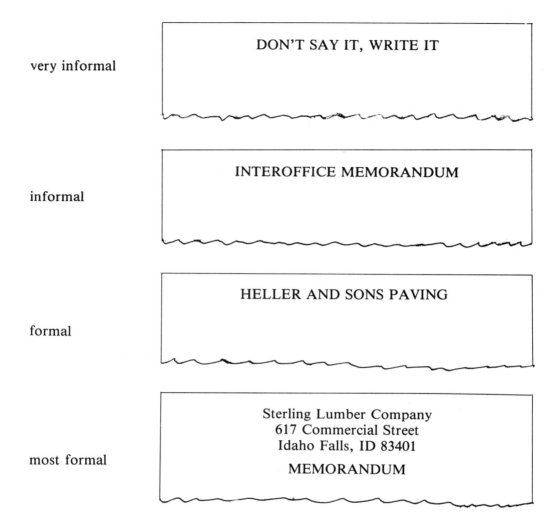

very informal

DON'T SAY IT, WRITE IT

informal

INTEROFFICE MEMORANDUM

formal

HELLER AND SONS PAVING

most formal

Sterling Lumber Company
617 Commercial Street
Idaho Falls, ID 83401

MEMORANDUM

All these types of preprinted letterheads are common in the workplace. Some companies provide employees with paper that can be inserted into computers that has the company logo and the word *Memorandum* preprinted across the top, as in the last example above. In actual practice on the job, many employees omit the letterhead and the word *Memorandum* at the top and begin immediately with the heading so they can save time.

Below the letterhead, the heading of every memo you write will have at least four parts. These parts are often called *lines* because many memo forms include a printed line for you to write information on. The four parts of the heading are usually called the **date line**, the **"to" line**, the **"from" line**, and the **subject line**. The following memo heading shows these parts.

```
+------------------------------------------------------------+
|                    MEMORANDUM                              |
|                                                            |
|                                      Date:                 |
|                                                            |
|   To:                                                      |
|                                                            |
|   From:                                                    |
|                                                            |
|   Subject:                                                 |
+------------------------------------------------------------+
```

Although the order of these lines in a heading will vary from company to company, every heading must have at least these four parts. The following memo heading is another typical arrangement.

```
+------------------------------------------------------------+
|                    MEMORANDUM                              |
|                                                            |
|   Date:                                                    |
|                                                            |
|   To:                                                      |
|                                                            |
|   From:                                                    |
|                                                            |
|   Subject:                                                 |
|                                                            |
+------------------------------------------------------------+
```

The preprinted heading at the top makes it easier to distinguish between the standard heading and what you have inserted on each line. Neither of the heading arrangements above is more correct than the other; company policy determines correctness. In addition to these two, there are many other heading arrangements that you will encounter, all equally correct as long as they include the four basic parts.

The essential four lines in a heading contain the following information:

• The **date line** always includes the day, month, and year. This may be written **6 May 1993** or **May 6, 1993**, depending on company policy; rarely would company policy allow **5/6/93**.

• The **to line** will include the name of the person to whom the memo is being sent. If you are familiar with the person you are sending the memo to, and if the memo is very informal, you MIGHT address it directly to your friend by using only his or her first name. Excessive familiarity, however, is often discouraged in large companies because such ''to'' lines produce poor records. You would probably be wise to ignore this very informal memo completely. The second level of familiarity, normally referred to as informal, addresses the intended receiver with both the first and last names. Since information is more complete in this "to" line, such a memorandum is preferred by most organizations. Even more commonly, you will write a more formal memo, especially if you are writing to a superior or to someone in another department of your company. In such a case you would use not only the addressee's full name but also that person's title. Observe the following examples of "to" lines.

Very informal	To:	Jack
Informal	To:	Jack Williams
Formal	To:	Jack E. Williams, Senior Engineer

Notice that the informal "to" line may use a nickname even though it also uses the person's last name. Do not use **Mr., Mrs., Miss, Ms.,** or any other personal title before the name.

• The **from line** is for your name. As in the "to" line, the form of your name will vary according to the level of formality you want to communicate. The "from" line must, however, be on the same level of formality as the "to" line.

• The **subject line** introduces the subject of the memo. The subject is not elaborated upon at this point; it is merely introduced as in the following examples. As with the "to" and "from" lines, the writer can express varying levels of formality by making the subject more or less complete.

Very informal	Subject:	Feasibility study
Informal	Subject:	Staff meeting, Friday, May 4
Formal	Subject:	Inspection report on Job #28-03

Any of these subject lines would be adequate because each instantly informs the reader of the topic to be discussed in the memo. The last one would be considered the most formal because it contains the most specific details.

Optional Items

• The **reference line** may be used to identify the exact item to be discussed. If the memo you are writing will become part of a permanent file, a reference number will help to ensure the proper filing of your memo. It will also help the recipient of your memo identify the exact job you are discussing.

• **Initials** of the author of a memo may be handwritten at the end of the "from" line to authenticate authorship. Memos are not usually signed at the bottom.

• A **steno line** is used when the author of the memo has someone else type up the final copy. The initials of the author and the person who typed the memo appear at the lower left, two spaces below the last line of the text. These initials are used only if someone other than the author of the memo typed it and are, in fact, rarely encountered.

• **A cc line** will appear two spaces below the initials line if copies are sent to individuals not listed in the "to" line.

Examine the following memo to see what the optional lines would look like in practice.

INTEROFFICE MEMORANDUM

To: Ray Wong   Date: July 12, 1993

From: Bill Harris *BH*   Reference: P.O. #321

Subject: Order from Piedmont Tool Company

I wanted to call this order from Piedmont Tool to your attention. This is the account we spoke of last week that always complains about our slow service.

I knew you would want to follow this one personally. I'll let you know if I hear any more complaints.

BH: jhp

cc: Raymond P. Henry, Manager

Memos that travel up the chain of command to superiors or down to subordinates are said to travel vertically. Those memos sent to coworkers of equal status travel horizontally. This distinction may be important; although you can write informal memos to your peers, you should always write formal memos when they are to travel vertically. It is also customary to use titles when writing to someone in another department if you are writing about a matter of significance. The appropriate level of formality is based on company practice; notice the memos written by other employees, and you will quickly develop a picture of what your memos should look like.

Exercise 5.2

Assume that you are working for a large heating and air conditioning company that has eight mobile crews. As a foreman of Crew #2, you need to write a memo to Richard Pederson, the foreman of Crew #7, about the availability of electrical supplies. Write three headings for that memo, each according to the level of formality requested. Be consistent within each memo.

INTEROFFICE MEMORANDUM

Date: _____

To: _____

From: _____

Subject: _____

very informal

INTEROFFICE MEMORANDUM

Date: _____

To: _____

From: _____

Subject: _____

informal

INTEROFFICE MEMORANDUM

Date: _____

To: _____

From: _____

Subject: _____

---

formal

Have your work checked by your instructor or a tutor.

Body of the Memo

Your goal must be the same in every memo you write: to communicate clearly in the fewest words possible. The first step in communicating clearly is to avoid confusion by making the body of your memo consistent with the heading. If the heading is very informal, the body should also be very informal, as in the following example.

INTEROFFICE MEMORANDUM

Date: August 10, 1993

To: Jack

From: Cindy

Subject: Lunch

Is our luncheon meeting with Mr. Parella still on

for this Friday? Shall we meet at your office and

ride to the restaurant together?

This memo about a business meeting leaves little doubt that Jack and Cindy are well acquainted. In a situation like this, you could use a very informal memo. Notice that the heading and the body are both very casual. In actual practice this memo would only be written if one of the people was normally working in the field and didn't have a mobile telephone. Here the informal tone would be fine, but you will find few situations like this where you can expect to write such a casual memo.

The very informal memo above illustrates another important characteristic of memos: they are written quickly and structured so readers can read them quickly. Even the longer memos that you will normally write will be written without wasting time, and that desire to write quickly will be evident in the structure of every memo. The structure of the memo must be direct. That is, you must present your major point first and give your reasons afterwards. For example, if you were a department supervisor calling a meeting, you would begin the memo by announcing the time, date, and place of the meeting and follow that information with what would be discussed.

Getting Ready to Write

Before you begin writing your memos, you must ask yourself four questions:

1. Why should this memo be written?
2. With whom am I communicating?
3. What does my reader (or readers) need to know?
4. What do I want from my reader?

Asking yourself these questions and writing down the answers to each question is the developmental stage of memo writing. These four questions should become a standard procedure for you to follow as you write memos. As you examine each of these questions carefully, you can see how they will help you develop your message.

• *Why should this memo be written?* This is just another way of forcing yourself to focus on what you want to have someone else do or what you plan to do that other employees must know about. The following are examples of typical answers to this question:

1. Department heads will need to submit their year-end reports early because the company office is going to be closed between December 23 and January 2. I will need the reports by December 15 so I can develop the year-end report for the owners before we shut down on December 23.

2. I want all of the sales staff to attend the weekly meeting next Monday morning. I want all sales personnel to understand that these meetings are important because this is how new sales strategies are developed and how enthusiasm is generated for our products. I also want to make it clear that the owner does not consider these meetings optional.

• *With whom am I communicating?* This question is more complicated than it would at first appear. Simply writing down all department heads or all sales personnel won't help. Think concretely of the people you are writing to before you go any further. If you were going to write to the department managers, for instance, you would find that you were not actually thinking of more than five or six people. If you don't treat them as individuals, you will probably alienate some or all of them. Before you begin writing, therefore, you should write the name of each so you can avoid stereotyping. For example, you will quickly offend the women in your organization if you use the masculine pronoun to refer to all department heads, even though two are women.

You should also be careful to consider how much each of these managers knows about the subject at hand. If you write the memo as if they were all new company employees who knew nothing about company policy, you would be adopting a condescending attitude that would alienate them all. On the other hand, if you assumed they all understood more than they did, you would confuse them all. Only if you consider the people you are about to write to as individuals will you be able to communicate effectively.

At this point you will also become aware of a political problem if you are writing a memo that will move vertically. If you are going to be addressing a superior in the company, you will want to be sure you write a formal memo; if you use an informal tone, you might very well offend. Similarly, if you are writing a memo to employees that you supervise, you should avoid using an informal tone as this will suggest an overly familiar relationship that could work against you.

• *What does my reader need to know?* At this point you list every item you can think of that you might want to cover in your memo. You should list even those items you suspect you won't want to include in your final draft because they will help you remember others. By listing the topics you might want to discuss in your memo, you free your mind up and allow it to explore the possibilities. Also, once you can see the list on paper, you can begin to visualize what your memo is going to look like. Furthermore, this will enable you to look at some of the ideas and put them in a logical sequence.

It is at this point that you will begin to ask yourself which ideas are the most important. These will appear at the beginning of your memo. They will be followed by the second most important ideas and so forth until you get down to the least important.

• *What do I want from my reader or readers?* When you ask this question, you are ready to write the memo. Your answer will probably be evident to you when you consider the list you created in step three. You will simply have to read over the list and state clearly what you expect the reader to do with the information you present. The answer to the question may be as simple as, "All employees must attend the weekly sales meeting on Monday mornings," or a more complicated, multiple-step procedure you want them to follow.

Exercise 5.3

Assume you are going to write a memo to inform the employees in your department about the following problem. You are the department head of a civil engineering division, and you have seventeen employees in your area, eleven men and six women. Those employees include engineers and aides; all must submit written reports which they prepare on computers in the staff workroom when each job is completed.

The problem you must inform your employees about is the temporary closure of the staff workroom, beginning one week from next Monday. You know the employees of the department are not going to be happy about the closure because they are accustomed to working there. However, the company management has decided the workroom must be remodeled because there is asbestos tile on the floor and asbestos insulation wrapped around the heating ducts in the ceiling; both present potential health risks. Also, the furniture is old and in such a poor state of repair that it is an embarrassment to the owners every time a client visits the facility.

The computers from the workroom will be temporarily moved to the lunch room. Although space will be limited and noise will be a factor, the work will be completed in one week so staff members will only be inconvenienced a short time.

The remodeling will result in a much more attractive environment. The asbestos floor will be removed and replaced with carpet. The walls will be repainted and the cabinets newly varnished. The furniture will all be replaced by chairs and tables that are more comfortable and attractive. In short, the workroom will be a room everyone can enjoy.

Complete the following worksheet.

1. Why should this memo be written? _____

_____

_____

2. With whom am I communicating? _____

_____

_____

3. What facts do my readers need to know? _____

_____

_____

4. What do I want from my readers? _____

_____

_____

Have your work checked by your instructor or a tutor.

THE BODY OF THE MEMO

When you are writing on the job, you can expect to use short paragraphs, usually not more than three or four sentences long. Each paragraph should discuss only one idea. Do not indent paragraphs when writing a memo, unless your organization specifically requires that you do. Writing that does not use indented paragraphs is called **full block style**, which is faster to write and has a less formal appearance. The following is a typical informal memo.

INTEROFFICE MEMORANDUM
BLUEWATER YACHTS

Date: September 10, 1993

To: Herb Williamson, Sales Manager

From: Dave Hickman, New Boat Salesman

Subject: Bay Area Fall Boat Show

Due to the complexities of coordinating our program at
the fall boat show, I will leave for Berkeley Thursday
evening. If you need to contact me, I will be staying
at the Marriott Inn, Berkeley, in the evening. During
the day I will be near my mobile phone most of the time.

As I mentioned to you at the sales meeting yesterday,
our booth at the show will include the following at-
tention-getting features.

- Slide presentations by Wayne Carlsen and Harry Hen-
  son, factory representatives for Classic Yachts. We
  have had tremendous interest in their presentations.

- Five boats in the water for public inspection.

- An extensive display of color pictures that show
  our boats under way around the Bay Area.

I will have a complete report covering our success at the
show on your desk by noon Monday.

Notice the spacing in the sample memo from Bluewater Yachts. The heading is double-spaced and is separated from the body by triple-spacing. Here the body is single-spaced because the message is fairly long. However, if the body portion of your memorandum is quite short, you might want to double space to make it appear longer. To separate paragraphs when using block style, skip an extra space. In the preceding memo, which is single-spaced, double-spacing is used to separate paragraphs. Notice also the ''bullets'' in front of the items being presented as features at the show. These bullets are commonly used in memos on the job to make items in a list stand out.

Most memos address only a single subject. But occasionally you will want to give a list of directions or a series of conclusions about the subject in the memo. When you do so, you will normally use an outline or list format. This is especially important when a procedure must be followed, as in the following memo:

INTEROFFICE MEMORANDUM
WHIDBY ISLAND MANAGEMENT CORPORATION

Date: July 1, 1993

To: All Personnel Using Computers in the Workroom

From: Marlene Ortmann, Office Manager

Subject: Proper sequence to follow when turning on computers

With over 65 employees in our office now, the new computers in the workroom have been receiving more use than anyone expected. As many of you have noticed, however, some intermittent problems have kept us from making full use of the computers.

The support staff from Cascade Computers spent part of the day with us yesterday searching for the problem. They found out that we are the problem! We are apparently not following the correct sequence when we turn on the machines at the beginning of each day.

To avoid the problems that we have experienced too often, we will need to be certain to follow these steps in the sequence listed:

1. Before starting up any machines, be sure to load the paper bins on each of the laser printers.

2. Turn on each of the laser printers and check the test copy that is automatically run to be sure the toner cartridge has enough toner. The printed page will have light and dark streaks if it must be replaced.

3. Turn on the computer that is marked SERVER. **Note.** After it is turned on, you must wait at least two minutes for the machine to check all its systems before you go to the next step.

4. Turn on each of the six computers.

5. When each of the computers is on line, open the hard disk and clean off any reports remaining from the previous day.

Please follow these procedures exactly. If these steps are taken out of sequence, the printers will not operate correctly and in some cases the computers will not work.

Exercise 5.4

Write the memo for the outline in Exercise 5.3. Do your work on notebook paper and write the final copy below, carefully handwritten in ink, or do your work on a typewriter or computer.

INTEROFFICE MEMORANDUM

Date: _____

To: _____

From: _____

Subject: _____

_____

_____

_____

_____

_____

_____

_____

_____

_____

_____

_____

_____

_____

_____

_____

_____

_____

Use the following checklist to make sure your memorandum is correctly written before you show it to your instructor or a tutor.

MEMORANDUM WRITING CHECKLIST
1. At least four parts in the heading?
2. Complete date line?
3. Same level of formality in all parts of memo?
4. Reference line needed?
5. Consistent tone used in body?
6. Only one idea in each body paragraph?
7. Paragraphs short?
8. Block style used in paragraphs?
9. Final copy edited?
10. Body paragraphs properly spaced?
11. Spelling checked with dictionary or computer?

Exercise 5.5

Select two topics from the list below and write memos for them. Submit your memos carefully handwritten on notebook paper, or prepare them on a computer or typewriter.

1. You are the supervisor of several clerks at one branch of the city library. There have been complaints from patrons about the improper and sloppy shelving of books. Write a memo to the clerks reminding them of the correct procedures to follow in shelving books. All books to be shelved must be separated according to call number and placed on a cart. Then they must be put on the shelf in the proper numerical order. At the same time, adjacent books on the shelf should be checked to be sure they are also in the correct order. Books must not be put on the shelf upside down. Finally, all books on the shelf should be pulled out to the edge and held upright by the bookends. Once a week all shelves should be dusted. Have your memo typed by the office clerk, Betty Jo Howard.

2. You are one of six department secretaries in an accounting firm. Your boss has asked you to coordinate an advanced training class in word processing for the six of you at the Wilson Office Equipment Company, dealers for the word processors you use. Write a memo to the other department secretaries informing them that they will report to the Wilson Office Equipment Company on a particular day next week from 8 a.m. to 5 p.m. Include the location of the company (make it the same as your work or home), and tell them that they will receive $7.00 for lunch expenses and $.27 cents a mile for travel.

3. As a salesperson for a paper products company, you attended a three-day convention in a nearby city (your choice but name it) two months ago (establish the dates). You turned in all expense receipts the Wednesday following the conference, together with your expense claim voucher, but you have not been paid yet. Write a memo to Chris Mitchell, the clerk in payroll, reminding her of this and asking when you will be reimbursed the $352.50 you spent at the conference.

6

Writing Business Letters

When you have completed this chapter, you will be able to—

1. Distinguish between memorandums and business letters.
2. Use the proper tone in letters.
3. Avoid excessive use of passive voice.
4. Write directly to the reader (using *I* and *you*) to avoid coldness.
5. List the seven standard parts of a business letter.
6. List the five optional parts of a business letter.
7. Use the correct spacing between parts of a business letter.
8. Address the envelope for a letter.
9. Distinguish between full block, modified block, and semi-block formats.
10. Properly plan and set up a business letter.
11. Write and revise a business letter.

As important and effective as memos are for communicating within a company, they are simply too informal for use between companies. Because the writer of a memo deliberately makes the message as brief as possible, the potential for misunderstanding is great unless the subject is very clear to both parties. Business letters can include more complete and detailed information. Letters, therefore, are used for almost all communication with customers, suppliers, and business associates in other companies.

Many people think that all letters are written by secretaries, but that simply is not the case today. In fact, you may be expected to write your own letters as part of your job. The secretary's job, when a secretary is available, is to type what you have written, exactly as you have written it. Some companies, however, only have a *typing pool*—a group of typists who do nothing but type letters for all company personnel. In this case, you will send all messages that you want typed to the typing pool. But typing pools are becoming a part of the business world of the past.

Computers are perhaps the most important development of the twentieth century. They have influenced every aspect of American life. Personal computers are used for entertainment, finances, education, correspondence, and a multitude of other purposes. Computers do many labor-saving chores in retail businesses: billing, inventory, ordering, payroll, and correspondence. It would be difficult to identify any profession unaffected by the computer. It follows, then, that your career in the "real world" will be affected by the computer. You can assume employers and society will expect you to be computer literate; indeed, you should be more than computer literate since that term refers to only a very generalized knowledge of computers. The job with the most potential in the future will require you to tap more than the basic functions of computers.

As a beginning employee with a company, you may be expected to use a computer to write letters. Word processing software is available for virtually every computer. Letters written on computers look better and cost less to write, so you can logically expect your employer to have installed these machines in every office. You will almost certainly get the opportunity to write business letters when you begin with a large company.

This does not mean that you will spend all your time on the job writing letters. Actually, a very small portion of your time will be spent writing. However, the letters you write are extremely important because they are the primary method you have of communciating with many customers and suppliers. The impression your letters create in these people's minds will influence their attitude toward you and your company. If your letter is sloppy and hastily done, the person who receives that letter will get the same impression about your company.

WHAT IS A BUSINESS LETTER?

A business letter and a memo have many of the same features in the heading and body. The major difference between these two common forms of communication is that the letter is more formal in appearance. The heading of a letter provides a complete address for the person to whom you are writing; the body of a letter is much more extensive. As a rule, you will attempt to say everything in a memo in one or two short paragraphs; by contrast, the rule for writing business letters is to write at least two, preferably three or more paragraphs in the body.

A second difference between a memo and a letter is in the level of formality. Informality in a business letter would be offensive to many people. Addressing someone you barely know in another organization by a first name or a nickname would make that person wonder about your motives and sincerity. This difference in formality can also be seen in the physical preparation of the letters you write. Although a memo might be casually written in longhand, a business letter is always carefully typed or printed. The final copy of a letter should be as nearly perfect as you can make it.

Using an Appropriate Tone

The attitude you express toward your subject and audience in anything you write is known as the *tone* of the writing. While the tone of your memos should be casual, the tone of a business letter should be businesslike, yet natural. On the other hand, you must avoid being too cold in your letters. If you are too businesslike and unfriendly, you may create a threatening tone that could make the person who receives your letter angry and difficult to deal with. For some writers, an effective tone comes easily; for others, it must be carefully developed. There are two techniques you can use to make the tone appropriate in your letters.

1. **Avoid passive voice.** One way to avoid being too cold is to avoid the passive voice. Overuse of passive sentences can create a cold, impersonal letter. *Passive* sentences are those in which the subject *receives* the action of the verb. The following are examples of the passive voice:

> **Passive:** The road's condition was studied by the engineers.
>
> It has been recommended by Mr. Price that you make a decision as soon as possible.

Notice how much more positive and direct these passive sentences sound when they are converted to active sentences.

> **Active:** The engineers studied the road's condition.
>
> Mr. Price recommends that you make a decision as soon as possible.

The passive voice creates serious problems for some writers because they overuse it. To convert passive voice to active voice in your writing, decide which noun is doing the action, and make that noun the subject of the sentence.

> **Passive:** The house was being eaten **by termites.**
> **Active:** **Termites** were eating the house.
>
> **Passive:** The Pinto was hit on the left front side **by the Buick.**
> **Active:** **The Buick** hit the Pinto on the left front side.

Use of the passive voice is not necessarily bad; however, overuse creates a feeling of excessive formality and coldness.

2. **Speak directly to your reader.** Another technique writers use to avoid coldness in their letters is to deliberately speak directly to the reader. By using the pronouns *I* and *you*, your writing will sound natural, like a conversation.

> **Don't say:** The **company** wants to help all dissatisfied **customers.**
> **Do say:** **We** want to help **you.**

Exercise 6.1

Answer the following questions as briefly as possible.

1. List three basic differences between memorandums and business letters.

   (1) _____

   (2) _____

   (3) _____

2. What is the difference between the audience for memos and the audience for business letters?

   _____

   _____

3. Define the word *tone* and explain what the proper tone is for most business letters.

   _____

   _____

4. Convert the following sentences from passive to active.

   Passive: Bill was hit by the falling rafter.

   Active: _____

   Passive: The order was taken by me.

   Active: _____

   Passive: The message was read by the speaker.

   Active: _____

   Passive: A new custodian has been hired by our company.

   Active: _____

   Passive: The coffee pot must be unplugged by the person who goes home last.

   Active: _____

   _____

5. Convert the following impersonal sentences into ones that speak directly to the reader.

   Impersonal: The company wants the customer to be satisfied.

   Personal: _____

   _____

Impersonal: Each employee is hereby requested to submit inventory sheets to this office.

Personal: _____

_____

Impersonal: The applicant must forward the completed document to this office within three days.

Personal: _____

_____

_____

Check your answers with the Answer Key.

THE PARTS OF A BUSINESS LETTER

Each letter you write will have at least seven distinct parts, and each part will have a specific location in the letter.

The Seven Essential Parts

1. **The letterhead** will always be professionally printed at the top of the stationery. Normally, it includes your company's name, address, state, ZIP code, and telephone number. If letterhead stationery is not available, you will need to type the information at the top of plain white bond paper. When this information is typed in, it is called a *heading*. Compare the following letterhead to the typed heading.

Letterhead

JAMES

Fred S. James & Co.   230 West Monroe Street, Chicago, Illinois 60606   312 346-3000 Telex 255121

June 11, 1993

Typed Heading

```
                              Fred S. James & Co.
                              230 West Monroe Street
                              Chicago, IL 60606
                              June 11, 1993
```

Note that, with the exception of the telephone and telex numbers, both the preprinted letterhead and the typed heading contain the same information.

The first line of the typed heading must be started one inch below the top of the page. The heading may be placed at the right or left margin, depending on the format you use. (If the heading is at the right margin, try to locate your heading so the longest line ends at the right margin. Normally, this means beginning all lines of the heading approximately in the center of the page.) Do *not* type your own name at the top; only company names are placed there.

2. **The date** is placed two lines below the letterhead if you are using preprinted stationery. If you type the heading on plain paper, the date is the last line of the heading. As the heading example shows, there is no space between the address and the date. The date never contains abbreviations; write out the month and year.

> **Not:**   Sept. 27, 1993
> **Not:**   Sept. 27, '93
> **Not:**   9/27/93
> **Always:**   September 27, 1993 **or** 27 September 1993

3. **The inside address** lists the name and address of the person or organization you are writing to. Unlike almost every other part of the business letter, the inside address does not have a fixed vertical location. If your letter is very short, you should start the inside address as many as eight lines below the date. For a long letter, however, you should start only two lines below the date. In medium length letters you would start the inside address somewhere between two and eight lines below the date, as required to center the letter vertically.

The inside address must be exactly the same as the address on the envelope. It contains the person's name, street address, town, state, and ZIP code. Often it also includes the name of a company and the person's title at that company.

> Ms. Roberta L. Mitchell
> 2617 South Pleasant Street
> Scottsdale, AZ 85251
>
> Roberta L. Mitchell, Editor
> Arizona Parklands Magazine
> 2617 South Pleasant Street
> Scottsdale, AZ 85251

Note that the names of states and personal titles are abbreviated, but everything else is spelled out. Although the personal titles **Ms., Mrs., Miss, Mr.,** or **Dr.** are not always included, it is still correct to place them before a person's name in the inside address. All other titles that come before a person's name must be spelled out.

Professor Richard A. Cross
Reverend Albert C. Evers
Governor June Kennedy
Senator Mary L. White
President Harold Warner

When you are writing to a company, you may not know the person who will read your letter. In this case, address your letter to the company.

The David White Company

Patterson Automotive Company

If you wish to communicate with the person holding a specific position within that company, you can address the letter to the job title.

Personnel Manager
The David White Company

Parts Department Manager
Patterson Automotive Company

Dean of Student Personnel
University of Alabama

Addressing a letter to an unknown person who holds a specific position fails to create the personal connection you should always attempt to achieve. People respond better when addressed personally; it's as simple as that. *Dear Ms. Keller* certainly sounds better than *Dear Personnel Manager.* For this reason, you should only address a letter to a position if you are unable to discover the name of that person. One way to learn the name of the person you want to write to is to call the company. The person who answers the phone will probably be able to give you the desired name or will transfer you to the department in which the person works.

4. **The salutation** is your greeting to the person who receives your letter. It is placed two lines below the inside address. A colon concludes the salutation (except for the most informal greetings, after which a comma may be used).

If you are addressing a known individual, there are many different levels of formality possible.

Sir:
My dear Sir:
Dear Sir:
My dear Professor Cross:
Dear Professor Cross:
My dear Richard:
Dear Dick,

Sir, of course, is very formal and *Dick* very informal; the others range in formality according to their position on the list. Although there may be more than one correct greeting for a given letter, use the most appropriate salutation. For instance, you should avoid the very formal and very informal in most situations. Excessive formality or informality can offend the reader. Normally, when you are addressing a letter to a particular individual, you should also greet that person by name in the salutation. If your letter were addressed to Professor Richard A. Cross, the salutation would be *Dear Professor Cross*, unless you knew him well enough to address him as *Dear Dick*, or unless you wished to be formal and address him as *My dear Professor Cross*.

Notice that the first word in the salutation and the nouns are always capitalized. The other words are never capitalized.

You will have some difficulty choosing a salutation when you write to an unknown person because you cannot know whether the recipient is a man or a woman. It might seem incorrect to use the salutation *Gentlemen* in a letter to the David White Company; however, that is correct usage. In an attempt to avoid use of sexist words, more and more letter writers have adopted other words for the salutation. When the letter will be read by an unknown person, writers are increasingly using one of the following:

> Dear Sir or Madam:
> Ladies and Gentlemen:
> Gentleperson:

5. **The body** of a business letter should begin two lines below the salutation. As you write the body, you should make your paragraphs short and your message perfectly clear. Long paragraphs tend to bore the reader in a letter, and confusing messages make it worthless.

If possible, write your letter so there are at least three paragraphs.

> (1) an **opening paragraph** that gives background information
> (2) a **body paragraph** that gets down to business
> (3) a **concluding paragraph** that sums up your point

Use single-space between lines in the paragraphs and double-space between paragraphs in an average or long letter. If your letter is exceptionally short, use double-space between lines and triple-space between paragraphs.

6. **The complimentary close** is placed two lines below the last line of the body. It should be aligned with the date at the top. Capitalize the first letter of the first word in your close but not the others. Like the salutation, there are various levels of formality; the close should be approximately the same formality as the salutation.

> Very respectfully yours, (very formal)
> Respectfully yours,
> Yours truly,
> Very truly yours,
> Sincerely yours,

    Sincerely,
    Cordially,
    Warmest regards, (very informal)

As you examine the list, observe that it begins with the most formal and works toward the least formal. Your complimentary close should be followed by a comma.

    7. **A signature** must appear below the complimentary close. Your name should be typed four lines below the complimentary close. You should then sign your name neatly between the two.

    Sincerely yours,

    Richard L. Hogue

    Richard L. Hogue
    Director, Marketing Research Division

Note that the title of the person who wrote the letter appears immediately below the typed name. The department or division sometimes appears on the same line.

Exercise 6.2

In the blanks on the left, write the number of lines each item should be placed below the previous item.

```
                              Rockford Public Works Department
                              3213 Taft Street
                              Rockford, IL 61107
```

One 0.   Example   March 10, 1993

_____1.   Joseph L. Adams

_____2.   714 Bedford Lane

           Rockford, IL 61111

_____3.   Dear Mr. Adams:

_____4.   This letter is in response to your telephone
           complaint regarding the overflowing of Pizer Creek in
           your neighborhood during the recent record rainstorm.

_____5.   Your home is located within a portion of the city
           where drainage ditches and creeks are not maintained by
           the Public Works Department. Clearing them has been
           the responsibility, therefore, of the residents in the
           area. To correct this situation, the city is
           considering the formation of a new assessment district,
           Zone 15-D. The formation of this district is dependent
           upon approval by a majority of the property owners in
           the November election.

                We are now preparing to initiate preliminary
           technical aspects of the new district so that this
           issue qualifies for the November 1993 General Election.
           Should Zone 15-D be approved, the average home will be
           assessed approximately $30 per year. This money will
           be used by Public Works to maintain the storm drainage
           system. Older drain lines will be replaced, for
           example, and adequate drainage inlets will be
           installed.

                You will have ample time between now and November
           to discuss and review this matter. If you desire
           additional information, don't hesitate to phone me at
           423-5651.
```

_____6.         Sincerely,

_____7.         James Kirkpatrick
                Administrative Assistant

Check your answers with the Answer Key.
```

Optional Letter Parts

Several additional parts of a business letter are optional. All optional letter parts have a colon separating the heading and the notation.

1. **The attention line** is rarely used. You may occasionally use it when you know only the last name of a person in a company. More commonly, however, you will use the attention line to direct your letter to an unnamed person who performs a certain function. The following are typical attention lines.

> Attention: Credit Manager
> Attention: Personnel Director
> Attention: Sales Manager
> Attention: Loading Dock Supervisor

When you do use an attention line, it should appear two lines below the inside address.

> Kittering Welding Company
> 3180 Airway Avenue
> Costa Mesa, CA 92626
>
> Attention: Sales Manager
>
> Ladies and Gentlemen:

Observe that the correct salutation would not be *Sales Manager* but *Ladies and Gentlemen* because the letter is actually addressed to the Kittering Company.

2. The **subject line** or **reference line** is commonly used by many companies. Insurance companies, for instance, normally use a policy number or claim number in their letters; other companies may use the **Re: line** to refer to a previous letter. This line is commonly placed two lines below the salutation, but be aware that other companies may place it two lines above the salutation.

> Betty L. Winkler
> Myriad Fashions
> 3698 Shaddelee Lane
> Fort Meyers, FL 33907
>
> Dear Ms. Winkler:
>
> Subject: Your letter of January 16, 1993

3. **The stenographic reference line** identifies the person who wrote the letter, and the person who typed the letter. If you are the writer and you also typed the letter, there is no need to include a reference line. The reference line appears at the left margin, two lines below the typed signature line at the bottom of your letter. The writer's initials appear in capital letters, and the typist's in small letters.

Sincerely yours,

Adrian Bell

Adrian Bell

AB:jem

4. The enclosure notation is used when you include something in your letter: an insurance policy, a sales brochure, a photocopy of an earlier letter, or an order would all be common enclosures. Type the word *Enclosure* two lines below the stenographic reference line if there is one, or type it two lines below the typed signature line if you haven't used a reference line.

Sincerely yours,

Adrian Bell

Adrian Bell

AB:jem

Enclosure: (1) contract

Many companies require their employees to make a note of what the enclosure is, such as a contract. It is not uncommon, however, to simply write *Enclosure* and not identify what is being enclosed. Company policy dictates correctness on this item.

5. The carbon copy notation line is placed two lines below the enclosure line. Use a carbon copy line whenever you are sending out copies. List each person who will receive a copy of the letter.

Enclosure: (1) contract

cc: Mr. H. Willis
      Ms. R. Mendoza

Exercise 6.3

Correctly place the following additional letter parts in the letter that follows.

1. The letter was dictated by Martha Albin to a secretary named Harriett Johnson.
2. The subject of the letter is the inferior service at the St. Louis store.
3. A copy of this letter is to be sent to the St. Louis store manager.
4. With the letter, you will enclose a copy of the estimate.
5. You will send the original letter to the main office but call it to the attention of the Vice President in Charge of Complaints.

1331 Platte Road
St. Louis, MO 63136
May 13, 1993

Busby Stores Incorporated
1742 Pritcher Avenue
Iowa City, IA 52240

Ladies and Gentlemen:

Normally the service at your St. Louis store is good and the employees trustworthy. I have been a satisfied, regular customer, in fact, for almost six years. My credit account should instantly reflect the frequence of my visits.

A recent incident, however, has left me deeply disturbed with the store. I visited the service center to purchase a new set of radial tires and have my car's alignment checked. When I left my car in the morning, the estimated cost for the service was $180.00. When I arrived to pick up my car, the alignment was not done because an additional $50.00 worth of parts would have to be installed before the alignment could be performed, according to the service manager. He insisted that the worn parts would wear out the tires within a few months. Unconvinced, I paid for the tires and departed.

Subsequently, I took my car to two competing service centers that specialize in analyzing suspension systems. The specialists informed me that there were absolutely no worn parts in my car's suspension.

Suspecting that someone was attempting to take advantage of me, I spoke to the complaint department at the local store. They listened halfheartedly, as if it was expected of them. Because of this token attention, I decided to write to you before I completely rejected all further dealings with your company. I expect nothing more than an assurance that this practice of recommending unnecessary repairs on trusting customers' cars will be stopped immediately.

Sincerely yours,

Martha Albin

Martha Albin

Check your answers with the Answer Key.

The Envelope

Addressing the envelope should be easy once you have written the letter. The next step is to type the name and address of the person to whom you are writing. Normally, the name and address of the person you are writing to is begun halfway between the top and bottom of the envelope, approximately one-half inch to the left of the center of the envelope. The address should be single spaced.

As you address your envelope, you should be aware that the United States Postal Service is becoming increasingly dependent on machines to sort mail and that those machines tend to dictate the way you address your envelopes. Most corporations have long advised employees to address their envelopes exactly the same as they typed the "to" block or inside address of the letter. While the authors of some business letters still follow that advice, others are changing to the newer Postal Service recommendations. Compare the following envelopes:

```
Neptune Nautical
613 Waterfront Way
Miami, FL 33101




                         Ms. Harriet A. Murchison
                         Piedmont Marketing Corporation
                         2617 West Kenneth Avenue, Suite 7
                         Richmond, VA   23227



```

Traditional Format Envelope

In its most recent recommendations, the Postal Service requires all of the same information, but some differences are readily apparent. Consider the following envelope:

```
Neptune Nautical
613 Waterfront Way
Miami, FL 33101




                         ATTN HARRIET A MURCHISON
                         PIEDMONT MARKETING CORPORATION
                         2617 W KENNETH AVE STE 7
                         RICHMOND VA   23227



```

New Postal Service Envelope

The recommendations of the Postal Service were designed to move the mail quickly. When people don't follow these recommendations, the automated sorting machines cannot function properly and workers have to sort the mail by hand, which slows everything. The following recommendations are from the Postal Service:

- Type or machine print the address.
- Use all capital letters.
- Use no punctuation.
- Use standard abbreviations (RM for room, STE for suite, APT for apartment, ST for street, AVE for avenue, DR for drive, LN for lane, PL for place, RD for road, CIR for circle, etc.).
- Always use your return address.
- Attention line is placed above the name of the firm.
- The last line is reserved for the city, state and ZIP code.

You will occasionally include three optional items on envelopes. When you need to make a special notation such as *Personal* or *Please Forward*, it should be placed two lines below your return address. If you want to call attention to a particular individual in a large company, type ATTN and the person's name on the first line of the address block and the company title on the second line. (Notice that the attention line is above the name of the company.) Finally, if you are going to send the letter *Special Delivery* or *Registered*, you type that notation in caps just below the stamp position in the upper right corner.

The following envelope shows the new format recommended by the Postal Service.

```
NEPTUNE NAUTICAL
613 WATERFRONT WAY
MIAMI FL   33101


                                              SPECIAL DELIVERY
PERSONAL



                        ATTN HARRIET A MURCHISON
                        PIEDMONT MARKETING CORPORATION
                        2617 W KENNETH AVE STE 7
                        RICHMOND VA   23227
```

Note that the envelope above has all capital letters. By contrast, only one envelope on page 136 has all capitals only in the addressee's block. Those envelopes are typical of the ones you will write on the job if you work for a company with the company name preprinted in the upper left corner. If your company does not use preprinted envelopes, however, the final copy will look like the one above.

Exercise 6.4

In the following space, address an envelope for the letter in Exercise 6.2. After the envelope, specify whether you have used the traditional format or the new Postal Service format.

Check your answer with the Answer Key.

FORMATS

Every business letter must follow a *format*—a plan that determines where each part of the letter is placed. You must deliberately decide which format to use for every letter you write. Some companies make the decision easy by specifying the format you should use; other companies ask you to make that decision. The format must, above all else, consistently follow some recognized plan. The various formats should not be mixed at random. Select a format and follow it closely.

Although everyone has a favorite letter format, no format is more correct than the others. Four formats are commonly encountered in business letters: *full block* format, *modified block* format, *semi-block* format, and *simplified* format. Each differs in some fashion from the others.

1. **The full block format**—Every line in the letter—heading, date line, inside address, salutation, body, closing line, and signature line—begins at the left margin. Paragraphs are not indented.
2. **The modified block format**—The heading, date line, closing line, and signature line begin approximately in the center of the page. All other lines begin at the left margin. Paragraphs are not indented.
3. **The semi-block format**—This format is exactly like the modified block format except that the first sentence in each body paragraph is indented.
4. **The simplified format**—This format is the same as the full block format except that the salutation and closing lines are omitted.

The differences among the four formats, fortunately, are easy to see. In the sample letters that follow, pay close attention to the placement of the various letter parts in relation to the margins.

LETTER TYPES

You will encounter a vast number of different reasons for writing business letters. Each of these reasons produces a letter type slightly different from all others. These letters are named for their purpose: **adjustment** letters, **application** letters, **claim** letters, **complaint** letters, **rejection** letters, **request** letters, and **sales** letters are all very common. Note, however, that the letters vary only slightly in overall appearance.

The following sample letters illustrate some different letter types as well as the four different formats. It is not necessary to write any particular letter in a specific format.

Full Block Format Notes:

1. All lines in the letter begin at the left margin; paragraphs are not indented.
2. The full block format is easiest to remember and fastest to set up. Some employers do not like it, however, considering it too informal in appearance.
3. As with all other letters, the full block letter is single spaced but double spaced between paragraphs.

Request Letter Notes:

1. Request letters ask for a response, usually for information or an action. These are one of the most commonly written letters in the business community.
2. Begin your request letter with enough background information so the recipient of your letter will understand why your request is being made.
3. After you have given enough background, explain the options available to the person to whom you are writing.
4. You should end your letter with an invitation to contact you if more information is needed.

Sample Full Block Letter Notes:

1. This letter illustrates a typical letter sent between offices in the business community.
2. One reality you must accept is that while overall letter format remains constant, minor deviations in format are common from company to company. This is not wrong; it is a company's choice to deviate from the standard format. As an employee, you will be expected to follow the pattern preferred by your employer. Observe how the letter on the right differs from the recommended format:
   a. The **RE** line is placed above the salutation rather than below it,
   b. The salutation is followed by a colon rather than the comma that is customary in a letter with an informal tone,
   c. The spacing between the title of the person who wrote the letter and the steno line is four lines here rather than the customary two lines, and
   d. The company's address and phone number are at the bottom rather than the top of the letter as is customary.

All of these deviations are minor. The letter is forcefully written, and it communicates perfectly. If the company has chosen to make these minor changes, no one in the business community is going to find fault with those changes. As an employee of a company, you should gladly follow any format the company's officers prescribe.

REQUEST LETTER IN FULL BLOCK FORMAT

Better Homes® Realty, Inc.

Mr. Tony Spagnuolo
Better Homes Realty
1185 Branham Lane
San Jose, CA 95118

Re: RENEWAL OF BETTER HOMES REALTY FRANCHISE AGREEMENT

Dear Tony:

Your current Better Homes Realty Franchise Agreement, dated September 29, 1987, has been in existence for almost five years. As provided for in this Agreement, you may, at your option, renew for an additional five year increment. The renewal will be subject to present terms and conditions and no additional franchise fee will be charged.

Should you choose to exercise your option for the additional five year term, please find enclosed for your review and signature two current, original Franchise Agreements.

Please sign and date both originals where indicated and return both to Better Homes Realty, Inc., for Ron Morck's signature. An original will then be returned to you for your files.

If you should have any questions, please contact our office. A self-addressed, stamped envelope is enclosed for your convenience.

Very truly yours,

Florence Stevens
Vice President of Operations

FS:jag
enclosures

Franchisor of Independently Owned and Operated Better Homes Realty offices.

National Headquarters: 1556 Parkside Drive • Post Office Box 8181 • Walnut Creek, CA 94596
Telephone (510) 937-9001 • (800) 642-4428 • Fax (510) 937-9006

Modified Block Format Notes:

1. Heading is considered a separate block. The longest line in the heading ends at the right margin of the letter. All other lines in the heading align with the beginning of the longest line.
2. The paragraphs are not indented. Spacing between paragraphs and parts is the same in all formats.
3. Complimentary close begins five spaces to the left of center.

Claim Letter Notes:

1. A claim letter should begin with a paragraph giving the reader enough background to understand the problem. For instance, if the claim involves an order, you should state the order number and the particular item you want to discuss. If the claim involves an item that has not performed adequately, identify the item at the outset.
2. The claim letter should then go on to describe the problem in some detail. Don't write an angry letter. Angry letters make readers angry, and angry people do not react the way you might want. Be thorough as you explain, and be firm.
3. If you have been inconvenienced by the product or service in question, be clear as you explain the embarrassment, injury, or fear.
4. Finally, close your claim letter with a clear statement describing what should be done to correct the problem. You should not be apologetic as you ask for a replacement item, an apology, immediate action, or better service. Just remember not to write an angry letter.
5. This letter is often called a complaint letter because it typically complains about a product or service.

CLAIM LETTER IN MODIFIED BLOCK FORMAT

6306 Palm Drive
Carmel, CA 93921
July 19, 1993

Western America Bank
Consumer Credit Division
San Francisco Service Center
2963 Businesspark Drive
San Francisco, CA 94101

Attention: Bookkeeping Department Manager

Dear Sir or Madam:

Subject: Loan #292-136042

When my husband and I bought our new home seven years ago, we arranged for a fixed rate mortgage with Western America Bank. Since we did not want to be forced to write a check every month, we opted to have the bank deduct the amount of the payment from our savings account each month. That arrangement has worked well for seven years.

Last month we received a letter from your office showing that our account had incurred a $3.73 shortage. We ignored that notification, assuming it was simply a clerical error. This month we were notified that our account was past due $3.73. We can't understand how this could be. We checked with our local branch of Western America Bank, and they informed us that $502.24--the amount specified in our original contract--has been withdrawn each month. Our bank suggested we contact you directly and ask you to research the problem.

Please notify us after you have investigated the problem so we will know how to proceed. We take pride in our good credit rating and wish to preserve it.

Sincerely,

Maxine L. Holloway

Semi-Block Format Notes:

1. Heading and complimentary close are placed the same as in modified block format.
2. The only difference between this format and the modified block format is that the paragraphs in the body are indented.

Adjustment Letter Notes:

1. Adjustment letters that say "yes" are easy to write provided that you begin by admitting your mistake. After you have briefly explained how the error occurred—without blaming anyone personally—you must end with a clear statement that tells exactly what will be done to correct the problem.
2. If you are denying a claim, the letter is more difficult to write. You must attempt to keep the customer happy, so you will have to write the refusal without offending the reader. Your letter should begin with a short paragraph saying you are glad to hear from the customer but sorry to hear about the problem. You must explain clearly and in depth why you must refuse the claim. You must then end your letter in a friendly way.
3. End both letters by focusing on the solution rather than on the problem—be positive. And, finally, make your reader aware that you are glad he or she took the time to write.

ADJUSTMENT LETTER IN SEMI-BLOCK FORMAT

Western America Bank
Consumer Credit Division
2963 Businesspark Drive
San Francisco, CA 94101

August 27, 1993

Maxine L. Holloway
6306 Palm Drive
Carmel, CA 93921

Dear Mrs. Holloway

Subject: Loan #292-136042

We have completed our research regarding the "past due" amounts appearing on your recent bills. This discrepancy is due to a problem with our computer billing system.

You are correct in stating that you are not past due for $3.73. However, the error was not corrected in time to affect the billing you will receive for your payment due on September 4, 1993. Please disregard the amount due of $505.97 as shown on the statement. Your account will be debited for only the current amount due of $502.24.

Thank you for your patience. If you should have further questions, please feel free to contact our Customer Service Department at (415) 422-7092.

Sincerely,

J. S. Stillson
Operations Officer
Customer Service

JSS:vlw

Simplified Format Notes:

1. All lines in the letter begin at the left margin, exactly like the full block format.
2. The salutation and complimentary close lines are omitted completely.
3. The subject line replaces the salutation, but the word "subject" is omitted. All letters in the subject line are capitalized. The subject line is not underlined and no colon follows it. It is typed two spaces below the address and the body is typed two spaces below the subject.
4. Type the name of the person who wrote the letter four spaces below the body of the letter, omitting any complimentary close. The signature is then placed just above the typed name.
5. **This letter format is not widely accepted. Although its popularity is growing in some areas because it saves time, you should not use it until you have checked to make certain it is permissible where you work.**

Inquiry Letter Notes:

1. Begin an inquiry letter by telling your reader why you need his or her assistance.
2. If you do not know the name of a contact person, use an attention line to direct your letter to a particular department.
3. Use outline format in the body to identify questions you want answered. Giving the reader a list of questions makes answering your letter easy and eliminates the chance of overlooking an important point.
4. Most inquiries require information about products or services, and availability.

INQUIRY LETTER IN SIMPLIFIED FORMAT

Silver Leather Products, Inc.
3001-11 Kensington Avenue
Philadelphia, PA 19134
(216) 659-0444
July 13, 1993

Mr. Michael Wooten
MicroPro International Corporation
33 San Pablo Avenue
San Rafael, CA 94903

WORDSTAR SOFTWARE

We have a Macintosh LC computer in our office and find it
a wonderful machine. It is used for inventory control,
employee records, and communication. The computer is, in
fact, the busiest employee at Silver Leather Products. And
that's the problem.

As our business grows, the number of letters flowing out of
our office grows in proportion. We have been advised that
we can speed up our output by replacing our present word-
processing software with the most recent WordStar software.
Our local Macintosh dealer does not stock such a package
and appears uncertain whether one has been developed. We
enjoy the many unique features of the Macintosh LC and would
only be interested in WordStar if it takes advantage of
those features.

You can help us, Mr. Wooten, by answering the following
questions:

1. Is WordStar available for the Macintosh LC?

2. Is it available in a recently revised edition?

3. Is it available in a "professional" version?

4. Where can we obtain a copy?

5. What is the price?

A quick response would be sincerely appreciated, as we are
rapidly outgrowing our present word-processing software.

Nita B Hornsby
Nita B. Hornsby
Accounting Department Supervisor

WRITING A BUSINESS LETTER

By using a four-step method, you can write effective letters without wasting time. The four steps are—

1. planning the letter
2. writing a rough draft
3. revising the rough draft
4. preparing the final copy

This four-step method must become a matter of habit so that you automatically follow each step as you write. As you write more and more letters, your speed will increase dramatically until you hardly realize that you are following steps. At first, however, each step will be a separate operation. The following explanation illustrates the four-step method. The exercises that follow ask you to develop your own letter using this method.

Step 1 Planning the Letter

You must begin each letter with a plan. After you become an experienced letter writer, you may omit writing out the plan for short letters; but you will still use the plan mentally as you develop the letter. The following sample shows how to use a list of basic questions to develop a brief plan:

Plan for Unsatisfactory Fishing Boat Letter

Why write a letter? Dealer won't repair flaws
Who to? Jack Patton, Complaints Department, Bartleby Aluminum Boat Company
What to say? Please encourage boat dealer to repair or replace boat
Tone? Firm but confident
Format? Modified block
Letter type? Complaint

Your plan actually need be no longer, unless you want it to be more complete. The best length depends on you; if you write better from a long plan or a formal outline, you should develop one. The plan in the preceding sample is the shortest one you should use.

Exercise 6.5

Select a topic from the following list, and develop a plan using the questions provided.

1. a defective piece of merchandise (real or imaginary)
2. poor service at a store or on repairs (real or imaginary)
3. a request for information

Letter topic: _____

Why write a letter? _____

Who to? _____

What to say? _____

Tone? _____

Format? _____

Letter type? _____

Have your work checked by your instructor or a tutor.

Step 2 Writing a Rough Draft

A rough draft is merely the first version of a letter. A rough draft is usually the handwritten copy from which the author or typist types the finished copy of the letter. Refer to your plan as you write your rough draft. Although you may choose not to use a plan after you have become experienced at writing letters, you may find it helpful to use one at first. Whether or not you use the plan, rapidly write the first copy of the letter, filling in all information as you go. The following letter about the unsatisfactory fishing boat was developed from the sample plan.

8119 Raley Street
New Hope, Pa 18938
August 2, 1993

Jack Patton, Complaint Department
Bartleby Aluminum Boat Company
382 Whitney Road
Houston, TX 77016

Dear Mr. Patton:

On February 15, 1993, I purchased a Bartleby Model ST14 aluminum fishing boat from Riveredge Marine Supply. At the time of the purchase, I was assured that your company unconditionally guarantees all products it manufactures.

From the first time I used the boat, it has consistently leaked around the transom. Granted, it leaks slowly; but in the course of a day's fishing, the water reaches a depth of three to four inches in the bottom of the boat. I have contacted Riveredge Marine Supply about the problem three times. They acknowledged the leak, but they argued that it is common for aluminum fishing boats to leak slowly. They insist that the boat is perfectly safe in spite of the leak. At my insistence, they attempted unsuccessfully to stop the leak with marine seal on my second visit. On my third visit, however, they bluntly told me they could do nothing to solve the problem.

In every other way, the Bartleby boat is excellent. It is a smooth-riding craft with exceptional stability. I do feel, however, that the operator of a new boat should not have to suffer wet feet every time the boat is used. Please advise me how I can get my boat repaired or replaced.

Sincerely yours,

Malcolm W. Fisher

Exercise 6.6

Write the rough draft of a business letter from the plan you developed in Exercise 6.5. (Do your work on notebook paper before copying it here.)

_____

_____

_____

_____

_____

_____

_____

_____

_____

_____

_____

_____

_____

_____

_____

_____

_____

_____

_____

_____

_____

_____

_____

Have your work checked by your instructor or a tutor.

Step 3 Revising Your Rough Draft

After you have written your rough draft, you can easily revise it before typing a final copy. The following Business Letter Checklist will guide you through the revision.

BUSINESS LETTER CHECKLIST

1. Does the letter have all seven essential parts?
2. Have you avoided abbreviations (other then states and titles)?
3. Are the salutation and complimentary close consistent in formality?
4. Have you avoided using passive voice excessively?
5. Do you use an appropriate tone in your letter?
6. Do you speak directly to the reader (using I and you)?
7. Are all words spelled correctly?
8. Is punctuation correct?

Exercise 6.7

Revise your rough draft from Exercise 6.6 before typing the final copy. Use the Business Letter Checklist as a guide.

Step 4 Preparing the Final Copy

The final copy of a business letter should be a computer printout or an error-free typed page. Avoid using lined binder paper. You should also avoid any typing paper except white (unless your company uses colored letterhead stationery).

Letter Placement In order to achieve maximum impact upon your reader, the final copy of your letter must be placed properly on the page. A short letter, for instance, would look strange if it were placed at the top, leaving the lower half of the page completely blank. As you set up your letter, you can vary these four areas to change the overall appearance of the letter.

1. **The top**—If you use typing paper that has a printed letterhead, you cannot move the top margin. However, if you are typing a heading on your letter, you can raise or lower the entire letter by raising or lowering the heading. On a very short letter, you might choose to begin the heading as much as one-quarter of the distance down the page.

2. **Inside address**—As indicated earlier, you can vary the spacing between the date and the inside address from two to eight spaces. This is the most commonly accepted technique used to center a letter on the page.

3. **The margins**—The margins on each side may also be modified to make the letter look smaller or larger. Normally, business letters have a sixty-space line length on an elite typewriter. If you have an exceptionally short letter, the line

length could be decreased to fifty spaces without making the letter appear to be squeezed in.

4. **Spacing**—If your letter is no more than two paragraphs in length, it is acceptable in some companies to use double-space between the lines of the body. Since letters are normally single-spaced, however, your double-spaced letter will look less professional than a single-spaced one.

The overall purpose of deliberate letter placement is to produce a letter with equal margin widths at the top, bottom, and sides so the letter will appear centered and balanced.

REMINDERS FOR TYPING THE FINAL COPY OF A LETTER

1. **Make sure format is consistent. (Don't combine two or more letter formats.)**
2. **Make sure placement is correct. (The final copy must be placed in the center of the page.)**
3. **Make sure spacing is correct. (The various parts of the letter must be the proper distance from one another.)**
4. **Make sure the letter is neat.**

As you write business letters, use the state abbreviations set forth by the U.S. Postal Service. Be sure to add the zip code on all correspondence.

STATE ABBREVIATIONS

Alabama	AL	Montana	MT
Alaska	AK	Nebraska	NE
Arizona	AZ	Nevada	NV
Arkansas	AR	New Hampshire	NH
California	CA	New Jersey	NJ
Colorado	CO	New Mexico	NM
Connecticut	CT	New York	NY
Delaware	DE	North Carolina	NC
Dist. of Columbia	DC	North Dakota	ND
Florida	FL	Ohio	OH
Georgia	GA	Oklahoma	OK
Hawaii	HI	Oregon	OR
Idaho	ID	Pennsylvania	PA
Illinois	IL	Puerto Rico	PR
Indiana	IN	Rhode Island	RI
Iowa	IA	South Carolina	SC
Kansas	KS	South Dakota	SD
Kentucky	KY	Tennessee	TN
Louisiana	LA	Texas	TX
Maine	ME	Utah	UT
Maryland	MD	Vermont	VT
Massachusetts	MA	Virginia	VA
Michigan	MI	Washington	WA
Minnesota	MN	West Virginia	WV
Mississippi	MS	Wisconson	WI
Missouri	MO	Wyoming	WY

Exercise 6.8

Write a business letter that uses the seven basic parts plus any two optional parts. Use one of the following topics.

1. Complain about a product or service
2. Inform another company about the progress your company has made on a job
3. Request information on a product or service

Choose one of the letter formats and use it consistently. Although you will normally type your letters, in this exercise write your letter in the space provided below. Note that the lines are provided to help you achieve proper spacing. (Outline, write, and revise your letter on notebook paper before copying it into the space here.)

_____

_____

_____

_____

_____

_____

_____

_____

_____

_____

_____

_____

_____

_____

_____

_____

_____

_____

_____

_____

_____

_____

_____

_____

_____

_____

_____

_____

_____

_____

_____

_____

Have your work checked by your instructor or a tutor.

Exercise 6.9

Write business letters on any *two* of the following topics. Submit your letters neatly computer printed or typed, making certain the format and spacing are correct.

1. **Rejection Letter**—Semi-Block Format

Assume you are the manager of the Tower Apartments. Recently, Charles Reynolds moved out of Apartment 67, leaving it dirty and badly in need of repair. Three window screens had been torn, the towel bar had been torn off the wall in the bathroom, the closet door had a hole in it, and the carpet was badly soiled. In fact, you have had to pay out a total of $321 to return the apartment to the condition it was in when Mr. Reynolds moved in. Today, you received a request from Mr. Reynolds for a refund of the deposit he paid when he moved into the apartment ten months ago. He points out in the letter that you told him the deposit was refundable when he moved into the apartment. You must write a letter rejecting his request. His address now is 113 West Capital Avenue, St. Paul, MN 55108. Use your address for the address of the Tower Apartments.

2. **Claim Letter**—Full Block Format

Six months ago you bought a goose down jacket from the Arctic Comfort Company, Box 5413, Troy, NY 12180. Since you bought the jacket in the fall, you had little opportunity to wear it for the first three months you owned it. When winter arrived, however, you wore it frequently for at least two months, enjoying being truly warm in sub-zero weather for the first time in your life. But every time you have worn the coat during the last month, you have been uncomfortable because all of the goose down has shifted from the shoulders to the bottom of the jacket. Upon examining the coat closely, you have discovered the stitching that should keep the goose down in the upper part of the jacket has failed. You have decided to write to the Arctic Comfort Company and ask them to repair or replace the jacket. You called the company and found that you must write to a Ms. Marianne Cohen, Adjustment Department Manager.

3. **Adjustment Letter**—Modified Block

You are the Service Manager of the Travelite Bicycle Company, the manufacturer of a popular line of bicycles designed for recreational riding. A Mrs. William R. Bly has written you a letter in which she complains that the 10-speed bicycle she bought from one of your dealers has a broken frame. Your bicycles all have a one-year guarantee against such breakage, but she has owned the bicycle now for almost 18 months. She attempted unsuccessfully to get the local dealer to repair or replace the frame. Since the bicycle has been used only about once a month, according to Mrs. Bly, she feels it should be repaired or replaced. After considering the situation, you have decided that the potential for bad publicity far outweighs the cost of repairing the bicycle. You will, therefore, write Mrs. Bly a letter, agreeing with her that the bicycle should certainly last longer without major problems. Explain to her that you will send a new frame for her bicycle to her local dealer, The Bicycle Cottage, by the fastest means. Tell her the dealer will install the frame as soon as possible and send the bill to the factory. Have a letter typed by Bill Schoff and sent to Mrs. Bly at 4701 Cedar Street, Fremont, OH 43420. Send a copy of the letter to your dealer in Fremont, The Bicycle Cottage, so he will know what to expect. Use your home address for the Travelite Bicycle Company.

7

Writing the Resume

When you have completed this chapter, you will be able to—

1. Develop a work history for yourself.
2. Develop an education history for yourself.
3. List possible employers, contacts, and leads.
4. Select the most effective ordering technique for work and educational backgrounds.
5. Write a resume using the most effective ordering technique.
6. Prepare a cover letter to introduce your resume.

THE RESUME DEFINED

A resume is basically a listing of your educational and work experiences. Although it will not get you a job, a resume can get you the interview that will get you the job. If you write a good resume, the personnel manager or business owner who receives it may be impressed enough to interview you.

The people who do the hiring are busy and do not have time to interview everyone who applies for a job. To save time, they frequently require job applicants to send them a resume with the job application. This is logical when you stop to think of it. Conducting an interview takes about thirty minutes; reading an application and resume only takes about one minute.

The process of filling a job vacancy involves many steps and much of the employer's time. As you might well imagine, anything that will save the employer time will create a favorable impression. The employer's first step in filling a vacancy is to identify the job specifications, which involves the listing of everything the employee will be required to do. Second, the job profile must be written. This often involves very complex considerations such as how much and what type of education or experience the prospective employee should have. At this point, the employer would also consider affirmative action quotas. Such quotas are important because businesses should have a balance of men and women, as well as a balance of the various races or ethnic groups that make up the community.

The third step in the hiring process is advertising the position, which is where you become involved. When you see the advertisement of the position and decide to apply, you can assume you are one of perhaps dozens or even hundreds of applicants. And that is where the resume becomes important. To apply for most jobs, you must fill out the company's standard job application form, which gives the employer some basic information about you. But everyone else who applies for the same position will complete the same application. The function of the resume is to give the employer more specific information about you so that you will have a much better chance of acquiring an interview.

HOW A RESUME HELPS YOU

Reading through your resume, the employer learns much about you. In fact, the resume reveals much more than just what jobs you have held and what schools you have attended. Those who submit a resume without being asked are obviously self-starters, and employers look for people who can do things without being told. If you can develop a good, clear resume, you are also demonstrating organizational skills. Employers recognize the skill needed to put all of your life's education and job experiences onto paper in an organized fashion. They logically want employees who have highly developed organizational skills.

Consider, too, how dramatically the resume demonstrates your ability to communicate on paper. The resume and cover letter clearly reveal how well you can write. If they are neat and prepared in a professional manner, you can also impress prospective employers with your potential. Indeed, the appearance of the resume often tells more about you than what the words on the paper say.

Some people are tempted by the slick ads of "professional" resume writers. They will often write your resume for fifteen or twenty dollars. As tempting as such offers sound, that shortcut defeats many of the purposes of submitting a resume. To begin with, inexpensive resumes written by professionals are easily recognized by employers. Such resumes use identical format and words for every customer, changing just enough to put your name and some personal details in. Worse yet, these resumes tell the reader that you were too lazy or unable to write your own resume, a message you definitely don't want to communicate.

This chapter will lead you through the various steps required to produce the best possible resume. As you work through the lessons, assume that you are actually going to send the final product to a prospective employer. If you **are** going to do so, find and use the correct name and address of the personnel manager in your cover letter. If you are not planning to send your resume to an employer, choose a company in your area and write the cover letter as if it were to be sent to that company.

PREPARING TO WRITE YOUR RESUME

Because the resume is so important, you should plan to write it carefully and thoughtfully. A carelessly written resume will most likely fail to get you the interview you want. A good, effective resume begins with careful preparation. Before actually writing your resume, you will need to make a list of your qualifications. Since the kind of job you're seeking will influence what information you put into your resume, you should also think about possible job sources before writing. Thinking carefully about your past jobs and education will also help you prepare for your interviews by forcing you to recall names, dates, and places.

Listing Your Qualifications

Planning your resume begins with a long, time-demanding listing of your qualifications. Put thought into compiling this list. You may never use every detail from this list in your final resume, yet being able to pick and choose what you will put in the final draft will help produce a complete, effective resume.

WORK HISTORY   You will need to list all of your present and past jobs, including details about your experience in those jobs. For some young job seekers who have little or no job experience, this section may be not more than a line or two long. However, those who have had many work experiences may take two or three pages to complete this section. Resumes begin with the current job and work back to the first.

Deciding how many jobs to list on the actual resume comes later. For now, list everything you have ever been paid to do. Even babysitting, yard care, and paper routes can be important in some instances.

Exercise 7.1

Compile your work history. For each job you have had, list the following:

- name of company
- address of company
- job title
- job duties
- special skills and talents developed on the job
- length of time on the job
- who could give you a reference

Job 1 (most recent or present job)

_____

_____

_____

_____

_____

Job 2 (job held before present one)

_____

_____

_____

_____

_____

Job 3 (job before job two)

_____

_____

_____

_____

_____

Job 4 (job before job three)

_____

_____

_____

_____

_____

Job 5 (job before job four)

_____

_____

_____

_____

_____

(Use additional sheets of paper if necessary to list other jobs.)

Have your work checked by your instructor or a tutor.

EDUCATION   Next you should make a list of your educational qualifications. List all schools you have attended, including high school, college, and any business, vocational, or other professional training. This list will include details about your course of study, as well as any special honors and extracurricular activities.

Exercise 7.2

List all schools you have attended, beginning with the most recent. For each school, include the following:

- school attended
- dates of attendance
- degrees earned
- grade average

- major subjects
- subjects you liked best
- honors, clubs, and scholarships
- special skills you learned

School 1 (most recent or present school)

_____

_____

_____

_____

_____

School 2 (school before present one)

_____

_____

_____

_____

_____

School 3 (school before previous school)

_____

_____

_____

_____

_____

(Use additional sheets of paper if necessary to list other schools.)

Have your work checked by your instructor or a tutor.

POSSIBLE JOB SOURCES   Once you have listed your qualifications, you will need to think about where you might apply those skills. You may already know of particular companies that have the job you are seeking. However, you should think of other possible job sources—friends, business associates, or employment agencies that could lead you to the job you want.

Exercise 7.3

Make a checklist of possible job sources or contacts. Consider the following as you make your list:

- firms that may have the job you want
- business associates
- personal friends or relatives
- employment agencies
- professional organizations

Your Job Sources Checklist:

_____

_____

_____

_____

_____

_____

_____

_____

_____

_____

_____

_____

_____

_____

Have your work checked by your instructor or a tutor.

THE PARTS OF THE RESUME

As you begin organizing the material for inclusion in your resume, you can assume you will not use everything you included in Exercises 7.1, 7.2, and 7.3. In fact, you will vary the details used from resume to resume, depending on the person or organization the final resume is to be sent to. For instance, if you were planning to send the resume to a company that would be more concerned with your school background than your work history, you should stress your educational experiences. You would do this by placing your Education History before your Work History; be certain to list such things as your grade point averages and any honor societies to which you belonged. By contrast, if you wished to stress your work experiences, you would go into detail as you explained the duties and positions you held while working for previous employers.

Organizing your material into its most impressive form is important. Develop an outline before you attempt to prepare the first draft. The following outline form is merely a suggested one; if you have good reason to do so, you can certainly deviate from this form. Most resumes include the following sections:

> Heading
> Job Interest and Goal
> Work History
> Education History
> Special Skills
> Personal Data
> References

Heading   Give complete names. "J. R. Ewing" might look good on television, but it looks careless on a resume.
> Name
> Address
> Telephone (include area code)

Job Interest and Goal   This is often called the *Career Objective* or *Job Objective* because it should present both your immediate and long-range job goals. Explain exactly the job or field of work you want. If you want to be considered for more than one job, list them, but be specific. Don't give the impression you are so desperate for work that you will accept a job doing anything. Such an attitude would make any employer suspicious.

Use words such as "career," "permanent," "long-range," and "continuing" to indicate your desire for lasting employment. Employers do not want to hire people who only plan to work for them long enough to get some money or experience before moving on. It costs a company money to train an employee; if you expect to get hired, you will have to convince the personnel director or business owner of your desire to stay with the company for more than a few months or a year. The following job objective statements indicate a desire for permanence:

1. To do my best in the electronics field as a technician with a career-oriented company offering advancement potential, and to earn a Masters of Science degree in electrical engineering.

The fact that this person mentions a desire to continue learning would also be helpful as many companies encourage advanced degrees.

2. A responsible and challenging position with an established company that rewards dedication, creativity, and ability with advancement potential.

3. My immediate goal is an entry-level position with an aircraft manufacturing company that would value my experience and education in aviation. By continuing to study at local schools, I plan to make myself even more capable, eventually joining the management staff of a progressive company.

The above job objective statements vary. Some are composed of fragments; others are complete sentences. Some are one sentence while others are two. None is more correct than the others. The only thing to remember is that this is the only place in the resume where you have the opportunity to tell your reader what kind of an employee you will be.

Work History   Put this section before the Education History section if you have a more impressive work history. Younger applicants typically put the Education History first because they have more education than job experiences. The opposite is true of older applicants. List each job you have had (most recent first). Include:

dates of employment
employer, address, type of business
name and title of supervisor
position you held
salary (if important)

Describe for each job:

job title
job duties
responsibilities
accomplishments (if noteworthy)

Be careful not to make your work history excessively long. Your entire resume should be no longer than two typed pages; one is usually long enough. If your recent jobs have all been significant but your earlier ones unimportant, omit the earlier ones from your work history. If the only jobs you have had are delivering papers for three years and waiting on customers in a donut shop for two years while you worked your way through college, put them in your work history, but put your work history after your education history.

Education History   List each school you have attended, giving the most recent or current school first. (This section should come first if you have never worked or if the work history section of your resume lists only part-time or insignificant jobs.)

college—major subjects, degree, date received, and GPA (if your GPA is exceptional)

high school—date graduated, subjects (if related closely)

additional training (correspondence courses, professional training, or vocational schools)

professional certificates or licenses held

internships or apprenticeships

scholarships or honors

extracurricular activities (if significant)

Military Experience (if relevant)

length of service and branch

job training or special skills learned

Special Skills, Licenses, or Memberships

foreign languages you speak or write

job-related skills, such as highly technical machines

job-related achievements or awards

memberships in professional organizations

Personal Data   Although information about your age, height, weight, marital status, and health is optional, it helps give the prospective employer a better knowledge of who you are. If you would rather not include it, you can't be forced to. The decision is yours.

References   Giving references is truly a matter of choice. If you are certain that you will gain something because you list references, then you should include them. Most resume writers, however, do not include them. As a rule, experts cite two reasons for not sending a resume with references at the bottom. First, if a significant percentage of those who receive resumes call the references listed, these friends and associates will be unnecessarily bothered by calls. Second, it is extra work for the person who sends out the resume because every person listed as a reference should be contacted before his or her name is given out as a reference. Standard practice is simply to note that you will send out references "On Request."

Exercise 7.4

Write a resume outline.

_____

_____

_____

_____

_____

_____

_____

_____

_____

_____

_____

_____

_____

_____

_____

_____

_____

Have your work checked by your instructor or a tutor.

WRITING YOUR RESUME

Converting your outline into an impressive resume requires serious thought and careful attention to detail. Above all, be honest as you list the courses you have taken and people you have worked for. Facts and names are easily checked by a thorough personnel manager. Errors and discrepancies between your resume and the information supplied by schools or past employers will make you look careless or dishonest.

The appearance of your resume will vary greatly depending on your job record, what effect you want to achieve, and your personal opinion of which format looks most pleasing. Resumes fall into two categories: chronological and functional. Chronological resumes are far more common and are generally used when work experience is limited or you are applying for your first job. The emphasis is on dates and places. List the jobs you have held and your educational background with the most recent events first. On the other hand, the functional resume is used to emphasize more effectively a wide range of work experiences that may span several years. For those having an excessive number of job changes or several lapses in employment, the functional resume has a number of advantages. Frequent job changes or lapses in employment can be deemphasized in the functional resume.

The format you use to structure your resume is not as important, perhaps, as the content or length. Your resume's basic purpose is to clearly tell the reader of your job experiences and education. Be aware that a resume can easily become too long. A resume should be one page for a young person, and not more than two pages for an older person who has had many different jobs and extensive education. Remember that employers are busy people who do not have time to read long resumes. If your resume is over two pages in length, it probably won't get read.

Before you begin the final copy of your resume, examine the following sample resumes very closely. You should immediately observe the tremendous variety in format exhibited in the samples. No one format is correct. Part of your responsibility is to decide which shows off your qualifications and experiences best. You may need to write both a chronological and functional resume to discover the right format for you.

Garcia Resume Notes

This is an example of a resume using chronological development. Note that it begins with the most recent job (here her only job) and the most recent school attended. This format allows the reader to see at a glance how many jobs she has had and how many schools she has attended. The chronological format is used far more commonly than the functional.

The resume on the opposite page was written by a young woman who began working for a personnel agency as a receptionist/bookkeeper immediately after graduation from high school. After two years on the job, she felt she had learned as much as she could in that position. Encouraged to do so by her company's president, Louisa Garcia wrote and submitted her resume, hoping to get the office manager position which had just become vacant.

Her **job objective** clearly states she wants a *permanent position* as a *personnel agency office manager*. As with most job objectives, Louisa's is a fragment rather than a complete sentence. Complete sentences are unnecessary in a resume and take up too much valuable space.

Even though Louisa has had only one job, she listed it first because her two years of experience in a personnel agency office would presumably be more significant to her employer than her part-time attendance at the local junior college.

Many people like the dates of employment and attendance in the left margin because it allows the reader an opportunity to observe dates of employment and attendance at a glance.

SAMPLE RESUME 1 — Chronological

Louisa B. Garcia
5261 Explorer Drive
Fort Lauderdale, FL   33316
(305) 764-2180

JOB OBJECTIVE: Actively seeking permanent position as
                        personnel agency office manager

EXPERIENCE:

  April 1992   Receptionist/Bookkeeper--Point West Personnel
    to
  present   Duties: As receptionist, my duties include
                        greeting clients, handling the phones, trans-
                        cribing and typing all correspondence for the
                        agency. Bookkeeping duties include all
                        aspects of that area (accounts payable and
                        receivable, payroll, etc.).

                        Salary Received: $600 per month: $50 auto
                                          expenses; 3% profit sharing

EDUCATION:

  1992-present   Florida Junior College, Jacksonville, FL
                        Majoring in secretarial practice (part-time)

                        Special Classes or Training: Regional
                        Opportunity Program (ROP); worked with word
                        processors and spread sheets

                        Special Awards: Gregg Filing Award in May
                        1986

  1988-1992   St. Francis High School, Jacksonville, FL

PERSONAL DATA:

                        Age: 20
                        Height: 5'2"
                        Weight: 110
                        Health: Excellent
                        Marital Status: Single

REFERENCES: Provided upon request

Patton Resume Notes

To save space and improve the overall visual balance of his resume, Jerry Patton moved the Personal Data section of his resume to the top of the page.

The Job Objective here becomes the Occupational Goal—merely another way of indicating the same thing. This is a matter of choice.

Jerry achieved a totally different appearance for his resume by changing format. Although this presents his experience chronologically, it appears quite different from Louisa's.

Under Qualifications, this resume lists the machinery and concepts Jerry learned in his classes at Tacoma Community College. He chose this approach to demonstrate his familiarity with high-tech terminology because he was applying for a job with an electronics firm. He then went on to list many unique skills he possessed under Special Skills.

SAMPLE RESUME 2 — Chronological

Jerry Patton
9625 Bradhugh Court
Bellingham, WA 98225
(206) 676-4812

Age: 22
Health: Excellent
Marital Status: Single
Height: 6' 1"
Weight: 190 lbs.

OCCUPATIONAL GOAL

To do my best in the electronics field as a technician, with a
career oriented company offering advancement potential, and to
earn a Masters of Science degree in electrical engineering.

EDUCATION

1990 to present, Tacoma Community College, Tacoma, WA
Degree: Associate of Arts
Major: Electronic Computer Technology; Microwave Communications
G.P.A.: In major 3.6, overall 3.5

QUALIFICATIONS

Microprocessors, 8080/8085 systems: RAM, ROM, EPROM memory, A/D
and D/A converters, input and output devices, control lines, tri-
state buffering devices, memory systems, decoding systems,
combining hardware and software techniques and interfacing,
switching speed and timing criteria, multivibrators, flip-flops,
counters, operational amplifiers, timers, phase lock loops,
decoders for multiplexers and machine language.

Communications: transmission lines, power measurements, gain,
noise and bandpass of RF circuits, spectrum analysis of RF
signals. Additional subjects covered include broadband
amplifiers, YIG, Gunn and BWO oscillators, frequency response,
gain and radiation patterns of antennas, plus modulation and
demodulation of AM, FM, and pulse signals.

SPECIAL SKILLS

Operate various types of test equipment, oscilloscopes, system
analyzer, DMM, VTVM, power supplies, frequency counters and gener-
ators; Emergency Medical Technician; operate heavy equipment.

EMPLOYMENT HISTORY

11-92 to 6-93	Mr. B's Liquors Duties: Clerk
5-92 to 6-93	Sutter Moving and Storage Duties: Driver and mover
5-91 to 8-91	Crowley Maritime Corporation Duties: Various labor work with subsidiaries

References: Upon request

SAMPLE RESUME 3 — Chronological

Paul M. Poulus
1037 McClain Road
Carmichael, CA 95608
(916) 991-3649

EMPLOYMENT OBJECTIVE: Actively seeking permanent position as a construction manager. Objectives are to be part of an established organization that offers advancement opportunity and rewards innovation and dedication.

WORK HISTORY:

1-1-90
to
present

Lexington Homes, 7700 College Town Drive, Sacramento, CA 95864
Job Title: Head of Project Bidding Department
Duties: Schedule bids for projects, input data on computer spreadsheet, develop budgets for small and large projects.
Salary: $1,800 monthly

1-15-86
to
1-1-90

Akropolis Construction, 6519 Fern Way, Castro Valley, CA 94546
Job Title: Superintendent of Construction
Duties: Schedule subcontractors' work, work with architect to develop plans, run large crews on projects, apply for and obtain all licenses and permits, schedule inspections.
Salary: $1,550 monthly

3-1-82
to
1-1-86

Shield Healthcare, 2860 Dwight Way, Berkeley, CA 94550
Job Title: Purchasing Agent
Duties: Keep stock of medical supplies on hand, take inventory of entire stocks, keep supply close to demand and not overpurchase supplies, develop inventory schedules to keep up with demand, manage all warehouse employees.
Salary: $1,150 monthly

Resume - Paul M. Poulus (continued)   2.

EDUCATION: American River College, Sacramento, CA   95841
                  Degree: Associate of Arts   (6-1-93)
                  Specialization: Business Operations

Major Subjects	**Minor Subjects**
1. business law	1. history
2. management	2. English
3. business environment	3. accounting
4. political science	
5. communications	

                  Castro Valley High School, Castro Valley, CA   94545
                  Graduated (June 17, 1980)

SPECIAL SKILLS: Dance instructor
                        Contractor's license
                        Read and speak Greek
                        Type 40 wpm

PERSONAL DATA: Date of birth: August 16, 1962
                       Marital status: Married--no children
                       Height: 5' 7"
                       Weight: 155 lbs.

REFERENCES: Upon request

Poulus Resume Notes

This chronological resume written by Paul Poulus highlights his work experience. He has clearly worked his way up in the business community. In addition, Paul has gone back to school and earned a degree while working, which clearly demonstrates his willingness to work to improve himself.

Although Poulus's resume includes the exact salary received on his past jobs, most job applicants do not provide this information unless a prospective employer specifically asks for it.

Poulus's resume also differs from most written today in that it simply states that references are available "On request." Most applicants now list three or four references on their resumes. (Note! Be certain you inform the people you list as references before you send your resume out.)

Functional Resume Notes

The functional resumes on the following pages differ radically from the previous resumes. Rather than emphasizing dates of employment, both stress jobs held or accomplishments. This type of resume was chosen by Kimberly Lyons because she had moved from job to job and from town to town frequently. Her resume now emphasizes her abilities rather than her frequent moves, a fact most employers would consider a sufficient reason not to hire her. Employers who read a functional resume may notice missing dates and suspect the applicant is prone to frequent moves, but the positive presentation of accomplishments might persuade the employer to offer an interview and discuss these points.

Functional resumes need concrete facts to be effective. Observe the details offered in the resume by Bhyers on pages 174-175. His resume is convincing because he uses dollar amounts saved, years in business, and numbers of people supervised.

Richardson's resume on pages 178-179 clearly emphasizes what she has done on the job rather than the dates of her employment. Her development as an employee is clear. By adding the dates of employment, she has emphasized how quickly she has progressed as a manager.

SAMPLE RESUME 4 — Functional

KIMBERLY L. LYONS
6442 HIGHVIEW LANE
CITRUS HEIGHTS, CA 95610
(916) 961-3015

POSITION

Office manager for well-established insurance agency in medium-sized rural town

EXPERIENCE

Analyst

AMERICAN GENERAL (CAL-WESTERN) LIFE INSURANCE – 2020 L Street, Sacramento, CA 95814: Policyowner Services Analyst - Duties include servicing policyowner and agents' requests, maintaining good customer and agent relations by explaining products and procedures. Requires analytical skills, organization, patience, and ability to handle stressful situations.

Auditor

VAL-U INN - Missoula, MT: Desk clerk and night auditor - Duties included making reservations, checking guests in and out, and answering the telephone. Balanced daily books two nights a week. Position required a strong sense of responsibility and maturity.

Manager

GOLD TRAIL MOTOR LODGE - Placerville, CA: Relief manager - Duties included running motel while manager was gone, including supervising housekeeping staff, light maintenance, bookkeeping, and customer relations.

Researcher

SACRAMENTO HISTORY CENTER - Sacramento, CA: Research Associate - Duties included researching the history of the Scandinavians in Sacramento, using traditional methods and oral interviews. Wrote and presented a paper at a conference of peers and ethnic community leaders.

EDUCATION

Life Office Management Institute (LOMA): Courses 1 and 2.

California State University Sacramento: B.A. in History in 1982, with Honors; 9 graduate units.

Sacramento History Center: Archivist Trainee - Learned to catalogue, organize, and preserve historical documents.

American River College: A.A. in 1971.

MACHINES

IBM CRT	MICROS Cash Register
IBM PC	OMRON Dial Terminal
CALCULATOR	MITEL Phone System

REFERENCES

On request

SAMPLE RESUME 5 — Functional

RAYMOND L. BHYERS
1243 Tarkiln Hill Road
New Bedford, MA 02745
(617) 995-2776

JOB OBJECTIVE:

A responsible and challenging position in which training, skills, and ability will be effectively applied in an atmosphere conducive to professional growth.

SUMMARY OF
QUALIFICATIONS:

Educated and experienced in modern personnel and administrative practices. Experienced in budget development and implementation, training, and management of mechanized data systems. People-oriented, shirt-sleeve manager specializing in administrative procedures, training, counseling, and supervising personnel. Ability to analyze and accurately grasp overall concepts as opposed to single facets, which increases productivity.

CREDIT
ADMINISTRATION:

Associate Credit Manager for a multibillion dollar lumber and retail sales organization. Responsible for managing 5000 contractor customers with annual credit sales of $46 million. Assisted in the reduction of delinquency from $1.86 million to $826,000 in FY '82, a 46% reduction. Solely responsible for reducing bad debt from $724,000 to $382,000, a reduction of 53% for the same period. Jointly responsible for providing credit guidance and decisions to 23 lumber centers located in the four western states, with annual sales of $71 million and annual receivables of $78 million. Provided supervision and direction to 23 credit administrators to establish credit limits, terms and delinquency control for individual contractor customers.

OFFICE
MANAGEMENT:

Performed extensive administrative functions for 23 years. Interviewed, selected, and trained assigned clerical personnel. Supervised flow of correspondence, files, and communications. Reorganized and redesigned administrative procedures, resulting in improved accuracy, greater efficiency, and increased production. Reduced error rate by 38%. Devised and improved form letters and

Raymond L. Bhyers   Page 2

check lists for four separate administrative
positions, which improved efficiency and
reduced workload.

PERSONNEL
MANAGEMENT: Extensive supervisory experience with
                    personnel in performance of their assigned
                    tasks. Interviewed, classified, and counseled
                    individuals on career development and
                    formulation of realistic goals. Responsible
                    for the presentation and management of a
                    career development and retention program for
                    a population of 7000 personnel. Coordinated
                    personnel actions to include work assignments
                    for five separate departments, comprising 25
                    personnel technicians at all levels.

ADMINISTRATIVE
AND TRAINING: Responsible for budget formulation and
                    control of an administrative staff of 21
                    employed in a 24-hour, 365-day operation.
                    Motivated employees to reduce sick leave by
                    50%. In a volunteer capacity have served on
                    Department of Defense Credit Unions, on Board
                    of Directors for two. During tenure on one,
                    increased assets from $5.5 million to $8
                    million.

HOBBIES AND
INTERESTS: Boy Scout Leader, Little League Baseball
                    Coach. Currently member of Toastmasters,
                    International.

EDUCATION: Northwestern University, Evanston, IL
                    M.B.A. 1981

                    Chicago State University, Chicago, IL
                    B.A. 1979, Major: General Business;
                    Minors: Finance and Sociology

                    Community College of the Air Force
                    A.A.S. 1977, Major: Resource Management

PERSONAL: Married, three children. Health excellent.

REFERENCES: Available upon request.

Arlene M. Richardson
3439 N. Flowing Wells Road
Tucson, AZ 85705
(602) 888-5134

PROFESSIONAL OBJECTIVE

A challenging position and active involvement in a progressive
company offering the opportunity to fully utilize proven property
management skills in the area of multi-family housing.

SUMMARY OF SUPPORTIVE QUALIFICATIONS

A results-oriented self starter with highly developed management,
problem-solving, and decision-making skills, including the
following: marketing rental space, expense analysis, financial
reports, supervising staff, and writing and implementing property
policies.

WORK HISTORY

PROPERTY MANAGER--Pen Real Estate Investors, Tucson, AZ
    April 1992 to Present. Manage sixteen properties with a
    total of 1123 apartment units. Duties include preparing
    annual budgets, supervising operating expenditures,
    interviewing, hiring, evaluating staff, keeping property
    records, preparing monthly owner statements, and improving
    tenant relations.

PROPERTY MANAGER--ECM Consultants, Phoenix, AZ
    August 1990 to February 1992. Managed over 3000 apartment
    units during a two year period for various owners, ranging
    from private investors to savings and loan companies.
    Properties were all in Chapter 13 bankruptcy. Managed
    properties under direct accountability to the bankruptcy
    courts, maintained strict operating cost inventories, hired
    staff and vendors, and oversaw major renovation on many of
    the properties.

PROPERTY MANAGER--Gene Martin Properties, Newport Beach, CA
    January 1988 to July 1990. Managed 11 distressed properties
    which had been through foreclosure. My duties were to
    restructure the properties' operating costs through
    reorganization of staffs and vendors. I was also
    responsible for preparing annual budgets, for investigating
    each property, and for developing a report on each property
    with recommendations for any needed improvements.

Arlene M. Richardson   Page 2

EDUCATION

Pima Community College, Tucson, AZ
  January 1993 to Present. Currently working on my
  undergraduate studies towards a Bachelors Degree in Business
  Administration.

American Schools, Phoenix, AZ
  September 1988 to January 1992. Certificate of completion in
  the following college level real estate courses: law,
  appraisal, economics, practice, finance, property management
  and office administration.

  April 1992--Arizona Real Estate Broker's License

TRAINING

Institute of Property Management, Newport Beach, CA
  February 1988 to March 1988. A one month, in-depth training
  program for property management, including the management of
  residential, commercial and industrial properties. Also,
  specialization training in the management of distress
  properties, HUD properties, and Chapter 13 properties.
  Received a certificate of completion.

PROFESSIONAL AFFILIATIONS AND DESIGNATIONS

  Certified Property Manager--since 1989.
  Tempe Apartment Association--since 1990.
  Pima County Board of Realtors--since 1987.
  Arizona Association of Realtors--since 1990.

PERSONAL ATTRIBUTES

  I feel very comfortable accepting responsibility and
  delegating authority. I work well with others and have
  excellent negotiating skills. I am a hard worker who
  believes in getting the job done with cost-effective
  results. I have a lot of common sense and a great sense
  of humor.

REFERENCES AVAILABLE UPON REQUEST

Exercise 7.5

Write a complete resume that you could use if you were applying for a job today. The final copy must be typed or done on a word processor, and it must be free of errors. Choose a format and follow it consistently. Your final copy will be submitted with the cover letter you write in Exercise 7.6.

DEVELOPING THE COVER LETTER

Every resume must be accompanied by a cover letter. The resume merely lists your qualifications for a job; the cover letter goes one step further to tell why the prospective employer should hire you. In short, the cover letter introduces you. Because the employer will read your cover letter first, it should be carefully written to create the best impression possible.

The cover letter should not include the same material as your resume. Rather, it should tell other interesting things about you that you want the prospective employer to know. These ideas should be presented in a very appealing manner. If possible, the cover letter should be addressed to a specific individual to make its impact certain. Of course, you will not always know the name of the personnel manager, but if you can learn it, use it. When writing the cover letter, observe the following general rules.

1. Your basic purpose is to tell the prospective employer what you can do for his or her company.
2. Be brief. A two-page letter is far too long; a three-paragraph cover letter is long enough in most cases.
3. State exactly which position you are interested in early in the letter.
4. Be sure to mention your resume so the employer will feel compelled to read it.
5. Make sure your tone is serious. Be clever and funny *only if* you are applying for a job as a clown.

SAMPLE COVER LETTER 1 — Full Block Format

2121 10th Street
Oronoco, MN 55960
May 4, 1993

Mr. John Wilcock, Manager
Sterling Lumber Company
547 Taft Street
Fond du Lac, WI 54935

Dear Mr. Wilcock:

The enclosed record of loyal, dependable service in the
lumber and building trades may be of interest to you.

My broad experience, covering all aspects of the trades from
working in the woods to working as a finish carpenter, will
require a minimal adjustment period.

My variety of experiences has been good, but I would like to
change from seasonal work to a permanent position with an
established firm such as Sterling Lumber Company. I would
like a full-time job that provides advancement
opportunities.

May I ask you to read my enclosed resume and to permit me to
call your office for an appointment. Thank you.

Yours truly,

Eugene M. Roberts

SAMPLE COVER LETTER 2 — Semi-Block Format

1243 Tarkiln Road
New Bedford, MA 02745
January 23, 1993

Rebecca Greenberg, President
New Century Electronics
1096 W. Third Street
Williamsport, PA 17701

Dear Ms. Greenberg:

Your advertisement in the Wall Street Journal caught my attention. I have the "extensive personnel administration and innovative ideas" you advertised for.

For over 20 years, I have worked with large corporations, managing personnel, credit, and clerical departments. The experience and skills I gained as I worked for them will be invaluable to your company. The improvements I have initiated while working for those companies improved their profit picture immensely. I would be delighted to bring my skill and creativeness to New Century Electronics.

In addition to having relevant experiences, I also earned an M.B.A. from Northwestern University. While working on my degree, I specialized in personnel management and have read widely to remain current for the past six years. I have many ideas for the improvement of personnel departments.

I would consider a position with your company a challenging professional opportunity with great benefits. My wife and I would like to leave the congestion of New Bedford and explore new areas and career possibilities. When you examine the enclosed resume, you will immediately see my experience, education, and enthusiasm all indicate that I am the best person for the position.

Thank you for your time. If I don't receive a call from you before next Monday morning, I will call you to arrange an interview. I am confident we would both benefit from such an interview.

Please feel free to contact me at home at (617) 995-2772, or I will contact you next week.

Sincerely yours,

Raymond L. Bhyers

Raymond L. Bhyers

SAMPLE COVER LETTER 3 — Modified Block Format

5261 Explorer Drive
Fort Lauderdale, FL 33316
May 6, 1993

Mr. Karl Dinse
Point West Personnel Agency
1900 Point West Way, Suite 111
Fort Lauderdale, FL 33316

Dear Mr. Dinse:

This letter is to inform you of my interest in the position of Office Manager at Point West Personnel Agency.

I believe that the position of Office Manager calls for a person who can perform well in certain areas:

1. Must be able to work effectively without supervision.

2. Must have the ability to supervise others.

3. Must be knowledgeable about office procedures and be prepared to act instantly to correct any problems that may arise.

I have these qualities. As a receptionist/bookkeeper, I have had the sole responsibility of running the front desk, including distributing the mail, answering phone calls, and directing them promptly and accurately to the counselors in the office; presenting a good company image to incoming clients; and effectively maintaining the books for the firm. I have been able to perform such duties without supervision and have become knowledgeable about office procedures. Although I have not yet had the opportunity to supervise others, I feel confident that my experience in dealing with fellow workers and clients will make me effective as a supervisor.

I am attaching a resume of my experience. You may contact me at any time for a personal interview by writing to 5261 Explorer Drive or telephoning me at (305) 764-2180. I look forward to hearing from you soon.

Sincerely,

Louisa B. Garcia

Everything in your cover letter must be as perfect as you can make it if you want to make the best possible impression. Consider the following checklist before you do Exercise 7.6. Then check the list again after you have written your cover letter.

COVER LETTER CHECKLIST

1. **Complete address and date, including state abbreviation and ZIP code**
2. **Correct spelling of names and address in the inside address**
3. **No abbreviations except for the names of states or normally abbreviated titles (Dr., Mr., Mrs., and so on)**
4. **No mixing of Full Block, Modified Block, and Semi-Block formats**
5. **Not too wordy; say it briefly**
6. **Neatly typed final copy**

What to do with your resume:

1. Proofread your resume carefully to be sure it does not have any errors.
2. Have a company print 100 copies of your resume.
3. Send it to companies that are advertising in newspapers or magazines.
4. Send it to companies that might have jobs for which you are qualified. This is the best use of the resume!
5. Send your resume to as many businesses as possible. The more people who read about you, the greater your chance of getting a job.
6. Whenever possible, personalize your cover letter. Do this by making certain the prospective employer knows exactly how well-suited you are for his or her *particular* company, not just any company. Point out how much you like the community where the business is located or how you have long wanted to work for that company.

What not to do with your resume:

1. Do *not* send it to anyone when it is in a rough and messy form.
2. Do *not* include false information in your resume.

Exercise 7.6

Write a cover letter to accompany the resume you wrote for Exercise 7.5. Type the final copy (or do it on a computer). Be sure it is your best effort. Check your cover letter against the Cover Letter Checklist before submitting it to your instructor.

8

Filling Out Standardized Forms

When you have completed this chapter, you will be able to—

1. List the common reasons for using forms.
2. Approach forms with a plan and with confidence.
3. Develop rough drafts to help you fill out forms.
4. Prepare for forms that must be filled out under time pressure.
5. Fill out forms without leaving any blanks.
6. Cope with difficulties commonly encountered when filling out forms.

Nearly everyone in this society will encounter some kind of standardized form. A standardized form is any preprinted form designed to be used by different people to convey a particular type of information. Grade report forms are a part of every class in our schools. Accident report forms are found in every truck and in every business where accidents can occur. And think of the number of report forms in hospitals, state office buildings, and police stations where precise records are necessary. The number of forms used in our society is incredible.

In fact, there are so many different report forms in this world that you cannot study one form or one type and know all about standardized report forms. All you can do at this point is learn the characteristics common to most forms and practice filling out some of those forms. The techniques you learn in this chapter will help you fill out any form you might encounter.

The reasons for learning to properly fill out forms are obvious. A recent study revealed that most employers complain that many job applicants are unable to correctly complete a basic job application form. As you might guess, if a prospective employee cannot fill out an application form, an employer might suspect that the person would also have difficulty accomplishing other job-related writing assignments.

WHY ARE STANDARDIZED FORMS USED?

To gain a thorough understanding of how to fill out forms, you must first know why companies develop so many of them. The most common reasons for using standardized forms are the following:

1. **To make information complete.** The basic reason for using forms is to make sure no information is overlooked. When people apply for jobs, for instance, they are almost always asked to fill out a long application form before they go in for the interview. Employers have found this necessary because applicants often accidentally or deliberately omit details about past employment and health. Yet these omitted details are important to the prospective employer. Standardized forms are also widely used to report accidents because people filing such reports are likely to forget details. These report forms deliberately ask every conceivable question to force the reporting person to think carefully about the accident.

2. **To save time.** The standard report form is also preferred because it takes much less time to fill out a form than it takes to write the same information in paragraphs. The average person should be able to fill out almost any standard form in minutes.

3. **To make information objective.** Forms remove much of the personal bias often found in written reports. When people are given a blank piece of paper and told to explain what happened, they often become bogged down with details that particularly impressed them but never really explain the issue.

An incident that dramatically illustrates this tendency occurred on Midway Island in the Pacific Ocean a few years ago. Nine men were working with a crane, picking up and stacking concrete blocks. The crane boom broke, fell across a tractor, and crushed the tractor operator. When the inspecting officer asked each man to write out an account of the accident, he discovered that no two people described the event exactly the same. In fact, he found it difficult to believe that all of them had been present at the scene of the same accident. In an attempt to understand what actually occurred, the inspector gave each worker a standardized form. When all the workers were forced to answer the same specific questions about the accident, the inspecting officer quickly learned what had happened.

4. **To place information in order.** Forms also force the person making the report to explain what happened in the proper sequence. That is, if the form asks the questions in a logical order, the person filling out the form cannot deviate from that order.

5. **To make information uniform.** Finally, the uniformity of standard forms aids the person who must read large numbers of reports. A personnel manager can save hours of time if all of the applicants for a particular job have filled out standard job application forms. For example, an engineering firm might be searching among a group of sixty-eight applicants for a civil engineer with hydrographic surveying experience in the tropics. Consider how much faster it would be to examine sixty-eight applications, looking only in one specific blank on each form, than it would be to read through all sixty-eight resumes.

Accident reports and job applications are just two of the many uses of standard forms. You will encounter sales forms when you go shopping or if you work in a retail store. If, for example, you work for a hardware store, you will most likely fill out an itemized sales form for each business transaction. In addition, you may complete estimate forms when you bid on a job for a contractor; inventory forms when you file a report of the stock on hand on a given date; loss forms when merchandise is stolen or destroyed; federal, state, and local tax forms stating your store's profit and loss; and many other common forms. Similar forms are a part of virtually every type of business.

Exercise 8.1

Answer each of the following questions.

1. List three of the forms you have recently encountered in your life.

   (1) _____

   (2) _____

   (3) _____

2. Briefly list five reasons employers use forms.

   (1) _____

   _____

   _____

   (2) _____

   _____

   _____

   (3) _____

   _____

   _____

   (4) _____

   _____

   _____

   (5) _____

   _____

   _____

Have your work on Item 1 checked by your instructor or a tutor; check Item 2 with the Answer Key.

THE TELEPHONE MESSAGE

No standard form is completed incorrectly more frequently than the telephone message form. Because the form used by most companies covers only a very small piece of paper and looks insignificant, employees become careless as they fill it out. If you consider the parts of the telephone form below, you can see the problem areas.

```
+-----------------------------------------------------+
|                   M E S S A G E                     |
| Date_____Time_____                   |
| To_____|
|               WHILE  YOU  WERE  OUT                 |
|                                                     |
| M _____|
|                                                     |
| of _____|
|                                                     |
| Phone_____|
|        AREA CODE        NUMBER        EXTENSION     |
|  +-----------------------+-----------------------+  |
|  | TELEPHONED            | PLEASE  CALL          |  |
|  | CALLED TO SEE YOU     | WILL CALL AGAIN       |  |
|  | WANTS TO SEE YOU      | RETURNED YOUR CALL    |  |
|  |         * URGENT      |    |                  |  |
|  +-----------------------------------------------+  |
| Message_____|
| _____|
| _____|
| _____|
| _____|
|                            _____      |
|                            TAKEN BY                 |
+-----------------------------------------------------+
```

You may have to take telephone calls for other employees when you are busy. That's when you are most likely to leave out important information. The top portion of most standard telephone message forms contains three essential items: the name of the person the caller wanted to speak with, the date, and the time. To avoid confusion, resist the temptation to omit the last name of either the person you took the message for or the caller.

Perhaps the best way to avoid problems with this shortest of all standard office forms is to leave no blanks and to be complete. This advice is particularly relevant to the message portion at the bottom. When the telephone interrupts what you are doing, you will occasionally have to force yourself to take the time to fill in the message portion. You may think the person for whom you took the message will quickly learn the message when he or she returns the call. The message portion, however, allows that person to be prepared mentally before returning the call.

FILLING OUT LONGER STANDARD FORMS

Forms intimidate some people unnecessarily, especially if they have never learned how to complete forms properly. A good form should be easy to fill out; it should include clear directions and require little thought. A poorly constructed form takes a little more thought, but you can learn to complete even a confusing form without extreme difficulty. You should approach all forms—good and bad —in the same way. Use the following steps as you fill out forms:

1. **Read the entire form rapidly** to see generally what types of questions are asked.

2. Read the form again, paying particular attention to the **directions**. Never begin filling out any form until you understand exactly what is expected of you. Be sure you know where your name goes; for instance, does it go above or below the word "name?"

3. If you have time, **make a rough draft** for longer forms. Obviously, you would never bother with a rough draft when speed is necessary. But when you have enough time and neatness could be a factor, don't forget to make a rough draft. Rough drafts are especially valuable when you are asked to fill out a complex form that has some items which you don't understand when you begin. As you work through a form, a later question will often help you answer an earlier question that caused confusion. Be sure you use a dictionary to check the spelling of all words you might have misspelled. Employers report that over half of all standard forms contain misspelled words.

4. Always fill out the form **in order**, beginning with the first blank and working your way through to the last. If you fill in blanks randomly, you run a high risk of forgetting something.

5. **Never leave an empty blank** on any standard form. You must write something in every blank. Even if the question asked in a certain blank does not apply to your situation, every blank must still be filled. For example, if you are asked how many children you have and you have none, don't simply leave that item blank; write "none." In other instances, standard forms will ask you for information that has nothing whatsoever to do with the situation. In such a case, you should write "NA" for "not applicable." When you write "none" or "NA" in a blank, your reader instantly knows you considered that point. The reader will not wonder whether you forgot to fill it in or deliberately avoided answering in an attempt to hide information.

6. Be as **brief** as you can. Most report forms have limited space to prevent the writer from becoming wordy and to make the reader's job easier and faster. Do not use long, elaborate sentences when filling out

report forms; you will only run out of space and lose your reader. However, do not give such brief answers that you fail to explain adequately. Try to say everything relevant to the question in the fewest words. Briefness is the ideal, but remember that omissions cause misunderstandings.

7. If the form you fill out has multiple copies, you will often be expected to **detach and keep one copy**. The directions telling which copy you are to keep usually appear at the bottom of each page.

Exercise 8.2

Use the following account of a boating mishap to fill out the California Boating Accident Report. Remember to write something in every blank. Write *NA* if the blank is not applicable. Write *UN* in the blank if the information is unknown.

SACRAMENTO RIVER TRAGEDY

The boating accident occurred under clear skies, three miles west of the town of Rio Vista, California, on the Sacramento River on July 17, 1985, just inside the border of Solano County. The boat named *Daffy Duck* (CF 9698 ER) was returning to the Pittsburg Marina at 4:33 p.m. after a day's fishing. The winds were blowing about 20 mph from the west, the direction the boat was traveling, and the water surface had become rough. The light aluminum Sharkcraft Model 14 boat, hull #1084, which was powered by a 65 horsepower Mercury outboard, was pounding badly. The operator, Jason Glout, 32, had about 30 hours of experience with open motorboats such as the one he rented on the day of the accident. The boat, which was 4'1" wide and 14'7" long, was only one year old. It was regularly inspected and in good condition. Because it was being pushed through the rough waters too fast, the boat turned over on a large wave and capsized. The owners of the craft, Pitts Marine, reported that Mr. Glout's signed rental agreement stated that he had completed the boating safety course offered by the U.S. Power Squadron one year earlier.

The two men in the boat at the time of the capsizing were thrown out as the boat sank. Neither man was wearing a lifesaving device at the time of the accident although there were four Coast Guard approved life preservers in the boat. Both men began swimming for shore in the 66 degree water immediately after the boat sank. Mr. Glout, of 3612 Creekside Blvd., Rio Vista, California 95002, was unable to reach shore and sank below the surface approximately ½ mile from the beach. Mr. William Ming, however, reached the shore and flagged down a passing motorist who called the Coast Guard. Search and rescue teams discovered Mr. Glout's body at 6:12 p.m., one mile downstream from the point where the boat capsized. Mr. Ming was taken to a hospital, treated for shock, and released the next day. Mr. Ming lives at the same address as Mr. Glout. His phone number is (707) 374-0942.

No other vessels were in sight at the time of the accident, and there were no witnesses other than Mr. Ming. The boat being operated by Mr. Glout has not been recovered and must be considered a total loss. Pitts Marine established a cost of $1,782.00 on the boat, motor, and equipment. The company's address is 290 East "B" Street, Benicia, California 94510.

IMPORTANT—It is mandatory that all items be completed when the information is available.

CALIFORNIA BOATING ACCIDENT REPORT

THE OPERATOR OF EVERY RECREATIONAL VESSEL IS REQUIRED BY SECTION 656 OF THE HARBORS AND NAVIGATION CODE TO FILE A WRITTEN REPORT WHENEVER A BOATING ACCIDENT OCCURS WHICH RESULTS IN DEATH, DISAPPEARANCE, INJURY THAT REQUIRES MEDICAL TREATMENT BEYOND FIRST AID, TOTAL PROPERTY DAMAGE IN EXCESS OF $200, OR COMPLETE LOSS OF A VESSEL. REPORTS MUST BE SUBMITTED WITHIN FORTY-EIGHT (48) HOURS IN CASE OF DEATH OCCURRING WITHIN 24 HOURS OF THE ACCIDENT, DISAPPEARANCE, OR INJURY THAT REQUIRES MEDICAL TREATMENT BEYOND FIRST AID. ALL OTHER REPORTABLE ACCIDENTS MUST BE SUBMITTED IN WRITING WITHIN TEN (10) DAYS. REPORTS ARE TO BE SUBMITTED TO THE DEPARTMENT OF BOATING AND WATERWAYS, 1629 S STREET, SACRAMENTO, CA 95814-7291, (916) 322-1833. FAILURE TO SUBMIT THIS REPORT AS REQUIRED IS A MISDEMEANOR AND IS PUNISHABLE BY A FINE NOT TO EXCEED ONE THOUSAND DOLLARS ($1,000) OR IMPRISONMENT NOT TO EXCEED SIX (6) MONTHS OR BOTH.

COMPLETE ALL BLOCKS (PRINT OR TYPE ALL INFORMATION. INDICATE THOSE NOT APPLICABLE BY "NA." THOSE UNKNOWN BY "UN."

1. OPERATOR'S NAME AND ADDRESS — AGE____
HOME PHONE (   )   WORK PHONE (   )

2. RENTED BOAT — ☐ YES ☐ NO

3. OPERATOR'S EXPERIENCE
THIS TYPE OF BOAT: ☐ UNDER 20 HOURS ☐ 20 TO 100 HOURS ☐ 100 TO 500 HOURS ☐ OVER 500 HOURS
OTHER BOAT OPERATING EXPERIENCE: ☐ UNDER 20 HOURS ☐ 20 TO 100 HOURS ☐ 100 TO 500 HOURS ☐ OVER 500 HOURS

4. OWNER'S NAME AND ADDRESS
HOME PHONE (   )   WORK PHONE (   )

5. NUMBER OF PERSONS ON BOARD

6. NUMBER OF PERSONS TOWED (I.E. SKIING ETC.)

7. FORMAL INSTRUCTION IN BOATING SAFETY
☐ NONE ☐ USCG AUXILIARY ☐ US POWER SQUADRON ☐ AMERICAN RED CROSS ☐ STATE ☐ OTHER (SPECIFY)

VESSEL NO. 1 (YOUR VESSEL)

8. BOAT NUMBER | 9. BOAT NAME | 10. BOAT MANUFACTURER | 11. BOAT MODEL | 12. MFGR. HULL IDENT. NO.

13. TYPE OF BOAT: ☐ OPEN MOTORBOAT ☐ CABIN MOTORBOAT ☐ AUXILIARY SAIL ☐ SAIL ONLY ☐ HOUSEBOAT ☐ RAFT ☐ CANOE ☐ KAYAK ☐ JET SKI/WETBIKE ☐ ROWBOAT ☐ OTHER (SPECIFY)

14. HULL MATERIAL: ☐ WOOD ☐ ALUMINUM ☐ STEEL ☐ FIBERGLASS ☐ RUBBER/VINYL ☐ PLASTIC ☐ OTHER (SPECIFY)

15. PROPULSION: ☐ OUTBOARD ☐ INBOARD ☐ INBOARD-OUTBOARD ☐ JET ☐ SAIL ☐ PADDLE/OARS ☐ OTHER (SPECIFY) — TYPE OF FUEL

16. BOAT DATA
NUMBER OF ENGINES ____ LENGTH ____
MAKE OF ENGINE ____ BEAM (WIDTH) ____
HORSEPOWER (TOTAL) ____ DEPTH (TOP OF INNER TRANSOM TO KEEL) ____
YEAR BUILT (ENGINE) ____ YEAR BUILT (BOAT) ____

17. PRIMARY BOAT USE: ☐ RECREATIONAL ☐ COMMERCIAL ☐ FOR-HIRE ☐ WORK BOAT

18. PREVIOUS ACCIDENTS INVOLVING THIS BOAT — DATES

VESSEL NO. 2 (OTHER VESSEL INVOLVED)

19. BOAT NUMBER | 20. BOAT NAME | 21. BOAT MANUFACTURER | 22. BOAT MODEL | 23. MFGR. HULL IDENT. NO.

24. NAME OF OPERATOR — AGE____
HOME PHONE (   ) WORK PHONE (   )

25. ADDRESS

26. NAME OF OWNER
HOME PHONE (   ) WORK PHONE (   )

27. ADDRESS

28. WITNESSES

NAME	ADDRESS	TELEPHONE NUMBER
NAME AGE____	ADDRESS	( )
NAME AGE____	ADDRESS	( )
NAME AGE____	ADDRESS	( )

ACCIDENT DATE AND LOCATION

29. DATE OF ACCIDENT | 30. TIME ☐ AM ☐ PM | 31. NAME OF BODY OF WATER / 32. LAST PORT OF CALL | 33. LOCATION (AS PRECISELY AS POSSIBLE)

34. STATE | 35. NEAREST CITY OR TOWN | 36. COUNTY

ENVIRONMENTAL CONDITIONS

37. WEATHER: ☐ CLEAR ☐ CLOUDY ☐ FOG ☐ RAIN ☐ SNOW ☐ HAZY

38. WATER CONDITIONS: ☐ CALM ☐ CHOPPY ☐ ROUGH ☐ VERY ROUGH ☐ STRONG CURRENT

39. TEMPERATURE (ESTIMATE) AIR ____°F WATER ____°F

40. WIND: ☐ NONE ☐ LIGHT (0 TO 6 MPH) ☐ MODERATE (7 TO 14 MPH) ☐ STRONG (15 TO 25 MPH) ☐ STORM (25 MPH AND OVER)

41. VISIBILITY: ☐ GOOD ☐ FAIR ☐ POOR

42. WEATHER ENCOUNTERED: ☐ WAS AS FORECAST ☐ NOT AS FORECAST ☐ FORECAST NOT OBTAINED

THIS **CONFIDENTIAL REPORT** IS USED IN RESEARCH FOR THE PREVENTION OF ACCIDENTS, AND A COPY IS FORWARDED TO THE UNITED STATES COAST GUARD.   (COMPLETE BOTH SIDES)

A-1 (REV. 11-83)   85 36095

ACCIDENT DATA

43. OPERATION AT TIME OF ACCIDENT

(CHECK ALL APPLICABLE)

- ☐ CRUISING   ☐ DRIFTING
- ☐ MANEUVERING   ☐ AT ANCHOR
- ☐ WATER SKIING   ☐ TIED TO DOCK
- ☐ TOWING   ☐ OTHER (USE ITEM 48)
- ☐ ACCELERATING

44. TYPE OF ACCIDENT

- ☐ GROUNDING   ☐ COLLISION WITH FIXED OBJECT
- ☐ CAPSIZING   ☐ COLLISION WITH FLOATING OBJECT
- ☐ FLOODING   ☐ FALL OVERBOARD
- ☐ SINKING   ☐ FALL IN BOAT
- ☐ FIRE OR EXPLOSION (FUEL)   ☐ PERSON(S) HIT BY BOAT OR PROPELLER
- ☐ FIRE OR EXPLOSION (OTHER THAN FUEL)   ☐ OTHER (USE ITEM 48)
- ☐ VESSEL(S) COLLISION

45. IN YOUR OPINION, CAUSE OF ACCIDENT

- ☐ WEATHER CONDITIONS   ☐ RESTRICTED VISION
- ☐ EXCESSIVE SPEED   ☐ FAULT OF HULL
- ☐ NO PROPER LOOKOUT   ☐ FAULT OF MACHINERY
- ☐ OVERLOADING   ☐ FAULT OF EQUIPMENT
- ☐ IMPROPER LOADING   ☐ FATIGUE
- ☐ HAZARDOUS WATERS   ☐ OTHER (SPECIFY)
- ☐ ALCOHOL
- ☐ DRUGS

46. PERSONAL FLOTATION DEVICES (PFD)

WAS THE BOAT ADEQUATELY EQUIPPED WITH COAST GUARD APPROVED PERSONAL FLOTATION DEVICES?
☐ YES   ☐ NO

WERE THEY ACCESSIBLE? ☐ YES ☐ NO

WERE THEY USED? ☐ YES ☐ NO

WAS THE VESSEL CARRYING NONAPPROVED

LIFESAVING DEVICES? ☐ YES ☐ NO

WERE THEY ACCESSIBLE? ☐ YES ☐ NO

WERE THEY USED? ☐ YES ☐ NO

47. FIRE EXTINGUISHERS

WAS APPROVED TYPE FIRE FIGHTING EQUIPMENT ABOARD?
☐ YES   ☐ NO

WERE THEY USED? (IF "YES", LIST TYPE(S) AND NUMBER)
☐ YES   ☐ NO

48. ACCIDENT DESCRIPTION

DESCRIBE WHAT HAPPENED AND WHAT COULD HAVE PREVENTED THIS ACCIDENT. (INCLUDE FAILURE OF EQUIPMENT. EXPLAIN CAUSE OF DEATH OR INJURY, MEDICAL TREATMENT, ETC. USE SKETCH IF HELPFUL. IF NEEDED, CONTINUE DESCRIPTION ON ADDITIONAL PAPER.)

49. POLICE REPORT TAKEN?

☐ YES ☐ NO AGENCY NAME: _____   TELEPHONE NUMBER ( )

50. DECEASED

NAME	ADDRESS	DATE OF BIRTH	VICTIM WAS—	CAUSE OF DEATH
			☐ SWIMMER ☐ NON-SWIMMER ☐ DRINKING ALCOHOL ☐ USING DRUGS	☐ DROWNING ☐ DISAPPEARANCE ☐ OTHER (USE ITEM 48.)
			☐ SWIMMER ☐ NON-SWIMMER ☐ DRINKING ALCOHOL ☐ USING DRUGS	☐ DROWNING ☐ DISAPPEARANCE ☐ OTHER (USE ITEM 48.)

51. INJURED (UNCONSCIOUS, GIVEN MEDICAL TREATMENT OR DISABLED OVER 24 HOURS)

NAME / TELEPHONE NUMBER ( )	ADDRESS	DATE OF BIRTH	NATURE OF INJURY / INJURED WAS—	
			NATURE OF INJURY INJURED WAS— ☐ DRINKING ALCOHOL ☐ USING DRUGS	☐ RECEIVED TREATMENT ☐ INCAPACITATED OVER 24 HOURS
			NATURE OF INJURY INJURED WAS— ☐ DRINKING ALCOHOL ☐ USING DRUGS	☐ RECEIVED TREATMENT ☐ INCAPACITATED OVER 24 HOURS

52. PROPERTY DAMAGE (ESTIMATE AND DESCRIBE)

THIS BOAT $ _____

TOTALLY DESTROYED ☐ YES ☐ NO OTHER BOAT $ _____ TOTAL BOTH BOATS $ _____ OTHER PROPERTY $ _____

53. PERSON COMPLETING REPORT

SIGNATURE OF PERSON COMPLETING REPORT

ADDRESS

DATE SUBMITTED

QUALIFICATION (CHECK ONE) ☐ OPERATOR ☐ OWNER

OTHER (SPECIFY)

TELEPHONE NUMBER ( )

SEND TO: DEPARTMENT OF BOATING AND WATERWAYS, 1629 S STREET, SACRAMENTO, CA 95814-7291

Have your work checked by your instructor or a tutor.

FILLING OUT FORMS WHEN UNDER PRESSURE

In some situations, you will have to fill out a form in a short period of time, even though you are totally unfamiliar with the form. This is especially true with job applications, driver's license applications, and other similar forms. Accuracy, speed, and neatness are important, especially in job applications where your prospective employer may be determining your fitness as an employee from the form. In such a situation, the ability to fill out a form quickly and properly could be very important.

Although each form is different, you can prepare yourself for filling out forms by following these steps ahead of time:

1. **Assemble dates, names, titles, and places** before you go to an interview where you might be asked to complete a form such as a job application. In a situation like a job interview, the pressure you feel might make you forget details—the titles of someone you worked for, an address, or the dates you worked for a particular organization. To avoid getting into an embarrassing situation like this, write out a job history exactly as you did for your resume in Chapter 7. Use the job history to help you fill out the application.

2. **Practice spelling difficult words or names** before you go to an interview where you might have to fill out an application under pressure of time. For example, if you fill out an application for a pest control company, be sure you know how to spell key words such as *extermination, debris,* and *fungus.* Even more important, be sure you know how to correctly spell the names of cities, streets, and people for whom you have worked.

You will find that many standard forms will have characteristics which will create problems for you. The most common problems and their solutions follow:

1. **Not enough space** to write an adequate response is undoubtedly the most common complaint about forms. When you find that you need more space, ask yourself first if you truly understand the question. You may find that you are attempting to answer more than the question is asking. If you recheck the form and cannot see any other possible interpretation, the next step is to shorten your response. Other obvious solutions to the problem are abbreviating commonly abbreviated words, writing smaller, and writing above or below the line. When you are certain that you need more room, use one or more of these techniques.

2. **Poor directions** are another common difficulty when filling out forms when under pressure. If you are confused about what is wanted, ask someone to explain it to you if possible. But if no one is available, look at the questions immediately above and below the troublesome directions. Usually a relationship will become obvious, providing a clue to what is being asked.

3. **Irrelevant questions** are found on almost every form, especially

employment forms. Whenever a form is designed to be used for more than one situation or for more than one person, extra items must be included. Again, the only solution to this problem is to write *NA* in the blank. Never leave the blank empty.

4. **"Write clearly,"** a very common message on standard forms, has two distinctly different meanings. In the most literal sense, "write clearly" warns you to make sure your reader can read your handwriting. You may need to print if your handwriting is not easily read. "Write clearly" also refers to pressing hard enough when filling out a standard form that contains multiple copies. An increasing number of forms make carbon copies as you write on the original page. To make sure your carbon copies are clear, you must use a ballpoint pen (or a pencil, if that seems appropriate). Felt-tip pens and fountain pens rarely make readable carbon copies.

JOB APPLICATION FORMS

Job application forms are important. Before employers even read your resume, they will carefully examine the application you filled out, looking for specific qualifications. If your application reveals careless preparation, misspelled words, blanks not filled in, vague information, or a missing signature, your name may be removed from the list of possible job candidates. The only way to be certain you will fill out applications properly in the future is to practice now, before you get in a situation where you will be asked to fill out an application on the spot.

Exercise 8.3

Complete the following application for employment.

APPLICATION FOR EMPLOYMENT
AN AFFIRMATIVE ACTION/EQUAL OPPORTUNITY EMPLOYER

APPLICANT'S NAME

DATE

MO	DAY	YR

LAST

FIRST

M.I.

POSITION DESIRED

PERSONAL INFORMATION

LAST NAME

FIRST NAME

MIDDLE INITIAL

SOCIAL SECURITY NUMBER

STREET ADDRESS

CITY   STATE   ZIP CODE

HOME PHONE   WORK PHONE   MESSAGE PHONE NO's.
(   )   (   )

DO YOU HAVE RELATIVES EMPLOYED AT BLUE CROSS? ☐ YES ☐ NO

ARE YOU UNDER AGE 18? ☐ YES ☐ NO

IF YOU ARE OFFERED A POSITION WITH BLUE CROSS OF CALIFORNIA CAN YOU SUPPLY PROOF OF YOUR RIGHT TO WORK IN THE U.S.A? ☐ YES ☐ NO

HAVE YOU EVER APPLIED FOR WORK AT BLUE CROSS? ☐ YES ☐ NO

HOW WERE YOU REFERRED TO BLUE CROSS?

HAVE YOU BEEN CONVICTED OF A FELONY? ☐ YES ☐ NO

POSITION INFORMATION

POSITION DESIRED

DATE AVAILABLE FOR WORK   SALARY DESIRED
/MO   /YR

PLEASE DO NOT COMPLETE SHADED AREA

TYPE	FULL TIME ☐	PART TIME ☐	CLASS	REGULAR ☐	TEMPORARY ☐
JOB CODE		W.C./C.C. NO.		REFERENCE	

SHIFT PREFERRED   ☐ 1   ☐ 2   ☐ 3   ☐ 4 W/E

ANSWER ALL QUESTIONS IN THIS SECTION IF POSITION APPLIED FOR REQUIRES DRIVING AN AUTOMOBILE OR A COMPANY CAR.

VALID DRIVER'S LICENSE?   IF YES, WHICH STATE?
☐ YES ☐ NO

UNDER WHAT OTHER NAMES HAVE YOU WORKED?

CONVICTION OF A CRIME IS NOT AN AUTOMATIC BAR TO EMPLOYMENT. ALL CIRCUMSTANCES WILL BE CONSIDERED.

EDUCATION

TYPE OF SCHOOL	NAME, CITY AND STATE OF SCHOOL	MAJOR	CIRCLE LAST YEAR COMPLETED	DEGREE
HIGH SCHOOL			FR SOPH JR SR	DIPLOMA? ☐ YES ☐ NO
COLLEGE			FR SOPH JR SR	DEGREE RECEIVED
GRADUATE, BUSINESS, TRADE, OR NIGHT SCHOOL				GRADUATED? ☐ YES ☐ NO

ADDITIONAL SKILLS OR TRAINING WHICH MAY BE APPLICABLE TO EMPLOYMENT AT BLUE CROSS

WHAT PROFESSIONAL LICENSES OR CERTIFICATES DO YOU HOLD?   VALID IN WHAT STATE?   DATE EXPIRES

LANGUAGES YOU READ, SPEAK OR WRITE FLUENTLY?

TYPING? ☐ YES ☐ NO WPM _____

SHORTHAND? ☐ YES ☐ NO WPM _____

WORD PROCESSING? ☐ YES ☐ NO (MODEL) _____

CRT? ☐ YES ☐ NO

MILITARY STATUS

ARE YOU A VIETNAM ERA VETERAN? ☐ YES ☐ NO

MILITARY TRAINING WHICH WOULD QUALIFY YOU FOR THE POSITION YOU ARE APPLYING FOR.

HEALTH STATUS

DO YOU HAVE ANY PHYSICAL CONDITION OR HANDICAP WHICH MAY LIMIT YOUR ABILITY TO PERFORM THE JOB APPLIED FOR? ☐ YES ☐ NO

IF YES, WHAT CAN BE DONE TO ACCOMMODATE YOUR LIMITATIONS?

OFFICES STATEWIDE

Bakersfield	Los Angeles	San Francisco	Santa Monica
Burbank	Sacramento	San Jose	
East Bay (Emeryville)	San Bernardino	Santa Ana	
Fresno	San Diego	Santa Barbara	

PER-5 SW (Rev. 1/85)

EMPLOYMENT DATA	List all previous employment. Include military service. Account for any periods of time not covered by stating nature of your activities. Use separate sheet of paper if necessary. LIST YOUR MOST RECENT EMPLOYMENT FIRST.
	May we contact your present employer? ☐ YES ☐ NO

DATES	COMPANY NAME AND ADDRESS	JOB TITLE/DUTIES	BASE SALARY PER MONTH	REASON FOR LEAVING
TO			FINAL $	
FROM			STARTING $	
SUPERVISOR NAME AND TITLE			PHONE ( )	
TO			FINAL $	
FROM			STARTING $	
SUPERVISOR NAME AND TITLE			PHONE ( )	
TO			FINAL $	
FROM			STARTING $	
SUPERVISOR NAME AND TITLE			PHONE ( )	
TO			FINAL $	
FROM			STARTING $	
SUPERVISOR NAME AND TITLE			PHONE ( )	

CERTIFICATION

APPLICANT: PLEASE READ THE FOLLOWING CAREFULLY BEFORE SIGNING THIS APPLICATION FORM

1. I declare my answers to the questions on this application are true to the best of my knowledge and belief. It is understood that any false statements appearing on any employment form will be sufficient reason for dismissal from the service of .
2. I understand that my pre-employment qualifications are subject to investigation and I hereby authorize (company) to conduct any necessary inquiries. And, I hereby release any former employers from all liability for any damages resulting from information furnished by them.
3. I also understand that a pre-employment physical examination may be required and is performed by a medical doctor selected by (company) without cost to the applicant. I agree to submit to this procedure with the knowledge that the results of this examination are a determining factor in obtaining employment with the above-named organization.
4. If employed, I will abide by the existing rules of (company) and such rules and regulations as may become effective while employed by said organization.
5. Your potential employment with (company) will be voluntarily entered into and you are free to resign at any time. Similarly, the Company is free to conclude an employment relationship where it believes it is in the Company's best interests at any time. While we hope our relationship would be long and mutually beneficial, it should be recognized that neither you, nor we will have entered into any contract of employment, express or implied. Our relationship is and always will be one of voluntary employment "at will."

I HAVE READ AND UNDERSTAND THE ABOVE

_____
SIGNATURE OF APPLICANT   DATE

TO BE COMPLETED UPON DATE OF HIRE

PERSON TO BE NOTIFIED IN EVENT OF EMERGENCY	ADDRESS	PHONE NO. ( )	APPLICANT'S BIRTHDAY MM DD YY

DO NOT WRITE BELOW THIS LINE

V: 1. 2. H: V. H. O. F. A. S: M. F. R: W. B. A. I. H. A: Y. N. C: 1. 2. 3. 4. 5. 6. 7. 8. 9.

INTERVIEW-1					INTERVIEW-2				
0 1	NAME	DATE M M D D	CC#	REQ.#	RTG	0 2 NAME	DATE M M D D	CC#	REQ.#	RTG

INTERVIEW-3					INTERVIEW-4				
0 3	NAME	DATE M M D D	CC#	REQ.#	RTG	0 4 NAME	DATE M M D D	CC#	REQ.#	RTG

TEST-1				TEST-2				TEST-3			
0 1	TYPE	DATE M M D D	RESULT	0 2 TYPE	DATE	RESULT	0 3 TYPE	DATE M M D D	RESULT

HIRE DATA

OFFER DATE	REQ.#	INT. I.D.	POSITION NUMBER	COST CENTER	STARTING SALARY	START DATE
JOB TITLE				HIRING SUPERVISOR		EXTENSION

Have your work checked by your instructor or a tutor.

PART THREE

Paragraphs:
Structures and Strategies

In the last few chapters, the memos, business letters, and resumes you wrote had short paragraphs that contained few sentences. Long paragraphs generally are not needed in memos and letters. The points being discussed in such business writing are frequently simple and direct enough so that a few sentences of explanation are sufficient. However, not all paragraphs you write will be so simple. In both the business and academic worlds, you will frequently find that you need to explain some very complex ideas. When you are faced with such explanations, the paragraphs you write will become noticeably longer.

When writing longer paragraphs, you may encounter problems that didn't occur when writing shorter ones. Minor questions, which can be easily ignored when writing short paragraphs, become major problems as paragraphs get longer. But when you thoroughly understand paragraph structure, you will have no trouble writing long paragraphs. As you work through the following chapters, you will discover that most paragraphs, regardless of their length, have the same basic structure.

In addition to knowing paragraph structure, you will have to know various methods—called **strategies**—of presenting ideas in order to write longer reports, research papers, and college essays. For every paragraph you write, there is a "best" arrangement. That is, there is always one most effective way to present your ideas. For this reason, you must know the various strategies if you want to achieve maximum impact.

CHAPTER

9

Writing Effective Paragraphs

When you have completed this chapter, you will be able to—

1. Select a topic to write on.
2. Develop a topic into a topic sentence.
3. Identify the controlling idea in topic sentences.
4. Develop topic sentences with simple and divided controlling ideas.
5. Write primary support sentences to explain topic sentences.
6. Write secondary support sentences that give examples of primary support sentences.
7. Identify topic, primary, secondary, and concluding sentences in paragraphs.
8. Write paragraphs using topic, primary, secondary, and concluding sentences.

A **paragraph** is a group of sentences that focuses on one specific topic. Although the paragraphs you write in memos and business letters may be no longer than a few sentences, paragraphs in more complex writing are normally between five and twelve sentences long. A longer paragraph is not necessarily better; it is just that a longer paragraph allows you more space to explain complex ideas. If an idea is very simple, a short paragraph is adequate. If an idea is very complex, you should write a long paragraph. Usually, topics differ in complexity from one paragraph to the next, so your paragraphs will often be of different lengths.

A paragraph is much more than a mere collection of sentences. A strong topic sentence, usually the first sentence, tells the reader exactly what the point of the paragraph is. After the topic sentence, you will write support groups to explain the topic sentence. These support groups may range in length from one to five sentences, depending on the complexity of the ideas. You may include as many support groups as you need to completely explain the topic sentence, although one sentence is usually not enough and more than four sentences usually develops into an excessively long paragraph. Support groups are made up of primary and secondary support sentences. Primary support sentences explain one part of the topic sentence; secondary support sentences give examples of what the primary support explains. Although this brief explanation of paragraph structure may sound complex, you will discover that writing is actually very easy if you keep these basic parts in mind and write carefully.

The following diagram illustrates the relationships of sentences in the basic paragraph. Refer back to the diagram as you work your way through the unit.

Topic Sentence _____

_____

_____. Primary Support 1 _____

_____

_____. Secondary Support _____

_____

_____. Secondary Support _____

_____

_____. Primary Support 2 _____

_____

Secondary Support _____

_____

_____. Concluding Sentence _____

_____

TOPIC SENTENCES

The **topic sentence** tells the reader the point of the paragraph. For that reason, you will normally place the topic sentence at the beginning of the paragraph. You can, if you wish, place the topic sentence elsewhere in the paragraph, even at the very end if you have reason to do so. Writing a paragraph in this way, however, is like serving dinner but refusing to identify the main course until after the meal is over. People may become too impatient. It is simply more practical to tell people what they are about to eat or read before they begin.

In addition to telling the reader what to expect, placing the topic sentence at the beginning of a paragraph has another distinct advantage. It keeps you from wandering off the subject as you write. By looking back at the topic sentence frequently, you can see when you begin to get away from the topic.

Choosing a Topic

The first step in developing a topic sentence is to select a topic. If you are writing on the job, topic selection is usually no problem; your topic will be selected for you by the situation that prompted you to write in the first place. You may, for example, write a paragraph in which you compare a new product with a product the customer has been using for years. In another situation, you may be required to explain the steps for carrying out a specific process. In such instances, you do not have to select the topic.

Occasionally, however, you will be asked to write a paragraph on a topic of your choice for a class exercise. When you are faced with such an assignment, always write on a topic you know well. Avoid selecting a topic because you think it will sound impressive. Writing on an unfamiliar topic could create problems for you. You may occasionally be tempted to say that you can't think of anything to write about, but such a comment is totally unjustified. Everyone knows enough about something to write a good paragraph. Here are some examples of everyday topics.

1. differences between your two favorite department stores
2. steps to follow when changing oil in a car
3. conditioning hair or giving yourself a permanent wave
4. definition of the term *drug abuse*

Exercise 9.1

Carefully consider the above list of topic possibilities. Then select three topic possibilities from your own work, school, or homelife.

1. _____

2. _____

3. _____

Have your work checked by your instructor or a tutor.

Writing a Topic Sentence

Once you have selected a topic, you are ready to develop a topic sentence. Effective topic sentences can be long or short, depending on you and the subject. Further, simple, compound, and complex sentences work equally well as topic sentences. But some topic sentences are better than others. As a general rule, you can assume that a more specific topic sentence will be better than a general one. That is, the most effective topic sentence is the one that clearly explains what is to be discussed in the paragraph. Consider the following topic sentences:

Weak: Adjusting brakes is easy.
Better: Anyone who can follow four steps can adjust automobile brakes.

The second example is a better topic sentence because it explains more precisely what is to be discussed: the four steps to follow to adjust automobile brakes. By contrast, the first sentence could go on forever discussing things that make adjusting brakes easy: proper tools, knowledge, helpers, procedures, good light, and on and on.

The Controlling Idea

Every good topic sentence should have a controlling idea. A **controlling idea** limits the paragraph by focusing on a specific aspect of the topic. Topic sentences without controlling ideas often wander aimlessly; the same sentence with a controlling idea guides the paragraph to the desired end. Suppose you have chosen the topic "jogging." Observe the following topic sentences:

> **Weak:** Jogging without proper shoes or loosening exercises can be very harmful.
>
> **Better:** Jogging without proper shoes or loosening exercises can be very harmful to knees and ankles.

The second topic sentence would be far more effective because it contains the controlling idea "to knees and ankles." That one phrase precisely limits what the paragraph can cover to a discussion of how jogging can be harmful to knees and ankles. Without that phrase, the paragraph would lack focus. In truth, wearing improper shoes and omitting stretching exercises can result in damage to feet, tendons, shins, hips, and thighs, as well as knees and ankles. By focusing your discussion on knees and ankles, as mentioned in the topic sentence, you can control the length of your paragraph. If you wanted to discuss potential damage to feet, tendons, shins, hips, and thighs, you would write about such problems in other paragraphs.

A controlling idea may be one or two words or even a series of words. When you are writing topic sentences with controlling ideas, always deliberately place the word or words you wish to discuss in the topic sentence. The controlling ideas in the topic sentences below are in bold type. Notice that each could be omitted from the sentence, and the sentence would still make sense, as is often the case.

Topic	Topic sentence
repairing your own car	Repairing your own car has **three** distinct advantages.
getting that first traffic ticket	Getting that first traffic ticket is an **embarrassing** experience.
Professor Stuart	Professor Stuart was an **intimidating** instructor.

Each of these topic sentences with a controlling idea will be far easier to develop into a paragraph. The first one, for instance, would be extremely difficult to make into a paragraph without the word *three*. If you fully explained all of the advantages people gain by repairing their own cars, your paragraph would be many pages long rather than 10 or 12 sentences long. The second example sentence above would also be excessively long without the controlling idea. If the paragraph did not focus on how it is an *embarrassing* experience, you would never know when to stop writing. After all, that first ticket is also an *expensive* experience, a *humbling* experience, a *learning* experience, and a *disturbing* experience. But those parts of the experience should be explained in other paragraphs.

Although one-word controlling ideas will often limit your paragraphs adequately, you will find multiple-word controlling ideas more useful in many of the paragraphs you write. Look closely at the following topic sentences.

Topic	Topic sentence
drought	The drought of 1986 was particularly devastating **to farmers in Georgia.**
dwarf lemon trees	Dwarf lemon trees, **because of their beauty and fruit,** are frequently planted in large, movable containers.
beginning college students	Beginning college students have an unreal concept of the **work required to get good grades.**

The controlling idea in each topic sentence limits the writer to a discussion of only that aspect of the topic.

Exercise 9.2

Underline the controlling idea in each of the following topic sentences.

1. IRA's provide extra money for a secure and comfortable retirement.
2. They gave the car an extensive examination before buying it.
3. One must admit that Medicare is good in that it aids in the prevention of fraud.
4. The emphasis on having a college degree has increased recently among the middle class.
5. *Dog Soldiers* is a depressing novel about drugs.
6. Children's values are easily influenced by poor role models presented on everyday television shows.
7. By exercising regularly, people can improve their health and control their weight.
8. The latest research implicates cholesterol as a leading risk factor in coronary heart disease.
9. Many married women want to help with the financial responsibilities it takes to raise a family.
10. Some politicians insist that the defensive-offensive satellites are crucial to our protection and safety.

Check your answers with the Answer Key.

Exercise 9.3

Write topic sentences with specific controlling ideas, developing the topic possibilities from Exercise 9.1. Underline the controlling idea in each sentence.

(1) _____

_____

_____

_____

(2) _____

_____

_____

_____

(3) _____

_____

_____

_____

Have your work checked by your instructor or a tutor.

Limiting the Controlling Idea

If a paragraph is to make sense and appear complete, it must thoroughly explain the topic sentence. To make certain the paragraph does not go on page after page, a controlling idea is carefully placed in that topic sentence. Your controlling idea must also be a topic small enough to be presented in one paragraph. You must limit the controlling idea. Consider the following example of a controlling idea.

Repairing your own car has many advantages.

This topic sentence, although it appears good at first glance, is actually too broad. *Many advantages* is the controlling idea, of course, but it is a very large topic. How many are *many* advantages? If you fully explained all of the advantages of repairing your own car, your paragraph could be many pages long. A better controlling idea would be the following.

Repairing your own car has three distinct advantages.

Here, your reader knows exactly how many advantages you will discuss because you have limited the controlling idea so it can be discussed in one paragraph.

Dividing the controlling idea requires little effort in this example sentence. In order to explain it adequately for your reader, you would merely explain any of the three advantages of repairing your own car. The following topics are similarly divided into subpoints.

Repairing your own car has **three distinct advantages**.

Point 1: pride of accomplishment
Point 2: knowing your car better
Point 3: saving money

Losing one's eyesight is a **frightening experience**.

Point 1: fear of being helpless
Point 2: fear of unknown
Point 3: fear of being pitied

People **who drive large cars and drive too fast** waste the earth's limited supply of fuel.

Point 1: large cars get poor mileage
Point 2: speed lowers mileage

As you examine the first of the three sample groups above, observe the relationship between the topic sentence and the points. In the first group, points 1, 2, and 3 merely explain *what* the *three distinct advantages* are. The second and third topics use words rather than numbers to limit the topic sentence. In such cases you might find it easier to make the topic sentence into a question and ask *how* or *why* the topic sentence is so. The second topic sentence can be broken up into points more easily by asking *why* losing one's eyesight is a *frightening* experience. The third example topic sentence can ask *how* fuel is wasted by driving large cars and driving too fast. The answers to that *how* become the subpoints you use to develop your paragraph.

Exercise 9.4

Divide the topic sentences you wrote in Exercise 9.3 into subpoints. If you need to revise them to improve the controlling idea, do so.

1. Topic sentence: _____

  _____

  Points: _____

  _____

  _____

2. Topic sentence: _____

  _____

  Points: _____

  _____

  _____

3. Topic sentence: _____

  _____

  Points: _____

  _____

  _____

Have your work checked by your instructor or a tutor.

PRIMARY SUPPORT SENTENCES

The next step in paragraph development is converting the subpoints of the controlling idea into sentences. These sentences are called **primary support sentences** because they directly explain the topic sentence. You must be certain the primary support sentences explain the topic in such a way that the reader can more clearly understand your point. The topic sentence about repairing a car can be used to show how primary support sentences are developed.

Repairing your own car has three distinct advantages.

Point 1: pride of accomplishment
Point 2: knowing your car better
Point 3: saving money

Converting the points into sentences results in the following:

> Repairing your own car has three distinct advantages. The pride of accomplishment you can feel from having changed a leaking water pump is immense. In addition, as you successfully perform more and more mechanical repairs, you will develop a thorough knowledge of the car. Finally, by doing your own repairs, you can save a tremendous amount of money.

This topic sentence and its primary support sentences form a basic paragraph that you can then develop into a more complete paragraph. (Note: Although the second-person writing used in the sample paragraph is effective for letters and memos, you should normally avoid it in paragraphs you write for college classes.)

Exercise 9.5

Develop the topic sentences and their divided points from Exercise 9.4 into basic paragraphs.

1. _____

_____

_____

_____

_____

_____

_____

_____

_____

_____

2. _____

_____

_____

_____

_____

_____

_____

_____

_____

_____

3. _____

_____

_____

_____

_____

_____

_____

_____

_____

Have your work checked by your instructor or a tutor.

SECONDARY SUPPORT SENTENCES

The basic paragraph containing a topic sentence and primary support sentences is rarely complete enough to stand alone. Usually you will need an additional explanation of the idea contained in each primary sentence. The sentences that explain or give examples of primary support sentences are called **secondary support sentences**. You can use many secondary support sentences if your primary sentence is particularly involved; you can use one or two secondary support sentences if your primary sentence is of average complexity; or you can use no secondary sentences if the primary sentence is perfectly clear by itself.

The basic paragraph about repairing your own car can be expanded to demonstrate how secondary support sentences make a paragraph complete. In this paragraph, the topic sentence is labeled **TS**, the primary support sentences are labeled **PS**, and the secondary support sentences are labeled **SS**.

TS Repairing your own car has three distinct advantages. **PS** The pride of accomplishment you can feel from having changed a leaking water pump is immense. **SS** Since most people know how to do little more than put gas in their cars, being able to replace engine parts puts you in a very special group. **PS** In addition, as you successfully perform more and more mechanical repairs, you will develop a thorough knowledge of the car. **SS**

This expanded understanding allows you to more fully appreciate driving. **SS** Further, knowing the car well helps you know when some mechanical part is wearing out; the part can then be replaced before it fails and leaves you stranded along a highway. **PS** Finally, by doing your own repairs, you can save a tremendous amount of money. **SS** For instance, installation of a replacement $18.50 water pump by a garage costs over $60.00. **SS** The owner who does his or her own work saves more than $40.00 in labor charges.

This example paragraph has nine sentences, making it about an average length paragraph for a complex subject. Notice that two of the primary support sentences required two secondary support sentences, while the other primary support sentence needed only one secondary support. You will find great variety in the paragraphs you write. Some paragraphs will have many primary support sentences with few secondary support sentences; other paragraphs will be just the opposite. Remember though, **primary support sentences must support the topic sentence** and **secondary support sentences must support the primary support sentences**.

Exercise 9.6

Label the topic sentences **TS**, the primary support sentences **PS**, and the secondary support sentences **SS** in each of the following student paragraphs.

I

(1)_____ More can be done to curb problems caused by teenage cruisers who spend their evenings driving around shopping centers. (2)_____ First, the existing curfew laws must be properly enforced. (3)_____ These curfew laws state that all citizens under eighteen years of age must be off the streets by 10:00 p.m., but these laws are rarely enforced. (4)_____ Teenagers as young as fourteen years old can be seen walking around the sidewalks at the shopping centers at midnight, and sixteen year olds "hot rod" their cars into the early hours of the morning. (5)_____ Second, more police officers must be hired to patrol the centers and their surrounding areas. (6)_____ Two hundred or more cars often cruise the shopping centers on Friday and Saturday evenings, but only five to seven policemen or security guards are on duty in the area. (7)_____ Third, in order to keep infractions of laws to a minimum, stricter penalties must be issued to offenders. (8)_____ At the present time, most teenagers caught breaking the law are given warnings, which are taken lightly. (9)_____ The penalties should be not only money fines but also labor fines or suspension of driving licenses.

II

(1)_____ Where the treatment of VD is concerned, there are five areas in the public health sector that need improvement. (2)_____ First, public health officials should become more sensitive toward the people they are serving, for many doctors have alienated large numbers of people in need of VD treatment. (3)_____ Second, the channels of communication between the general public and health workers should be opened; ideally, every town should have a "hot line" that would protect confidentiality while dispensing information. (4)_____ Also, all women undergoing pelvic examinations should be routinely tested for venereal disease. (5)_____ This precaution is especially needed because many women show no symptoms in the first stages of VD. (6)_____ Further, the clinics should be cleaner and more attractive. (7)_____ Currently, many people avoid the clinics because of the shabby buildings in which they are sometimes housed. (8)_____ Finally, more money is needed to increase the number of health care workers who follow through on investigating sexual contacts named by those who are treated for VD.

III

(1)_____ Although few people understand why, most coffee drinkers know gourmet coffee tastes better than that bought in grocery stores. (2)_____ To begin with, commercially packaged coffee is normally ground months or years before it is taken from the can and brewed. (3)_____ Every passing day between the time the coffee is ground and brewed results in decreased flavor. (4)_____ The particular type of grind also contributes directly to the flavor of the cup of coffee. (5)_____ If a coffee is ground too fine for the type of coffee maker, it produces a stringent, bitter drink. (6) _____ By contrast, an excessively coarse grind will produce a weak, flavorless coffee. (7)_____ Perhaps the most important factor determining the flavor of the final product is the coffee beans used. (8)_____ Canned coffees found on supermarket shelves are made from robusto beans, while gourmet coffees purchased in better coffee shops are made up of arabica beans. (9)_____ The arabica beans, grown at a much higher altitude, are far more expensive because of their rarity and superior flavor.

Check your answers with the Answer Key.

SUPPORT GROUPS

Support groups are primary and secondary sentence combinations used to support a topic sentence. A support group will always be composed of one primary sentence and all secondary sentences that support it. In those rare cases where you have no secondary support, each support group will be composed of just one primary support sentence. In no instance, however, will you have more than one primary support sentence in a support group. Observe the following student paragraph.

> **TS** Rather than discontinuing postal service on Saturdays, other methods of saving money should be considered. **PS** For instance, there is nothing wrong with setting postal zones for first-class mail such as those presently used with parcel post mail. **SS** Sending a letter across the country should cost the customer more than sending it across town. **PS** Further, the bulk service rates given to private business and the press should be reconsidered. **SS** While bulk rate is acceptable for charities, it appears that businesses should not be allowed to gain by extremely low-cost mailing rates unavailable to individuals. **PS** Limiting politicians' free mailing privileges also seems fair. **SS** Their extensive use of free mailing services costs the post office millions each year.

This paragraph contains three very simple support groups. Only rarely will you find a paragraph like this in which each primary support has only one secondary support sentence. More commonly, support groups vary in size within a single paragraph.

Exercise 9.7

Label the sentences in the following paragraph with **TS**, **PS**, and **SS**. When you have completed that, write the number of support groups in the blank at the end of the paragraph.

(1)_____ Many doctors complain that Medicare limits the authority of the doctor. (2)_____ To begin with, Medicare tells the doctors how long a patient can stay in the hospital. (3)_____ Medicare states that a patient who had an appendectomy can stay in the hospital four days. (4)_____ Medicare does not consider the age or the condition of the patient. (5)_____ Medicare does not consider the fact that a young patient would recover much quicker than a 70-year-old patient who obviously would need a longer period to recover. (6)_____ In addition, Medicare will not cover any care that administrators do not consider reasonable and necessary for the treatment of an illness or injury. (7)_____ Sometimes a doctor may recommend surgery to a patient when he or she feels it is needed to treat an illness or injury. (8)_____ If Medicare does not feel that surgery is necessary, however, the doctor will not be paid. (9)_____ Thus, the doctor is left with the choice of not doing the surgery or doing the surgery and not being paid for services rendered. (10)_____ If the doctor decides not to take the case, a patient may go without an operation, which may result in death at a later time.

The paragraph has _____ support groups.

Check your answers with the Answer Key.

Exercise 9.8

Add secondary support sentences to *any two* of the basic paragraphs you developed in Exercise 9.5. Label your sentences as *TS*, *PS*, and *SS*.

1. _____

_____

_____

_____

_____

_____

_____

_____

_____

_____

_____

_____

_____

_____

_____

_____

_____

_____

_____

_____

_____

_____

_____

_____

2. _____

_____

_____

_____

_____

_____

_____

_____

_____

_____

_____

_____

_____

_____

_____

_____

_____

_____

_____

_____

_____

_____

_____

_____

_____

Have your work checked by your instructor or a tutor.

CONCLUDING SENTENCES

The example paragraphs in this chapter were written by students. Some of the paragraphs are   better than others, of course, but all illustrate a solid understanding of paragraph structure. The example paragraphs were taken from full-length student papers, and they were selected because they did not have concluding sentences. You will, however, often need to use a concluding sentence in paragraphs you write, especially if you are writing one long paragraph rather than an essay composed of many paragraphs.

A **concluding sentence** is a one-sentence summary of what you said in the entire paragraph. By placing a one-sentence summary at the end, you have a perfect opportunity to emphasize the point you wanted to make when you decided to write the paragraph in the first place. Some of your paragraphs that are good without a concluding sentence will be even better with one. The following paragraph was used as an example earlier in this chapter without a concluding sentence. Notice how smoothly it ends when a concluding sentence is added.

> More can be done to curb problems caused by teenage crusiers who spend their evenings driving around shopping centers. First, the existing curfew laws must be properly enforced. The curfew laws state that all citizens under eighteen years of age must be off the streets by 10:00 p.m., but these laws are rarely enforced. Teenagers as young as fourteen years old can be seen walking around the sidewalks at the shopping centers at midnight, and sixteen year olds "hot rod" their cars into the early hours of the morning. Second, more police officers must be hired to patrol the centers and their surrounding areas. Two hundred or more cars often cruise the shopping centers on Friday and Saturday evenings, but only five to seven policemen or security guards are on duty in the area. Third, in order to keep infractions of laws to a minimum, stricter penalties must be issued to offenders. At the present time, most of the teenagers caught breaking the law are given warnings, which are taken lightly. The penalties should be not only money fines but also labor fines or suspension of driving licenses. **CS** Only by taking these three steps will the authorities ever decrease the problems caused by shopping center cruisers.

The concluding sentence in this paragraph effectively sums up the writer's message. By restating the overall point, that one sentence increases the chance of the reader remembering the writer's point.

Exercise 9.9

Write concluding sentences for the two paragraphs you wrote in Exercise 9.8.

1. _____

_____

_____

_____

2. _____

_____

_____

_____

Have your work checked by your instructor or a tutor.

CHECK YOUR PARAGRAPHS

When you write a paragraph, regardless of your purpose, you should deliberately follow the steps covered in this chapter. The following checklist will help you evaluate your paragraphs.

PARAGRAPH CHECKLIST

1. Topic sentence properly placed?
2. Controlling idea easily identified?
3. Primary support sentences explain controlling idea?
4. Secondary support sentences explain primary sentences?
5. Support groups all closely related to topic sentence?
6. Concluding sentence sums up message of paragraph?
7. First sentence of paragraph indented?
8. Variety of sentence structure used?
9. Transitions and conjunctive adverbs used?
10. Correct punctuation used?

Exercise 9.10

Label the sentences in the following student paragraph as **TS, PS, SS,** or **CS**.

Building a Covered Patio

(1)_____ As you begin building your covered patio, you will need to follow these steps to attach a 2″×6″ board, commonly called a ledger, to the outside wall of the house; later, you will secure the rafters of the new patio to this board. (2)_____ Begin by marking in several places 3 inches down from the bottom of the existing house rafters to indicate the location of the top of the ledger. (3)_____ The 3 inches will give you adequate space to work freely with the ledger and rafters, and the marks will guide you when attaching the ledger. (4)_____ Then you will need to locate the studs in the existing wall by using a "stud finder." (5)_____ Locating the studs is important because the bolts will need something solid to screw into when the ledger is being attached. (6)_____ After locating the studs, you will need to drill 5/8″ holes through the ledger and the wall and into each of the studs. (7)_____ These holes will be approximately 16 inches apart. (8)_____ Drilling the holes can be accomplished by using an electric power drill and a 5/8″ drill bit. (9)_____ When you have drilled the holes, attach the ledger to the wall with the lag bolts, using a ratchet. (10)_____ Use caution when attaching the ledger to the wall; make sure that the lag bolts have washers to prevent them from being pulled through the ledger. (11)_____ Using a ratchet to tighten the lag bolts will allow you to screw the bolts into the wall much more tightly and with less effort. (12)_____ When the ledger is bolted firmly in place, you can go on to the next step in the procedure.

Check your answers with the Answer Key.

Exercise 9.11

Write *one* paragraph on any of the following topics. Your paragraph must be at least eight sentences long, and each sentence must be labeled as **TS, PS, SS,** or **CS**. Do your work on notebook paper and check it against the *Paragraph Checklist* before copying it into the following space.

1. The value of an education for a person going into your field
2. The problems faced by people seeking employment in your field
3. What frightens people about growing old

_____

_____

_____

_____

_____

_____

_____

_____

_____

_____

_____

_____

_____

_____

_____

_____

_____

_____

_____

_____

Have your work checked by your instructor or a tutor.

CHAPTER

10

Explaining a Process

When you have completed this chapter, you will be able to—

1. Identify the two types of process writing.
2. Correctly order the steps in process paragraphs.
3. Develop limiting topic sentences for process paragraphs.
4. Write participation and observation process paragraphs.
5. Write for a specified audience.
6. Develop thesis sentences for long process descriptions.

Process writing may be the most commonly encountered professional writing in your everyday world. Examples of process writing—also called "assembly instructions," "application instructions," or just "instructions"— are all around you. When you purchase a can of paint, a bicycle, a car part, or a vacuum cleaner, you look for the "how-to-do-it" instructions. Consider the following instruction paragraph which accompanies a major company's automatic washing machine. (The numbers in parentheses refer to part numbers in a diagram in the instruction booklet.)

VII. hot water hose assembly

Insert flat hose washer (21) in the end of hose (20) that connects to hot water inlet valve on back of washer (see 'H' mark on cabinet for hot) (22). When connecting hose, be careful to screw the coupling on straight. Insert a filter washer (23)...screen side toward the faucet...to end of hose that connects to hot water faucet (24). Caution: do not deform filter washer screen. When connecting hose, be sure that it is connected properly from the hot water inlet on the washer (22) to the hot water faucet (24).

[From "Part VII hot water hose assembly," **How to Install Your New Kenmore Automatic Washer Booklet.** Courtesy of Sears, Roebuck and Co.]

This process paragraph is typical of those found in the directions accompanying many products. In brief, precise language the instructions give every step that must be followed to connect the hot water hose to the washer.

Like many process paragraphs, the preceding sample paragraph explains only one part of a complete process. In this case, the entire process is the installation of a new washer, and connecting the hot water hose assembly is only one step in that process. You will usually need to write several process paragraphs to describe the steps in a longer process. On rare occasions you may write only one or two process paragraphs within a longer paper that includes other types of writing (such as narration, description, classification, comparision, or definition).

WHAT IS PROCESS WRITING?

A *process* is a series of steps taken to produce a certain result. **Process writing** explains how to perform the steps in a process. There are two distinct types of process writing that can be easily identified.

Participation Process Writing

The first type—illustrated by the washing machine instructions—is how-to-do-it process writing. This type is called **participation** process writing because it asks the reader to follow a set of instructions. In this most common type of process writing, the writer explains directly to the reader in *second person* how to perform the required steps.

Observation Process Writing

The second type is called **observation** process writing. In this type, you objectively describe a process in *third person* as if you are watching the process occur while you write. The following paragraph objectively describes the process of connecting two pieces of PVC pipe.

> When a person connects a fitting to the section of PVC pipe, the first step is to make sure the end of the pipe is cut squarely. If the cut end is not squarely cut, the pipe may not enter the fitting far enough to produce an adequate bond. The second step is to thoroughly clean the end of the pipe and the inside of the fitting with a dry cloth. When the pipe and fitting are clean and dry, PVC cement is applied to both the end of the pipe and the fitting. Immediately after the cement is applied, the pipe and the fitting are pushed together with a twisting motion. In less than a minute the cemented joint will no longer need to be held together since the cement will be firm. Within an hour, water pressure can be applied to the pipe.

This paragraph does not *command* the reader to do anything; it merely describes the process used to cement a fitting to a piece of PVC pipe.

You will use participation process writing when you are giving your reader instructions. Use observation process writing when you are explaining a process. Remember, observation process writing just describes a process; participation process writing gives step-by-step instructions to the reader.

Exercise 10.1

Answer the following questions as briefly as possible.

1. What is a process?

_____

_____

_____

2. Describe the two types of process writing.

(a) _____

_____

_____

(b) _____

_____

_____

3. Give three examples of process writing that can be found around a home.

(a) _____

_____

(b) _____

_____

(c) _____

_____

Check your answers with the Answer Key.

Exercise 10.2

In the blank following each paragraph, identify the paragraph as either **observation** or **participation** process writing.

I

If someone in your boat falls overboard there are two basic methods you can use to get them back into the boat safely. The first is self-rescue. If somebody falls overboard the first thing to do is get something that floats into the water near the person that he can hang on to. A PFD is *best* but don't delay to hunt for one. An empty gas tank, a styrofoam icebox, an oar, all float and would help keep the victim afloat until you can get something better to him. Stop the boat dead in the water and have the person swim to the boat. He can see the boat, and with the motor turned off you can talk to him. If the person is hurt or unconscious, or for some reason can't swim to the boat, the second rescue method is used. Again, put something that floats into the water near the victim. Reduce speed of the boat and turn back to where the person is. Approach the victim with the bow into the wind or into the current. Shut off the engine completely because even in neutral the propeller can still spin fast enough to injure. When alongside, get a swim ladder over if you have one—if not, help the person back into the boat over the *stern*. If you must go into the water to help—put on a PFD first and hang onto a line.

> [The Skipper's Course—CG-433. Department of Transportation, United States Coast Guard, Office of Boating Safety. Washington, D.C.: U.S. Government Printing Office, 1972.]

I. _____ process writing

II

Felling a tree with an axe is a three-step process. In the first step, the axman carefully circles the tree to determine in which direction it leans. Then he makes an undercut on the trunk of the tree slightly less than waist high. The undercut is always made on the side toward which the tree leans and is cut to a depth equal to one-third of the diameter of the tree. The final step is to make the overcut slightly higher than the undercut on the side opposite the undercut. The axman cuts into this overcut until the tree falls.

II. _____ process writing

Check your answers with the Answer Key.

WRITING PROCESS PARAGRAPHS

Writing a good process description is a matter of planning. If you carefully follow a standard procedure, the reader will be able to perform the task you are describing.

Order the Steps

Chronological ordering of the steps in a process paragraph is extremely important. Because you want the reader to be able to follow the procedure, you must begin with the first step and describe each step in sequence until you reach the last step. Any deviation from chronological order will cause confusion at best and could be dangerous at worst.

The only exception to using chronological order occurs when you must warn your reader about a potentially dangerous step in the sequence. For instance, if you were writing a participation process description on the proper operation of a crane and failed to warn your reader to look carefully for power lines before moving the boom, someone could get killed. Warnings or cautions must be placed in the series at least *one step before* the potential danger occurs. Companies typically ask employees who write process descriptions involving dangerous machinery or procedures to list **warnings** and **cautions** so readers will be aware of all dangers before they begin. The reason for such concern is simple. Companies have been successfully sued after customers were injured or killed because of improperly written installation or use instructions. By making the dangers clear from the beginning, companies hope to avoid injuries and lawsuits.

A **warning** is included anytime a possibility of severe personal injury or loss of life exists.

A **caution** is included anytime a possibility of personal injury or equipment damage exists.

In longer process descriptions the warning is often inserted between paragraphs to attract attention. It is common to put the warning in capital letters and between rows of asterisks, as in the following:

* * * * * * * * * * * * *

WARNING
DO NOT POUR GASOLINE INTO
CARBURETOR OF ENGINE WHILE
CRANKING. BACKFIRE COULD
RESULT IN SERIOUS BURNS.

* * * * * * * * * * * * *

In the following installation instructions from a gas water heater, the warnings and cautions are placed in boxes *and* in bold print to get the reader's attention.

The pressure rating of the relief valve must not exceed 150 psi, the maximum working pressure of the water heater as marked on its rating plate.

The BTUH rating of the relief valve must equal or exceed the BTUH input of the water heater as marked on its rating plate.

Connect the outlet of the relief valve to a suitable open drain. The discharge line must pitch downward from the valve to allow complete drainage (by gravity) of the relief valve and discharge line and must be no smaller than outlet of the valve. The end of the discharge line should not be threaded or concealed and should be protected from freezing. No valve, restriction or reducer coupling of any type should be installed between the relief valve and the tank or in the discharge line.

> **WARNING: Tank MUST be full of water before water heater is turned on.**

4. **TO FILL WATER HEATER** — Make certain drain valve is closed. Open shut-off valve in cold water supply line. Open each hot water faucet slowly to allow air to vent from the water heater and piping. A steady flow of water from the hot water faucet(s) indicates a full water heater.

5. **GAS SUPPLY** — For the purposes of adjustment (with main burner on), the maximum and minimum recommended inlet and normal operating manifold gas pressures in inches of water column are:

		Max.	Min.			
Inlet	Nat.	7.0″	5.0″	Manifold	Nat.	4.0″
	L.P.	14.0″	11.0″		L.P.	10.0″

If high or low inlet gas pressures are present, consult the gas company for correction.

> **CAUTION: Do not attempt to convert this water heater for use with a different type of gas other than the type shown on the rating plate. Such conversion could result in hazardous operating conditions.**

The branch gas supply line to the water heater should be clean ½″ black steel pipe or other approved gas piping material, and should be pitched toward water heater. A ground joint union or ANSI design certified semi-rigid or flexible gas appliance connector should be installed in gas line close to the water heater, and a manual gas shut-off valve should be installed in the gas line prior to the union. The manual gas shut-off valve should be at least 5 feet above the floor and readily accessible for turning on or off. A drip leg should be installed at bottom of the gas line. Refer to Fig. 4.

Compound used on threaded joints of the gas piping should be of the type resistant to the action of liquefied petroleum gas. Care should be taken not to use an excessive amount of pipe joint compound at the pipe connection to the gas thermostat as it may be damaged.

6. **LEAK TESTING** — The water heater **must** be disconnected from the gas piping system during any high pressure (above 14″ W.C.) leak testing. Otherwise, damage to the gas valve may result. Perform a leak test at normal pressure on the remaining fittings after connections have been made and gas turned on. Soap test joints of gas line and fittings. Bubbles indicate leaks.

> **WARNING: Do not use open flame to test for leak.**

7. **VENTING** — This water heater must be installed with the factory supplied draft hood in place. Refer to Fig. 4. Vent connectors must be attached to the draft hood outlet to connect the water heater to the gas vent or chimney. The vent connector must be the same size (diameter) as the draft hood or larger, never smaller. For proper venting in certain installations a larger vent connector size may be needed. Consult Vent Tables in ANSI booklet Z223.1-1980 or NFPA booklet 54-1980. Horizontal vent connectors must be pitched upward to the chimney at least ¼″ per foot of length. All vent connectors must be at least 6″ from adjacent unprotected combustible surfaces. Joints of vent connectors shall be securely fastened by sheet metal screws or other approved methods.

INSTALLATION CHECK LIST

A. Water Heater Location

☐ Close to area of vent.
☐ Indoors and protected from freezing temperatures.
☐ Proper clearance from combustible surfaces observed and water heater not installed on carpeted floor.
☐ Sufficient fresh air supply for proper operation of water heater.
☐ Air supply free of corrosive elements and flammable vapors.
☐ Provisions made to protect area from water damage.
☐ Sufficient room to service heater.

B. Water Supply

☐ Water heater completely filled with water.
☐ Water heater and piping air vented.
☐ Water connections tight and free of leaks.

C. Relief Valve

☐ Temperature and Pressure Relief Valve properly installed and discharge line run to open drain.
☐ Discharge line protected from freezing.

D. Gas Supply

☐ Gas line equipped with shut-off valve, union and drip leg.
☐ Approved pipe joint compound used.
☐ Soap and water solution used to check all connections and fittings for possible gas leak.
☐ Gas Company inspected installation (if required).

E. Venting

☐ Flue baffle hung in top of heater's flueway.
☐ Draft hood properly installed.
☐ Vent connector(s) pitched upward to chimney (¼″ per foot of length minimum).
☐ Vent connector(s) securely fastened together with screws.
☐ Vent connector(s) at least 6″ from combustible material.

Limiting the Topic

Because process descriptions are usually several paragraphs long, you must carefully limit the portion of the procedure you cover in one paragraph. If you fail to limit the topic, your paragraph may be many pages in length or you might neglect an essential step in the process. The same limiting techniques you used in Chapter 9 will help you control your process paragraphs; you can use a word or a series of words as a **controlling idea** to limit what will be covered.

Structuring the Paragraph

Process paragraphs use the same basic paragraph structure that you learned in Chapter 9. Each primary support sentence explains an individual step involved in the process identified in the topic sentence. Secondary support sentences add details about the steps in the primary supports. Examine the following student-written participation process paragraph closely. Study the relationships between the topic sentence and the primary support sentences carefully.

> **TS** If the lawn is to be full and lush, you should follow a series of three steps to prepare the soil. **PS** You must first thoroughly loosen the soil to a depth of four to six inches. **SS** This loosening is usually accomplished by going over every inch of the area with a rototiller. **SS** Although it is more work, you can use a shovel in place of a rototiller if the area is small. **PS** The second step is to remove all debris from the area to be seeded. **SS** Clumps of dead grass, loose roots, rocks, and hard clods must all be removed prior to seeding. **SS** You can remove this debris most easily by repeatedly raking the soil in different directions. **PS** The final step in seedbed preparation is to level the surface of the soil. **SS** By using the back of the steel rake, you can smooth out ridges and gouges. **CS** If you carefully prepare the soil in this manner prior to planting, the sowing of the seed will be easier.

This paragraph follows logically from a carefully controlled topic sentence to primary support sentences and finally to secondary sentences. More important, however, the writer moves chronologically through the steps to be followed in preparing a lawn for planting. Notice also that the writer uses a concluding sentence very effectively.

Exercise 10.3

Write a process paragraph at least seven sentences long on any one of the following topics. Be sure to limit the topic. Make this a **participation** process paragraph, using second person.

how to make something   how to install something
how to repair something   topic of your choice

_____

_____

_____

_____

_____

_____

_____

_____

_____

_____

_____

_____

_____

_____

_____

_____

_____

Have your work checked by your instructor or a tutor.

Exercise 10.4

Convert the paragraph you wrote in Exercise 10.3 into an **observation** process paragraph, using third-person writing.

_____

_____

_____

_____

_____

_____

_____

_____

_____

_____

_____

_____

_____

_____

_____

_____

_____

_____

_____

_____

Have your work checked by your instructor or a tutor.

WRITING FOR A SPECIFIC AUDIENCE

Successful writing involves more than writing well-developed paragraphs. The most beautifully written process paragraphs using professional-level language and ideas often fail to communicate with the worker on the job. As a result, the worker may read the process description, misunderstand the instructions completely, and proceed to do the process incorrectly. In such a case, the writer of the paragraph is responsible for all misunderstandings and errors that occur.

Part of writing on the job—especially when writing process description—is being able to accurately predict the ability of your reader. That is, you must not use words or sentences more difficult than your reader is capable of understanding. Writing for a person with a particular ability is called **writing for a particular audience**. More than writing for a specific person, you must write for the average person who will be following the process you are describing. Many companies request their technical writers to explain at the outset for whom the instructions are written. The manual accompanying the water heater, which was mentioned earlier, contains the following paragraph at the beginning.

> The purpose of this manual is twofold; for the installing contractor, to provide requirements and recommendations for the proper installation and adjustment of the water heater, and for the owner-operator to explain the features, operation, safety precautions, maintenance and trouble shooting of the water heater.

This paragraph makes it clear that a contractor should be doing the installation. All installation instructions, therefore, can be in moderately technical language, but not more technical than the least knowledgeable plumbing contractor can understand.

Avoid falling into the trap of thinking of your reader as uneducated. In fact, your reader may merely be less informed about the subject than you are. Imagine, for instance, that you are working for an automotive ignition manufacturer and your assignment is to write a process description telling how to install a condenser in an auto distributor. You would have to assume that people from every profession—doctors, lawyers, teachers, mechanics, and nurses—would use your instructions to install your company's product. If you assumed that anyone who did not already know how to install a condenser was stupid, you would insult a large number of your company's customers. Such an attitude could lead to problems for your company and possible loss of your job.

Deciding how to write for a particular audience is easier than it sounds. Ask yourself what the least knowledgeable person who will use your instructions already knows about the subject, and when you have the answer you will be ready to write a process description. This is an important step because many of your decisions depend on the assumptions you make about your audience. For instance, you could use certain technical terms if you were a civil engineer writing for other civil engineers, but that same vocabulary would be inappropriate if you were writing for the average person. The following process description, written for plumbing contractors, would not be well understood by someone who does not know much about plumbing.

The branch gas supply line to the water heater should be clean ½'' black steel pipe or other approved gas piping material, and should be pitched toward water heater. A ground joint union or ANSI design certified semi-rigid or flexible gas appliance connector should be installed in gas line close to the water heater, and a manual gas shut-off valve should be installed in the gas line prior to the union. The manual gas shut-off valve should be at least 5 feet above the floor and readily accessible for turning on or off. A drip leg should be installed at bottom of the gas line. Refer to Fig. 4.

Compound used on threaded joints of the gas piping should be of the type resistent to the action of liquified petroleum gas. Care should be taken not to use an excessive amount of pipe joint compound at the pipe connection to the gas thermostat as it may be damaged.

These paragraphs were written for a limited audience: plumbing contractors. It does not matter that the average person cannot possibly follow the instructions. If plumbers can follow the procedure and correctly install a water heater, the instructions are successful.

Exercise 10.5

Write a process paragraph at least seven sentences long in which you describe how to perform some task. Identify your audience before you begin writing. Make sure that the words and sentences you use can be understood by your audience.

Topic _____

Audience _____

_____

_____

_____

_____

_____

_____

_____

_____

_____

_____

_____

_____

_____

_____

_____

_____

_____

_____

_____

Have your work checked by your instructor or a tutor.

WRITING LONGER PROCESS DESCRIPTIONS

The instructions for installing a water heater that you just read explained only part of the entire process. Process descriptions are usually several paragraphs or even pages long. When you describe a difficult or lengthy process that has many steps, you should include a separate paragraph of instructions for each step. You should also include an introduction to the instructions, a list of materials and tools needed, and a conclusion.

Selecting a Topic

You can write instructions for doing almost anything. In a job-related situation, the topic will normally be selected for you—by your boss. For the purpose of classroom assignments, though, you will be expected to select your own topics. Often the best topic for a process description is the one most familiar to you. Select something you do often or something you enjoy doing. The following are examples of good topics:

1. How to prepare a particular food in the kitchen
2. How to change a part on a car
3. How to plant a lawn or a shrub
4. How to serve in tennis
5. How to perform some task where you work

Exercise 10.6

Select a topic that you can write a process description on.

Topic _____

_____

Have your work checked by your instructor or a tutor.

Developing a Thesis Sentence

A thesis sentence is like a topic sentence. However, a *thesis sentence* states the topic of an entire essay. Just as the topic sentence controls the paragraph, the thesis sentence controls the entire essay. The only difference between topic and thesis sentences is that the thesis sentence covers a larger subject. If you were to write a complete set of instructions for changing a tire, you would create a thesis sentence like the one that follows.

Changing the tire on a car is effortless if you follow eight logical steps.

This thesis sentence tells the reader that you are going to present an eight-step procedure for changing a tire. The reader then knows exactly what to expect—probably eight paragraphs, with each paragraph describing one step. Write your thesis carefully, thinking ahead about the steps you will describe as you write the entire paper.

Exercise 10.7

Develop a thesis sentence with at least three steps. Use the topic you selected in Exercise 10.6.

Thesis sentence _____

_____

_____

_____

Have your work checked by your instructor or a tutor.

Writing the Individual Paragraphs

Most longer process descriptions have at least four different sections: introduction, materials, instructions, and conclusion.

Introduction paragraph   The introduction paragraph introduces the subject and explains why the reader would want to know how to do the process. Place the thesis sentence at the end of this paragraph.

Materials paragraph   The materials paragraph explains what tools and materials will be needed to perform the process. This list must be complete or the entire process will fail.

Process paragraphs   Each step in the process must have a separate paragraph. Your paragraphs will vary in length, depending on your subject, from five to twelve sentences. Occasionally, process analysis paragraphs contain only two or three sentences, as do some in the following paper.

Conclusion paragraph   A conclusion paragraph is not absolutely necessary, but it gives your process description a finished appearance. Use one whenever your description seems incomplete at the end of the last body paragraph.

The following student-written process description was written by an employee of a management company. Her process describes the steps apartment managers must go through to evict a tenant. As she wrote, the audience she kept in mind was anyone who owns an apartment or a rental house and has a problem tenant.

THE EVICTION PROCESS

1.   You have a problem tenant you must evict. A problem tenant never pays the rent on time, and rules, to the problem tenant, were intended for everyone else. Besides not paying the rent, the problem tenant has no respect for his or her fellow residents. You will usually have a file full of complaints against this tenant. Once you have made the decision to get rid of your problem tenant, whether you own a huge apartment complex or a small single family rental house, you will find, if you follow these three steps of eviction, that the whole eviction process will seem much less intimidating.

2.   Depending on the reason for the eviction, you will need to use at least one of two different forms: the Three Day Notice to Pay or Quit, or the Three Day Notice to Perform Conditions and/or Covenants or Quit. You will also need a Proof of Service form no matter which of the previously mentioned forms you use. These forms can all be purchased at most office supply stores. Something else you will need is a good real estate attorney. You can call a few of the large apartment complexes in your area, and the resident managers will usually be able to recommend an attorney who is experienced in eviction cases. Lastly, you will need to have replacement door locks on hand.

3.   First, you will need to make a decision on which form to use. If the tenant has not paid the rent, you should serve him or her with the Three Day Notice to Pay Rent or Quit; of course, if the tenant pays, and problem tenants usually do, you still have the problem tenant. Once the rent has been paid, therefore, you should serve the problem tenant with a Three Day Notice to Perform Conditions and/or Covenants or Quit. Remember to collect the rent first, if at all possible, because once you serve this form, you cannot collect the rent, unless the tenant performs what you have requested—which is not usually the case. Make sure you are very precise when filling out the forms. On the Three Day Notice to Pay Rent or Quit, you cannot add in late charges. The amount due must consist of rent only. On the Three Day Notice to Perform Conditions and/or Covenants or Quit, you should write out the entire paragraph on the lease agreement that pertains to the problem the tenant is causing. Also, write out precisely what you feel the tenant should do to comply with your notice. Whichever form you use, the person who serves the tenant will have to fill out and sign a Proof of Service form.

4.   Next, after the Three Day Notice has expired, providing the rent has not been paid or the conditions and/or covenants have not been performed, it is now time to take the paperwork to the attorney. However, you must give the tenant an extra day if the third day lands on a weekend or on a holiday. For example, if the third day lands on Sunday, the tenant will have through Monday to pay or perform. You

will need to provide the attorney with a copy of the tenant's application, lease agreement, any addendums, and the Three Day Notice. The attorney will do all the rest of the legal work involved.

5.   Finally, the sheriff's department will come out and post a writ, sometimes called a lockout form, on the tenant's door. This writ will have a lockout date which will be five days later. On that date the sheriff's officers will come back to the unit, and the deputies, if necessary, will physically remove the tenant from the unit. This can be a little unpleasant, but the deputies usually handle it quite well. If you decide to let the tenant remove his or her belongings from the unit, as opposed to your moving the belongings to a storage facility, you must take the door off the hinges. If the tenant gets back into the residence, shuts and locks the door, the tenant may actually be able to reclaim possession, and you will have to start the eviction process all over again. Once you do have possession, change all the locks in the unit immediately.

6.   Evicting a tenant is never a pleasant experience, so you will want to try to work with the tenant for a solution other than eviction. Sometimes, however, you will have no alternative. By following the steps given, you will make fewer mistakes, and that is important since mistakes can be very costly.

Caroline Widener

Exercise 10.8

Briefly but completely answer the following questions about the process description for evicting a tenant.

1. What sentence in the first paragraph is the thesis?

_____

2. Which paragraphs in the paper are not process description?

Paragraph numbers_____

3. Which paragraph is the introduction paragraph?

Paragraph number _____

4. Who is the intended audience? _____

5. Does the paper use *observation* or *participation* process description?

_____

6. Which paragraph is the materials paragraph? _____

7. Is this paper written primarily in first, second, or third person?

_____

Check your answers with the Answer Key.

Exercise 10.9

Write a *participation* process description that contains the following:

one introductory paragraph (include your thesis from Exercise 10.7)
one materials paragraph
at least three process paragraphs
one conclusion paragraph, *if needed*

Do your work on notebook paper and submit the final copy to your instructor. As you work, use the following checklist.

PROCESS DESCRIPTION CHECKLIST

1. Consistently uses either second person (if participation) or third person (if observation)?
2. Uses chronological order?
3. Includes any necessary warnings?
4. Can intended audience understand instructions?
5. Is thesis sentence clear?
6. Separate paragraph for each step in the process?
7. Each body paragraph has a topic sentence with controlling idea?
8. Good support clusters supporting each topic sentence?
9. Sentence variety?
10. Proper punctuation?

11
Classifying

When you have completed this chapter, you will be able to—

1. Classify large lists of items into smaller groups of similar items.
2. Arrange items in a group in a manageable, logical order.
3. Write topic sentences for classification paragraphs.
4. Write classification paragraphs using location order.
5. Write classification paragraphs using importance order.

When carpenters build a house, the framing materials normally arrive in one huge load. After the truck drives away, the carpenters are often faced with a pile of lumber in which the rafters, the last thing to be used, are on top; the ceiling joists, the next to last thing needed, are second down; the studs for the walls are next; and so on until they get to the bottom and find the heavy floor stringers and joists, the materials they need first. Obviously, carpenters cannot work with the materials in such a state of disorder. Before they can begin building the house, they must sort the materials into piles of similar items.

The same situation faces writers. They are faced with a large mass of ideas that must somehow be separated and rearranged into groups before they can write a logical, meaningful body of words about these ideas. It is at this point that writers use a technique known as classifying. Without classifying the materials first, neither a writer nor a carpenter can produce a usable product.

WHAT IS CLASSIFYING?

Classifying is the process of sorting through a large group of items and arranging those items into small groups according to similar qualities. Without thinking about it, you classify items every day. When you go to the mailbox, for example, you immediately begin classifying the contents. If there are four people receiving mail at your house, you have four major classifications. Each piece of mail could be sorted and placed in a stack for its addressee. This is only one broad example of classification.

But we don't stop there when classifying objects, people, or ideas. We frequently reorder the smaller groups again and again. After you have sorted out the mail for other people, you could then classify it according to other characteristics or qualities. Here are just three of the many possible divisions:

Possible Division 1	**Possible Division 2**	**Possible Division 3**
very personal mail	letters	desirable mail
bills	bills	mildly desirable mail
junk mail	advertisements	undesirable mail
	magazines	

Your reason for classifying and the objects that you classify will vary widely, but the process will be the same: grouping a number of items together according to some similarity.

Exercise 11.1

Classify the following list of vehicles into groups. Decide whether each is primarily a commercial, private, or emergency vehicle, and place it under the appropriate heading.

1. ambulance
2. bicycle
3. convertible
4. coupe
5. delivery van
6. diesel bus
7. dump truck
8. fire truck
9. flatbed truck
10. four-door sedan
11. heavy-duty pickup
12. imported economy car
13. milk truck
14. motorcycle with two-way radio
15. light-duty pickup
16. sports car
17. squad car
18. fuel tank truck
19. taxi
20. tow truck

Most commonly used as *commercial vehicles*	Most commonly used as *private vehicles*	Most commonly used as *emergency vehicles*
_____	_____	_____
_____	_____	_____
_____	_____	_____
_____	_____	_____
_____	_____	_____
_____	_____	_____
_____	_____	_____
_____	_____	_____
_____	_____	_____

Check your answers with the Answer Key.

DEVELOPING THE CLASSIFICATION PAPER

On occasion you will write a single paragraph of classification within a paper that contains other types of writing. Other times you will write a whole paper that classifies ideas or items into groups. But before you actually begin writing the paper—or even a single paragraph—you must think about the order you will use to present your ideas.

Ordering the Groups

Once you have classified the items of a large list into manageable groups, you begin the next step in the classification process—**ordering the groups**. Begin by selecting the best ordering technique. Before you can write about the items in a group, you must decide how they should be ordered so the reader can move from one item to the next without becoming confused. Although many different ordering techniques can be identified, three are most commonly used: chronological, location, and importance.

Chronological order requires you to arrange the items in the order they happened. This is the same order you used for describing a process. For instance, if you were working as an insurance adjuster, you might use this ordering technique to explain how an accident occurred. Use chronological order when you are writing about a series of events.

Location order is commonly used in reports written by employees. If you were working for a law enforcement agency and had to report on what you found at the scene of a crime, you might use location order to describe the scene you saw after entering a room. When you use this ordering technique, you must begin at a given point and move logically. For instance, when you are describing a room, start at the farthest point from you and move toward your position, describing everything between that far point and you. Or you could begin with what is closest to you and work toward what is farthest away. If you are describing a vertical surface, start at the top and work down, one object at a time. When describing items on a horizontal surface, such as a table top or counter, you could work from left to right.

Employees who write reports describing equipment in the company's inventory often use location order. A typical assignment is to describe all the office equipment a company has in service at a given time. You could order the items by location, starting at the farthest work area from your own location. All equipment in each work area would be classified into a group under a heading identifying that area (such as *supply room, shipping room,* or *typing pool*).

Importance order is another ordering technique. When you use this technique, you place items in order according to their importance, usually beginning with the least important and working up to the most important. Importance ordering is particularly useful when you have to write a report justifying a purchase or a plan of action. For example, if you were working with a fire department that needed a new truck, a justification report would have to be written and presented to the city council before funds for the truck could be allocated. You would begin by making a list of all the reasons why the department needed the truck, and then put those reasons in order of their importance, beginning with the least important and ending with the most significant. The resulting order might look like the following:

old truck looks run down
old truck costing too much for repairs
prices going up shortly
old truck breaks down often—could result in loss of life

Notice that the group ends with a suggestion that lives might be lost if the new equipment is not purchased, certainly the most moving argument. You should end with your strongest point because it is the last one your reader will read. This will leave the reader with a strong impression of your request.

Occasionally, you will encounter a situation in which you should reverse the importance ordering. That is, you should present your most important point first if custom demands it. When you are listing job titles, for example, it is customary to list the most important position first. Reverse the order if the situation appears to demand that you do so.

Exercise 11.2

Order each of the following groups, using the ordering technique specified.

Chronological Order

Subject: the accident

the trip to the hospital in an ambulance
the sound as the two skidding cars collided
the smell of gasoline from the ruptured tank
skidding sideways after losing control
watching the world spin as the car rolled over after impact
hearing ambulance attendants talk as they removed the injured from the wreck

_____

_____

_____

_____

_____

_____

_____

Location Order

Subject: landscaping a yard (You are standing at the back door of the house; start at the farthest point from you.)

plants immediately beyond fountain in center of yard
grassy area between fountain and back of yard
potted plants on patio against house
trees along back of property
ground cover in front of fountain

_____

_____

_____

_____

_____

Importance Order

Subject: jobs in a bank (most important first)

credit manager
assistant teller
teller
president
owners
teller supervisor

_____

_____

_____

_____

_____

_____

Check your answers with the Answer Key.

Writing the Classification Paragraph

After grouping the items you wish to work with into similar categories, you can begin developing paragraphs. If the items in a particular group are part of an obvious whole, write a single paragraph about them. For instance, you might write a single paragraph about the following group:

Subject: jobs in a hardware store
1. manager
2. assistant manager
3. sales clerk
4. stock clerk

Such a paragraph would begin with a topic sentence similar to the following:

A typical hardware store has four levels through which a beginning employee must plan to advance.

A paragraph built around this topic sentence would contain four support clusters—one for each job. It would almost certainly be eight or more sentences long if you provided an adequate number of examples to explain what the person in each position did.

If the items in a particular group are more general, each item would be developed into a separate paragraph. In such a case, the items you classified into groups would become paragraphs in a longer paper. Items about life as a ski patrol member might be classified as follows:

1. training for ski patrol duty
2. getting a position as a ski patrol member
3. the people ski patrols must deal with
4. situations normally encountered by ski patrols
5. clothes and equipment needed by ski patrols

These five ideas would be the groups of classified items and each would become a paragraph. The following student paragraph divides the third item into four types of people that ski patrol members must deal with.

The members of the ski patrol must deal with four types of men skiers who grace the slopes at the onset of each new ski season. One type is the turkey that goes to a resort solely for the nightlife. He dons the latest in ski fashions and uses the local lingo hoping to be recognized as a skier, although he has probably never descended a slope in his life. Another type is the basic beginner who is genuinely interested in learning the sport. His actions are easy to pick out as he falls down the slope with ski equipment projecting from every angle. A third type is the egomaniac whose sole purpose in life is to impress his friends and enemies on the slope. He crashes down the slope wildly with no regard for others while trying to show his skiing proficiency. The fourth type is the average recreational skier who is there only to enjoy the sport. He can be seen skiing rhythmically down the slopes and generally enjoying the day. Each of these distinctly different types must be recognized and handled without hesitation by the effective ski patrol member.

Notice that the author of this paragraph begins by dividing the group "the members of the ski patrol must deal with" into "four types of men skiers." By doing so, the writer can organize the paragraph in an orderly fashion.

Writing a classification paragraph is no more difficult than writing any other type of paragraph; it is just a matter of following a series of steps.

Step 1—Selecting a Subject When you are writing on the job, your subject will usually be chosen for you by a situation or your superior. In some instances, you may write a single classification paragraph about a subject; in other instances, you will write a number of paragraphs. But whether you are writing one or a series of paragraphs, the way you approach the task remains the same. The primary consideration in choosing a subject is to select something with which you are very familiar. The more familiar you are with your subject, the easier it is to write about. Your work, classes, or hobbies will provide you with a very workable subject. Consider the student paragraph which analyzed the skiers a ski patrol must deal with. Notice that the student was successful writing about what some people might consider a minor aspect of his work.

The following are good subjects for classification paragraphs:

1. the authority structure where you work
2. the structure of a classroom desk
3. bicycling as a sport
4. jibing a small sailboat
5. types of students who frequent the cafeteria
6. duties of someone holding a particular job

Exercise 11.3

Select a subject for a classification paragraph. It can be a subject from the preceding list, from Exercise 11.2, or any other topic you wish to write about.

Have your subject checked by a tutor or your instructor.

Step 2—Writing the Topic Sentence As with most paragraphs, the topic sentence of a classification paragraph is almost always the first sentence in the paragraph. But more important than the placement of the topic sentence is the proper construction of this sentence for a classification paragraph. The topic sentence for such a paragraph must do two things:

1. identify the subject
2. identify the classification principle (the characteristic shared by the parts being talked about, such as size, color, or function)

A topic sentence which does these two things is easy to write and also very easy for the reader to understand. Consider the topic sentence from the paragraph about skiers. It is a good topic sentence because it introduces the subject, "men skiers"; in addition, it identifies the classification principle, the ones "who grace the slopes at the onset of each new ski season." With such a clearly written topic sentence to work from, writing the paragraph is not difficult.

Exercise 11.4

Write three topic sentences for classification paragraphs. Write **sub** above the subject and **prin** above the classification principle.

1. _____

_____

_____

2. _____

_____

_____

3. _____

_____

_____

Have your work checked by your instructor or a tutor.

Step 3—Writing the Support Groups   Once you have developed an effective topic sentence, writing support groups is as simple as explaining each part of the division you identified in your topic sentence. If you have three major divisions, you will have three support groups. Begin by writing a primary support sentence for each major division. Look back at the student paragraph on the skiers and you will quickly see how obvious the four divisions of skiers are. The writer lists the skier who wants the "nightlife," the skier who is the "basic beginner," the "egomaniac," and the "average recreational skier." Each of these types is identified in a primary support sentence. Because additional information is needed, the writer provides secondary support sentences to give details about each type of skier. And because the paragraph became quite long, the writer added a concluding sentence to sum it up.

Exercise 11.5

Read the following student paragraph and answer the questions following it. The paragraph, part of a longer paper, has a clear classification structure.

Unfortunately, many elderly persons must attempt to financially support themselves with retirement pensions and social security payments which are drastically insufficient. Although some of the aged are fortunate enough to receive generous retirement pensions, most retired persons receive only a small percentage of the salaries they earned while working. For example, recent studies indicate that average retirement pensions amount to only twenty-eight percent of employees' working salaries. Additionally, most of these pensions are fixed and do not increase as the cost of living increases. Although helpful, social security payments are far from sufficient to support the elderly persons who are dependent upon them. The average social security payment, the basic income for most elderly persons, is $410.00 per month. But $410.00 per month is clearly inadequate to support anyone in this country. Thus, because pensions and social security payments are insufficient, the elderly are financially unable to provide themselves with even their most basic needs.

1. What is the subject identified in the topic sentence? _____

_____

2. What is the classification principle? _____

3. How many support groups are used in this paragraph? _____

4. What ordering technique is used in this paragraph? _____

_____

Check your answers with the Answer Key.

Before you submit any classification paragraph, you should use the following checklist to make sure your work is correctly done.

CHECKLIST FOR WRITING CLASSIFICATION PARAGRAPHS

1. Begins with strong topic sentence?
2. Topic sentence identifies the subject?
3. Topic sentence identifies the classification principle?
4. Primary support sentences clearly support the topic sentence?
5. Most effective ordering technique used?
6. Sentence variety used?
7. Correct punctuation?
8. Spelling of all unfamiliar words checked?

Exercise 11.6

Using **location order**, write a paragraph on one of the topic sentences you developed in Exercise 11.4. Make sure you select one with **at least** three divisions. If none of your topic sentences has a three-part topic, or if none lends itself to location order, modify one of them. Your completed paragraph must contain a minimum of eight sentences. Write your rough copy on notebook paper, revise according to the checklist, and write the final copy on the following blanks.

_____

_____

_____

_____

_____

_____

_____

_____

_____

_____

_____

_____

_____

Have your work checked by your instructor or a tutor.

Exercise 11.7

Using **importance order**, write a paragraph on a topic of your choice, or on one of the topic sentences you developed in Exercise 11.4. Choose a topic that could be presented well using importance order. Your completed paragraph must contain a minimum of seven sentences. Write your rough copy on notebook paper, revise according to the Checklist, and write the final copy in the following blanks.

_____

_____

_____

_____

_____

_____

_____

_____

_____

_____

_____

_____

Have your work checked by your instructor or a tutor.

WRITING LONGER CLASSIFICATION PAPERS

Writing full-length classification papers requires that you approach the project in an orderly fashion. Classification papers are among the easiest to write. You begin by identifying the subject and breaking it into its logical divisions. In the following classification paper the author has placed her thesis sentence at the end of the introductory paragraph. Her purpose in this paper was to explain why "this nation's elderly encounter serious financial difficulties." She wisely limited her paper to the major reasons for these difficulties. Notice the three divisions she identifies in her thesis: "limited incomes and increased medical and essential living expenses." Creating divisions will help you focus your attention on specific aspects of the overall subject. Such a thesis is called a divided thesis. Read the following paper to be certain you understand the structure of a classification paper.

Prison for the Aged

Old age is a living hell for many of America's elderly. Because they lack financial stability, almost sixty percent of this country's elderly are living in poverty and disillusionment. After years of earning and spending money without making plans for their futures, these elderly persons are completely unprepared for the financial burdens of their later years. Almost immediately upon their retirement, these elderly citizens begin to encounter money problems. Because they have limited incomes and increased medical and essential living expenses, many of this nation's elderly encounter serious financial difficulties.

Unfortunately, many elderly persons must attempt to financially support themselves with retirement pensions and social security payments which are drastically insufficient. Although some of the aged are fortunate enough to receive generous retirement pensions, most retired persons receive only a small percentage of the salaries they earned while working. For example, recent studies indicate that average retirement pensions amount to only twenty-eight percent of employees' working salaries. Additionally, most of these pensions are fixed and do not increase as the cost of living increases.

Although helpful, social security payments are far from sufficient to support the elderly persons who are dependent upon them. The average social security payment, the basic income for most elderly persons, is $410.00 per month. But $410.00 per month is clearly inadequate to support anyone in this country. Thus, because pensions and social security payments are insufficient, the elderly are unable to provide themselves with even their most basic needs.

In addition to pension and social security inadequacies, the aged encounter extensive medical expenses which tax their financial situations. A recent television documentary, *Growing Old in America*, explained that most elderly persons have very precarious health. As their health deteriorates, the aged encounter increases in pharmaceutical, physician, and hospital costs. These expenses include the escalation of the numbers of medical occurrences as well as the cost of each occurrence. Obviously, inflation is partially responsible for the increasing medical expenses. Unfortunately, these extensive medical costs are only partially paid for by Medicare or other health insurance plans: the elderly are financially responsible for any services not covered by medical insurances. Therefore, as their medical costs continue to escalate and their incomes remain inadequate, the elderly are placed in extreme financial jeopardy.

Although limited incomes and increased medical expenses are serious considerations, the constant increase in basic living expenses is the most financially devastating factor facing the elderly. According to information released by the United States Housing Administration, the cost of housing in most American cities has doubled in the last ten years. Consequently, the aged attempting to support themselves with limited incomes are overwhelmed by such inflated costs. Similarly, the cost of food has escalated by almost fifty percent over the last fifteen years, causing further demands on the finances of the elderly. All in all, the increases in necessary living expenses, such as housing and food, are primary causes of the desperate financial conditions of many elderly people.

After considering the income limitations and expense increases encountered in later years, there is little doubt regarding the seriousness of the elderly's financial difficulties. Without adequate incomes, the aged are unable to provide themselves with even their basic needs. Ultimately, these unfortunate people, who have lived and worked in this country for many years, are living substandard existences without hope for improvements. Thus, this tragic paradox exists: in this nation of freedom for all, many of the elderly are prisoners of poverty.

—Janet Speelman

Exercise 11.8

Write a classification paper that has *at least four paragraphs*. Each paragraph must have a minimum of *seven sentences*. Write on any of the following topics.

1. problems facing handicapped students on your campus
2. reasons some college students abuse drugs or alcohol
3. benefits of a consistent exercise program
4. characteristics of different types of bicycles
5. types of customers where you work

Submit your final copy written neatly in ink on notebook paper or typed (you may use a computer).

12

Comparing and Contrasting

When you have completed this unit, you will be able to—

1. Write comparison paragraphs.
2. Write analogy paragraphs.
3. Write contrast paragraphs.
4. Use point-by-point and block techniques to combine comparison and contrast in a single paragraph.

In longer college papers, research papers, and reports, you will frequently need to explain how two objects, ideas, or people are alike or different. Although you will rarely write an entire paper of comparison or contrast, you will often use one or more paragraphs to compare or contrast people or things you are analyzing or describing. After you have made your point by using this technique, shift to another type of writing.

Writing comparisons and contrasts is easy because they are a common part of your life. You automatically consider how things are alike or different many times during your day. Therefore, all you have to do is practice writing down the comparisons or contrasts that you normally make.

WHAT IS COMPARISON AND CONTRAST WRITING?

Anytime you explain how two or more items are alike, you are **comparing** them. Those items could be cars, boats, people, ideas, or other items. Usually, the items that are compared are at least somewhat similar. You could, for instance, compare a Volkswagen with a Cadillac because they both have wheels, doors, seats, and many other common features. You would have a very difficult time comparing an orange with a motorcycle, however, since they have little in common.

When you explain how two or more items are different, you are **contrasting** them. As with a comparison paragraph, the items being contrasted should not be too different, or you will have a difficult time describing their differences. When writing a contrast paragraph, you merely ignore the similarities and write about the differences.

Comparison Paragraphs

A comparison paragraph begins with a strong topic sentence that clearly states what two items, concepts, or people you intend to discuss. If you only mention one of the items in the topic sentence, you will confuse your reader when you introduce the second item. The controlling idea must directly state the relationship between the items. After you have written the topic sentence for a comparison paragraph, you must then offer support groups to explain the topic sentence. Consider the following comparison paragraph:

> In many ways, the German shepherd and the Doberman pinscher are alike. The most obvious similarity, of course, is size. Both dogs are tall and heavy, normally over two feet tall at the shoulder and frequently weighing in excess of one hundred pounds. For many people, however, the most significant similarity of these two dogs is their fearsome reputation. The average person considers German shepherds and Doberman pinschers to be unpredictable killers. Stories abound that tell of these dogs attacking defenseless children who had unknowingly invaded the territory of one of these dogs. Although not everyone realizes it, both dogs make extremely good pets. Loyal and loving, each breed tends to become a family member quite rapidly, even eagerly. When attached to a relaxed, even-tempered human, both breeds of dogs become unbelievably docile and lazy.

This paragraph is an example of the type of writing known as *pure comparison*. That is, the paragraph only explains how the two breeds of dog are alike; it completely ignores the differences between them.

The example paragraph is developed from a strong topic sentence that clearly states what two objects are to be discussed. Three support groups are used to show the three most significant similarities between the two breeds of dog. You don't necessarily need three support groups; the number of support groups depends on how complex the subject is and how much you have to say.

Exercise 12.1

Write one **comparison** paragraph on any of the following topics. Your paragraph must have at least seven sentences and at least two support groups.

    two instructors
    two television characters
    two cars
    two jobs
    topic of your choice

_____

_____

_____

_____

———————————————————————————————————

———————————————————————————————————

———————————————————————————————————

———————————————————————————————————

———————————————————————————————————

———————————————————————————————————

———————————————————————————————————

———————————————————————————————————

———————————————————————————————————

———————————————————————————————————

———————————————————————————————————

———————————————————————————————————

———————————————————————————————————

———————————————————————————————————

———————————————————————————————————

———————————————————————————————————

Have your work checked by your instructor or a tutor.

Analogy Paragraphs

The analogy paragraph is a special kind of comparison paragraph. The **analogy** explains one object that is unfamiliar to most readers by comparing it to something the readers are familiar with. Parents often use analogies as they attempt to convince their children to eat an unfamiliar food. You have probably heard someone say something like, ''You'll like frogs' legs; they taste like chicken.'' You have probably used analogies to explain what something looks, tastes, or smells like. For instance, if someone asked you what a food processor was, you might say, ''It's like a blender.'' Then you might go on to explain how a food processor is similar to a blender.

The analogies you use when speaking are essentially the same as those you write in paragraphs. The only difference between the spoken analogy and the written analogy is in completeness. Your spoken analogy would normally be shorter than a written one. As you speak, you can watch your listener's face to find out when you aren't communicating clearly. If your listener doesn't understand, you can give a more detailed explanation. But when you write an analogy, you must anticipate every question your reader could ask and write so clearly that those questions will never need to be asked. This means, of course, that a written analogy must be very complete and detailed. The following analogy paragraph illustrates how to explain an unfamiliar object by comparing it to a familiar object.

When it is on land, the blue-footed booby bird looks and acts like a clown. Both the clown and the booby bird have feet that are out of proportion with the size of the bodies they support. The clown, of course, is well known for huge feet that cause numerous falls. Because the booby is actually a seabird more at home in the water than on land, it falls over its feet whenever it attempts to hurry. Even when walking normally, however, the booby waddles like a clown, feet slapping the ground, looking as if it might fall at any moment. More than just looking like a clown, though, the blue-footed booby acts like a clown. Everyone laughs at the pratfall routines of clowns as they fall upon their backsides. As if imitating the clowns, booby birds devise the most creative falls imaginable. Ten booby birds and a television antenna can produce the best natural comedy act around. The ten birds (booby birds are almost as large as chickens) will all attempt to get on one antenna at the same time. The result, of course, is inevitable; they knock one another off again and again as the airborne clowns try to squeeze in. As logic would predict, the antenna eventually falls under the weight, and the feathered clowns flutter to the ground, protesting loudly as they fall. Although the blue-footed booby may at first look like just another large white bird, its blue feet and clownish antics will allow it to be readily identified.

An analogy such as this is almost never used alone; it is more commonly used as a supporting paragraph to complete the picture of a person, object, idea, or bird described in other paragraphs. When you are writing an analogy, be sure to continue comparing the unfamiliar object to the familiar object. If you mention the familiar object only in the topic sentence, the comparison will be confusing and unclear. To avoid incomplete analogies, you should include at least two support groups.

Exercise 12.2

Write an **analogy** paragraph on any one of the following topics. Your paragraph must be at least eight sentences long.

an object used in a class you are taking is like a ___?___
the heart is like a water pump
a topic of your choice

_____

_____

_____

_____

_____

_____

_____

_____

_____

_____

_____

_____

_____

_____

_____

_____

_____

_____

Have your work checked by your instructor or a tutor.

Contrast Paragraphs

Although you will often want to explain how two ideas, objects, or people are alike, you will more commonly want to show how they differ. You'll frequently point out differences to explain why one item is better than the other. For this reason, contrast paragraphs are more commonly encountered in writing than comparison paragraphs.

To develop an effective contrast paragraph, begin with a clearly stated topic sentence that explains exactly what two items are to be discussed. In the topic sentence, you must include a strong controlling idea that specifically states the contrast you wish to show. Each primary support sentence must directly support that controlling idea. Evidence and examples are then used to show how the primary support sentences are true.

In the following student paragraph, observe how smoothly the writer moves from the topic sentence to the first support group and then on to the second support group.

> Selfish parents encourage their children to become deeply involved in Little League baseball for two totally different reasons. Some parents pressure their children into playing so that they can use the Little League games and practices as a babysitter, a place to dump their children. These uninvolved parents are often no more than chauffeurs and contribute very little to the welfare and development of their children. Another group of parents becomes involved to an extreme. Such parents create pressure for their children by using the Little League as an arena in which they attempt to win through the triumphs of their children. These parents oftentimes frustrate their children by setting lofty goals of accomplishment that far exceed the children's actual talents and abilities. Social status, as measured by a child's abilities, is very much a part of the Little League game with the child's status on a team being conferred upon the parents. Accordingly, competitive parents feel that they gain personal status with the other parents when their children hit home runs or perform well in some other capacity; the same parents take it very personally if their children do not perform well or are pulled out of a game and benched. In the latter case, the children are frequently subjected to verbal abuse from their parents. Unfortunately, all of this adds up to a tremendous burden of pressure for the children who are supposed to be having fun.

Often you will find that a single paragraph of contrast is enough. Other times you may need two or more paragraphs to completely explain the differences between two ideas, people, or things. When you write additional contrast paragraphs, be sure each begins with a strong topic sentence.

Exercise 12.3

Write a **contrast** paragraph on any one of the following topics. Your paragraph must be at least seven sentences long.

two instructors
two politicians
two careers
an apple and an orange
a topic of your choice

_____

_____

_____

_____

_____

_____

_____

_____

_____

_____

_____

_____

_____

_____

_____

_____

_____

_____

Have your work checked by a tutor or your instructor.

COMBINING COMPARISON AND CONTRAST

You should now be writing comparison paragraphs and contrast paragraphs with ease. To show in one paragraph how two items, ideas, or people are the same (or different) requires only that you begin with a strong topic sentence and then follow with a number of support groups to explain your point. But you will often find it inconvenient to write paragraphs that separate the similarities from the differences. Many times it is more logical to combine your comments about the similarities and differences in one paragraph.

Combining comparison and contrast has the distinct advantage of helping the reader to follow your train of thought. When you write an entire paragraph of comparison followed by an entire paragraph of contrast, your reader can easily forget the similarities when reading about the differences. This creates an opportunity for confusion and error.

There are two basic ways of organizing paragraphs of combined comparison and contrast.

Point-by-Point

The most commonly used technique of organizing combined comparison and contrast paragraphs, point-by-point offers you good potential for adequately discussing complex topics. This technique is easy to master because it is the same cluster approach you used to write paragraphs in the last few chapters. To write a paragraph using this approach, begin by clearly stating the two objects or concepts you plan to compare and contrast. The topic sentence must also contain a controlling idea that explains what the paragraph will discuss. You then use a primary and secondary support cluster to explain each comparison or contrast you are making between the two items.

The most difficult part of writing a combined comparison and contrast paragraph is developing an effective topic sentence. Your topic sentence must indicate that both similarities and differences will be discussed. Consider the following topic sentences:

> For all their similarities, soccer fans and football fans have very different ideas on what makes a good sport.
>
> Although they have different engines, the two most popular imported pickups have almost identical cabs, beds, and handling characteristics.

Topic sentences such as these make it clear immediately that both similarities and differences will be discussed. But be aware that paragraphs developed in this way can be excessively long unless the topic sentence is carefully limited. Notice how the following paragraph moves from a clearly limited topic sentence through a series of clusters.

> The buoyancy compensator and the stabilizing jacket are both used by divers to accomplish identical functions, but they look and operate very differently. The buoyancy compensator, normally called a BC, and the stabilizing jacket, usually called a jacket, are designed to help support the weight of

a diver who is on the surface. Both do this by means of an air bag which the diver can put air into or take air out of at will. Aside from having an identical purpose, the BC and the jacket are very dissimilar, especially in appearance. The BC is shaped like a horseshoe that has been closed at the bottom; it is worn over the diver's head and strapped around the waist. By contrast, the jacket looks like a vest and is worn in exactly the same manner as a vest. More important than looks to the diver, however, is the difference in function between the BC and the jacket. Because the BC only covers the front of the diver's chest, it tends to force the diver's head and chest out of the water when inflated, making it difficult to snorkel while wearing one. The jacket, because its inflation is in the back, in the top, under the arms, and in the chest, allows the diver to snorkel long distances with less effort.

This paragraph describes the similarities and differences of two unfamiliar, rather complex pieces of equipment used by scuba divers. The point-by-point technique used is very effective. By explaining the two items in depth, one point at a time, the writer enables the reader to grasp the similarities and differences without causing confusion.

Block

The block technique of combining comparison and contrast within a single paragraph is the easiest to write for most beginning writers. The block paragraph is actually two short paragraphs compressed into a single paragraph. The first half of a block paragraph explains what one person, idea, or object is like; the second half explains the other item.

In some cases, the block technique is superior to the point-by-point technique. Using the point-by-point technique can be distracting to the reader if you are making extensive comments when comparing or contrasting. The block technique allows you to fully describe one item before describing the second item. Consider the following paragraph, which is developed using the block technique.

Susan and Sally are both excellent job applicants with approximately the same qualifications, but they are two totally different people. Susan has a degree from a major university and two years' experience. She has a professional appearance at all times, dressing conservatively and treating every subject with utmost sincerity. Her driving, determined attitude and her self-critical approach to everything she does leave little doubt that she would succeed at whatever she attempted. Sally, like Susan, has a degree from a major university and slightly more than two years' experience. She dresses stylishly rather than conservatively, but she does not wear exaggerated clothes. Sally is a friendly, light-hearted person who has no trouble meeting people. In fact, everyone who meets her is immediately impressed with her warmth and interesting personality. She, too, is determined to succeed in the business world and is willing to devote her complete attention to any task. With such similar backgrounds and abilities, the choice between the two applicants will be very difficult to make.

Exercise 12.4

Reread the two example paragraphs for the point-by-point and the block techniques. As you read, identify the support groups in each paragraph (make note of those groups in the left margin). When you have identified them, fill in the following blanks.

1. The "BC-jacket" paragraph has _____ support groups.

2. The "Susan-Sally" paragraph has _____ support groups.

Check your answers with the Answer Key.

Exercise 12.5

Reread the student paragraph on Little League parents and answer the following questions.

1. Is the paragraph pure comparison, pure contrast, analogy, or combined comparison and contrast? _____

2. Is point-by-point or block development used?

_____

3. How many support groups are in the paragraph?_____
Check your answers with the Answer Key.

Comparison and contrast paragraphs are easy to create because we often talk about how two items or people are alike or different. Before you consider any comparison, contrast, or analogy paragraph to be complete, however, you should use the following Checklist to be certain you haven't forgotten anything.

**CHECKLIST FOR WRITING
COMPARISON AND CONTRAST PARAGRAPHS**

1. Topic sentence clearly states both items being compared or contrasted?
2. Topic sentence has good controlling idea?
3. Primary support sentences clearly relate to controlling idea?
4. Secondary support sentences give examples for primary support sentences?
5. Transitions help reader move smoothly from one support group to the next?
6. Sentence variety?
7. Sentences properly constructed?
8. Proper punctuation?
9. Spelling correct?

Exercise 12.6

Using the **point-by-point** technique, write a combined comparison and contrast paragraph on one of the following topics. Your paragraph must be at least eight sentences long.

two objects used or produced where you work
two objects used in your favorite hobby
two objects used in a class on campus

Write your first draft on notebook paper. Use the Checklist to revise your rough draft. Then copy your revised paragraph in the following blanks.

_____

_____

_____

_____

_____

_____

_____

_____

_____

_____

_____

_____

_____

_____

_____

_____

_____

_____

Have your work checked by your instructor or a tutor.

Exercise 12.7

Using the **block** technique, write a combined comparison and contrast paragraph on one of the following topics. Your paragraph must be at least eight sentences long.

two people in your family
two friends
two people in your class

Write your rough draft on notebook paper. Use the Checklist to revise your paragraph before copying it in the following blanks.

_____
_____
_____
_____
_____
_____
_____
_____
_____
_____
_____
_____
_____
_____
_____
_____
_____
_____

Have your work checked by your instructor or a tutor.

13

Defining

When you have completed this chapter, you will be able to—

1. Use appositives to define terms.
2. Use synonyms to define terms.
3. Write formal one-sentence definitions.
4. Revise weak definitions into effective definitions.
5. Write extended definition paragraphs using examples.
6. Write extended definition paragraphs using partition.
7. Write extended definition paragraphs using analogy or contrast.

The need for defining is very real. In your daily conversations with other people, you regularly define terms without thinking about it. If you use an unfamiliar word, the person with whom you are talking may ask you to explain what you mean. This is an obvious clue that the person either does not understand the word or the context in which it is used. You will also recognize the need to define a specific word or term if the person you are talking with suddenly begins talking about something completely unrelated to what you were discussing. And, there are several less obvious clues that signal you to define a term more clearly. When these situations occur, you automatically stop, give a proper definition, and go on with the discussion, all without realizing it.

But when you are writing, you can't wait for the reader to ask questions or go astray before you define potentially troublesome terms. You must decide which words could prevent the reader from understanding what you are communicating and define them at the beginning. But that is where the difficulty begins: no two people understand all of the same words. Terms that cause total confusion for one reader may be easy for another reader to understand. Your constant challenge as a writer is to accurately estimate your reader's knowledge of the subject before you begin writing.

To estimate your reader's knowledge of a subject, you must make some basic assumptions. Although you will not be correct every time, you can learn to closely estimate your reader's ability. It is common for writers to overestimate the reader's knowledge of a subject since they often assume their readers know far more than they actually do. This usually leads to confusion on the part of the reader. The more practical approach is to estimate the reader's ability slightly lower.

When writing on the job, the difference between assuming too little or too much knowledge in your reader is the difference between long, detailed writing and brief writing. The less familiar the reader is with the subject, the more you will have to explain. Of course, you will run the risk of boring the knowledgeable reader by explaining too much, but having a bored reader is better than having a confused reader who makes a mistake after reading what you have written. In an on-the-job situation, failing to communicate is very serious; it can mean losing a sale or causing an expensive mistake—maybe even losing your job.

WHAT IS DEFINITION WRITING?

A definition can be anything that helps your reader understand or visualize what you are discussing. A definition can be a word, a few words, a sentence, a paragraph, or even a page or more. The length of a definition depends on the complexity of the term or concept you are defining. The length of the definition also depends on your reader's knowledge of the term or concept. When you wish to write only a short definition, you can use any of the following defining techniques.

A Word or a Few Words

When you use a simple word or term that your reader might be unfamiliar with, you can define it with a word or a few words. When you define an object, person, or idea in this manner, you can use an **appositive**, as in the following examples.

> His acrophobia, *a fear of high places*, prevented him from skydiving.
>
> She used a sextant, *a device for measuring the angular distance from the horizon to the sun*, to locate her boat's position in the ocean.

In each example, an appositive renames the noun that could be unfamiliar to the reader. Normally, appositive words and phrases are set off by commas because they are not essential to the basic message in the sentence. In the examples, the appositives offer helpful explanations for the reader, but they would be unnecessary if the reader were familiar with the subject being discussed.

A **synonym** can also be used to define a word or term when you wish to explain directly what something is. The following are typical sentences using synonyms to define terms.

> A monitor is the *video screen* on which you view text on a computer.
>
> The touring ski, *a cross-country ski*, is much narrower than a downhill ski.

Synonyms, as shown in the above sentences, can be used as direct explanations or as apposivites. The important point to remember is that the short definition, regardless of what it is technically called, is usually placed immediately after the word being defined.

One-Sentence Definitions

A one-sentence definition may also be used to explain an unfamiliar word. As with synonyms and appositives, use one-sentence definitions only when the reader is at least somewhat familiar with the term and the term is not excessively complex. Defining the theory of relativity to someone who has no concept of physics could not be done with a synonym or even one sentence. By contrast, explaining a "shotgun carriage" to a lumbermill worker in anything more than a sentence would be unnecessary and boring to the reader.

There are three different types of one-sentence definitions.

1. The **example** definition uses a real-life example that the reader is familiar with to define an unfamiliar word.

An example of a tragedy is *Romeo and Juliet*.

An example definition like the one above would appear in a paragraph and would only be used to prevent your reader from becoming confused by the term *tragedy*.

Exercise 13.1

Write two **example** definitions. Define terms used in your work or hobby.

1. _____

_____

_____

2. _____

_____

_____

Have your work checked by your instructor or a tutor.

2. A **dictionary** definition can also be used as a one-sentence definition. After you have used a new term, you can define that term in the sentence following with a definition from a dictionary. You may quote the dictionary if you identify the dictionary you used, or you may rewrite the dictionary definition in your own words. Avoid beginning a paragraph with a dictionary quote, however, as that tends to make the paragraph awkward.

According to the Random House dictionary, a theodolite is a "...precision instrument having a telescope for establishing horizontal and sometimes vertical angles."

[From *The Random House Dictionary of the English Language*, Revised Edition, Copyright © 1975, 1979 by Random House, Inc. Reprinted by permission.]

A dictionary definition can be quite effective if it is not excessively long and is truly relevant to the subject. Do not include a dictionary definition merely to impress your reader.

Exercise 13.2

Write two sentences using **dictionary** definitions. Define complex terms used regularly in one of your classes.

1. _____

_____

_____

2. _____

_____

_____

Have your work checked by your instructor or a tutor.

3. A **formal** definition is one that classifies the term being defined. In a formal definition, the term is placed in a general class. It is then separated from all the other items in that class by telling the characteristics that make it different from other items in that class. Dictionary definitions are formal definitions, but often you will prefer to write your own formal definition. The following outline demonstrates the three steps used to develop your own formal definition.

Step 1-Identify the term	Electronic mail is
Step 2-Classify the term	a message
Step 3-Separate the term	transmitted from one computer to another over telephone lines.

First, the term being defined is introduced (electronic mail). The second step clearly establishes what electronic mail is (a message). The third step then distinguishes electronic mail from all other messages by describing its special characteristics. This definition is good for an audience that already understands computers. If you were not familiar with computers, however, this definition would probably be confusing. This does not mean that the definition is faulty. It just suggests that it was written for a specific group of readers—those who already know about computers. Much of the writing you do on the job will be intended for a specific audience.

Exercise 13.3

Write two **formal** definitions. Make sure they would be understood by the reader specified in parentheses. Define terms from your classes, your hobby, or your work.

1. (for a reader knowing nothing about the subject)

Step 1 _____

Step 2 _____

Step 3 _____

_____

Write the definition in one sentence.

_____

_____

_____

2. (for a person with a basic knowledge of the subject)

Step 1 _____

Step 2 _____

Step 3 _____

_____

Write the definition in one sentence.

_____

_____

_____

Have your work checked by your instructor or a tutor.

Avoiding Weak Definitions

When writing one-sentence definitions, you must be constantly alert for some common defining errors.

1. Avoid using the term you are defining in the definition. If the reader doesn't know the term, using the word in the definition will only cause further confusion.

> **confusing**   Arc welding is welding with an arc.
>
> **confusing**   An electronic watch is a watch that is electronically powered.

Both of these definitions are weak because they fail to explain to the reader exactly what the terms mean. The following definitions would more effectively help the reader understand and visualize the terms.

> **clear**   Arc welding is fusing two pieces of metal with a rod carrying a heavy electrical charge.
>
> **clear**   An electronic watch is a watch powered by a battery rather than a wound spring.

Each of these improved definitions may need to be further improved for a specific audience. For a reader with virtually no knowledge of welding, for instance, the first definition would still be inadequate.

2. Avoid using "is when" and "is where" in your definitions because what follows these expressions is almost always a general description rather than a specific definition.

> **weak**   Soaring is where a person rides in a glider plane.
>
> **weak**   Aerating a lawn is when a person drills holes in the sod.

The "is where" and "is when" in these definitions describe an action; they do not define the term adequately. The following definitions are more effective.

> **clear**   *Soaring* is a *sport* in which the participant rides in an engineless aircraft and uses air currents to remain airborne.
>
> **clear**   *Aerating a lawn* is a *process* of drilling holes in a compacted sod so that water can penetrate to the roots.

Notice that these more effective definitions are also longer than the "is where" and "is when" definitions. As a general rule, short sentences do not adequately define complex terms.

Exercise 13.4

Revise the following weak definitions into effective definition sentences.

1. An attic fan is a fan installed in the attic.

_____

_____

_____

2. An electric mixer is a mixer that is electrically powered.

_____

_____

_____

3. Failure is when a person fails.

_____

_____

_____

4. A computer is a device used to compute.

_____

_____

_____

5. Working overtime is where a worker works overtime.

_____

_____

_____

6. Rafting is where a person rides in a raft.

_____

_____

_____

Have your work checked by your instructor or a tutor.

WRITING EXTENDED DEFINITIONS

Some terms can be defined in a word or a sentence, but not all. Many of the most important definitions you write can be a word or sentence in one instance, but will need to be much longer in another instance. For example, imagine you were writing letters as part of your job with a dairy, and you had to use the term "butterfat content." You would define that term much differently in a letter to a dairy owner than you would in a letter to a customer. For the dairy owner you would use no more than a sentence, if you decided to define the term at all. For the customer, however, you would want to write a far more extensive definition. Such longer definitions, called **extended definitions**, are at least a full paragraph long and are often two or three paragraphs long.

In developing an extended definition paragraph, you should use the techniques for paragraph writing that you have learned in earlier chapters. A definition paragraph usually begins with a strong topic sentence that is a formal, one-sentence definition in itself. The rest of the paragraph expands on that formal definition. Exactly how you expand your formal definition will vary from paragraph to paragraph. Three of the possible methods for expanding a definition follow.

1. **Examples**—One of the most natural techniques of developing a definition paragraph is to give examples of the topic sentence to explain it. The following student paragraph defines *bravery* by giving examples of the bravery of senior citizens.

> Bravery is an everyday action that raises older citizens above all other people in stature. Living on meager incomes, these "old folks" never know from month to month if they will have enough money to buy food or pay for clothing. Most watch in silent horror as their meager bank accounts disappear to cover hospital and medical costs, knowing that the savings which took a lifetime to gather will never be replaced. But worse than facing poverty, retired people face the prospect of seeing friends and loved ones die. As more and more friends and relatives leave this world, a growing sense of loneliness sets in, which is difficult to find courage enough to face. Being alone is worse than being poor, but many senior citizens hide this fear very doggedly to avoid being thought of as complaining persons. Facing such fearsome enemies as poverty, loneliness and death, senior citizens can certainly be classified as brave.

Defining a term by giving examples can be difficult if you fail to narrow the paragraph enough in the topic sentence. This paragraph works well, however, because the writer informed the reader at the outset that only the actions of older citizens were going to be used to define *bravery*. Had the writer neglected to narrow the definition to only one type of bravery, the reader would not be satisfied by the definition. The reader would think the definition was incomplete unless many paragraphs of varying examples of bravery had been given. As you write definition paragraphs, be careful to limit the term in the topic sentence.

Exercise 13.5

Write one extended definition paragraph using **examples**. Your paragraph must begin with a formal definition sentence and be at least seven sentences long. Define one of the following terms:

Yuppie   Depression
Failure   Liberated woman
Male Chauvinist   A term of your choice

_____

_____

_____

_____

_____

_____

_____

_____

_____

_____

_____

_____

_____

_____

_____

_____

_____

Have your work checked by your instructor or a tutor.

2. **Process**—You can also define a term by describing the **process** by which it works. The following paragraph defines the term *aerating* by explaining the two steps in the process of aerating a lawn. A definition paragraph developed in this manner is like the paragraphs you wrote in Chapter 10, in which you described a process.

> Aerating a lawn is a two-step process of sod treatment that includes breaking up the sod and spreading soil conditioner. The fundamental part of the process is opening up the packed sod that will not allow water to reach the roots of the grass. Although any number of devices can be used to penetrate this sod, the most common is to use an aerating machine which cuts ½'' round holes about four inches apart throughout the entire lawn. The second step in the process is to spread a thin layer of soil conditioner on the lawn and rake it into the holes punched by the aerating machine. This conditioner prevents the newly punched holes from plugging up once again and allows air and water to get through the top layer of sod.

Not only does this paragraph tell the reader how the aerating is done, but it also defines the term *aerating*. Therefore, this is considered a definition paragraph.

Exercise 13.6

Write one extended definition paragraph using **process**. Your paragraph must begin with a formal definition and be at least seven sentences long. Write your paragraph in third person. Define one of the following terms:

Cruising

Cheating

A process from your life at home or on the job

_____

_____

_____

_____

_____

_____

_____

_____

_____

_____

_____

_____

_____

_____

Have your work checked by your instructor or a tutor.

   3. **Comparison or Contrast**—Although not as commonly used, comparison or contrast can effectively define a term, provided that the comparison is stated in the topic sentence. Analogy paragraphs (one form of comparison) often give especially good definitions of a term or concept. Consider the development of the following analogy which begins with a carefully established comparison in the topic sentence.

> A library is an institution with purposes that are like those of a bank. Just as a bank exists to save people's money, the library exists to save people's ideas. Every book in a library represents some person's ideas. Some of those books are the result of profound thought; the ideas contained are monumental. Similarly, some bank accounts are impressive because they are so large. Libraries and banks can also be explained in terms of their circulating purpose. The library, like a bank, lends out what it protects. Books, the library's money, do no one any good while sitting on the shelf; therefore, library personnel are happy only when they have many books on loan.

   You can also write an extended definition of a term using contrast. The contrast development shows how the object being defined is *different* from an object well known to the reader. For instance, if you were to write a report for a purchasing agent of a company that already had a number of half-ton pickups that had had trouble with brakes, clutches, and transmissions, you could contrast the qualities of the three-quarter ton truck you wished to sell with those half-ton pickups, as in the following paragraph.

> The heavy-duty pickup differs in many respects from the half-ton pickup the company normally uses. The brakes on the heavy-duty model are far superior to the lighter half-ton model. Unlike the half-ton truck which has trouble stopping when heavily loaded, the heavy-duty model has adequate brakes to stop safely even under the heaviest loads. Most people assume that since the two trucks have the same size engine, they also have the same size clutch and transmission. This is not the case, however. The heavy-duty truck has a twelve-inch clutch. The larger clutch eliminates many problems when the vehicle is under heavy use. Similarly, the transmission of the three-quarter ton is actually a truck transmission that was designed to withstand heavy service. The slight additional expense of the heavy-duty model is more than compensated for by the extra service delivered.

   In this paragraph, the writer assumes that the purchasing agent is unfamiliar with the heavy-duty pickup. By contrasting that unfamiliar item with the familiar light-duty pickup, the writer has shown how the heavy-duty pickup is superior.

Exercise 13.7

Write one extended definition paragraph using **analogy** or **contrast**. Your paragraph must begin with a formal definition and be at least seven sentences long. Do one of the following:

Define **white collar crime** by contrasting it with other types of crime.

Define **drug abuse** by comparing it with the proper use of drugs.

Define a **technical term** from a class or your work by contrasting it with something very common.

_____

_____

_____

_____

_____

_____

_____

_____

_____

_____

_____

_____

_____

_____

_____

_____

_____

Have your work checked by your instructor or a tutor.

14

Narrating and Describing

When you have completed this unit, you will be able to—

1. Distinguish between first, second, and third-person writing.
2. Convert first-person to third-person writing.
3. Write narrative paragraphs using chronological order.
4. Write descriptive paragraphs that appeal to the five senses.
5. Describe events without omitting any details.
6. Describe an object using an appropriate order.
7. Combine narration and description to achieve more realistic writing.

The terms **narrating** and **describing** and the types of writing they represent are probably not new to you. **Narrating** is the act of telling—through speaking or writing—about an event that has occurred. The most common example of **spoken** narratives are encountered when one person tells another what happened that day at work or school. The most common **written** narratives are found in letters and books.

Although many think describing is the same as narrating, it is actually quite different. While narrating tells a story, the act of **describing** tells about a person, place, object, or condition so that the reader or listener can clearly imagine what or who is being written or spoken about.

A combination of narration and description is the most common type of writing people encounter. Almost every letter you write to a friend or relative contains both narration and description. When you write a letter, you normally write about what has happened to people you know or to yourself; in this way, you are writing narration. But when you tell exactly what a particular object or person looks like, you are writing description. In some college classes, you write lab reports in which you tell what you observed. Those reports narrate and describe your findings. And in the working world, every time you write an accident report, you are using narration and description. Since both writing techniques are commonly used, you should learn to use them well.

USING FIRST, SECOND, AND THIRD PERSON

When you are writing narration and description, you must be concerned with *first, second, and third person*. **First-person writing** refers to writing in which you speak in your own voice using the word **I**.

> **I** was turning into the yard when the accident occurred.
>
> **I** first swam in the Pacific Ocean at the Midway Islands.

Such writing is natural when you are writing a personal letter to a friend or relative. You often see first-person writing in newspapers and magazines when a writer explains a personal experience. In your job, you may use first-person writing to explain exactly what you saw or did.

Second-person writing is writing in which the writer speaks directly to the reader. In such writing, the pronoun **you** is used extensively.

> Where will **you** go for a vacation next summer?
>
> **You** should always leave **your** desk clean when **you** leave to go home.

Notice that the word **your** is used to show possession in second-person writing. Also remember that the word **you** can be understood in a sentence, as in the sentence "Always wax a car in the shade." Here the understood **you** is the subject of the sentence.

Second-person writing is less commonly used than either first or third person in an academic environment. Although you may not use it very often, you will see it used. Textbooks, for instance, use second person almost exclusively. In fact, most writers who are giving instructions use second person, as you learned in Chapter 10, simply because it is the most convenient way to explain how to do something. Notice that we are speaking directly to **you** as we explain how to write in this chapter.

In business, you may write a report in second person if you know exactly who will read the report. If you were to write for a magazine, you might also use second person. However, the most common occasion for using second person is when writing letters, either business or personal.

Third-person writing is commonly used in writing for school and work. Preferred because it is objective, **third-person writing** speaks clearly about something or someone else. In this type of writing, you will use the pronouns **he**, **she**, **it**, and **they** extensively. The following examples are written in third person:

> **He** is a senior vice-president for Intel Corporation.
>
> **They** plan to fly to New Zealand for a Christmas vacation.
>
> Because **it** is objective, third person is often preferred.

In letters, third person will help you explain events that happened.

We say that a paragraph is written primarily in **first person** if it expresses the writer's position or thoughts extensively. If a paragraph speaks directly to the reader, it is labeled **second person**. And if it speaks about someone or something other than the writer or the reader, it is called **third person**. Although a given paragraph might be primarily first, second, or third person, we rarely write an entire paragraph in any one person. Instead, we usually mix the various kinds of writing together. Many employers will require you to mix all three "persons" in your writing. Consider the following narration by a woman who remembers her mother very clearly.

THE NAP

I remember my mother for the naps she took. These naps stick in my memory because of the importance they held for my mother and how they affected the lives of my brothers and me. She was able to take naps every afternoon without worry as to what my brothers and I were doing because we lived in an area where we could find entertainment for ourselves without getting into trouble.

Our home was located five miles from the nearest town. It was set back from the main road about a half mile with our front yard situated between the road and the house. At the road edge of the yard there was an impassable row of shrubbery that prevented us from being harmed by the passing cars. The left side and back of the house were surrounded by trees, and to the right there was a field planted in corn. My brothers and I called the hills behind the trees mountains, but they were really just mounds of dirt left from the time when coal had been stripped from the ground. We spent many hours "exploring" in those mountains while my mother napped.

During my entire childhood and even after I left home, anyone could walk right into our home; the door was never locked. To enter the house it was necessary to walk around to the back and enter through the back door. My father had remodeled the house some time before I can remember and never got around to putting in a front door. Upon entering the house, I would find myself in the junk room. Beyond the junk room, the kitchen was on the left and the living room was on the right. Any day of the week, if the living room was entered between one-thirty and three-thirty in the afternoon, my mother could be observed fast asleep on the couch.

As children, we were not allowed to make any noise during my mother's nap time. If we were outside, we stayed out. If we happened to need or want to go inside, we had to whisper, tip-toe, and make sure the door didn't bang. Upon hearing any noise, my mother would yell, "Get outside!" Years later, one afternoon, my husband and I quietly entered the house and found my mother asleep on the couch. Seeing that she was asleep, we slipped back outside and waited for her to awake. Years of conditioning were still in effect even though I had been married for years, and we had just traveled over two thousand miles to visit her.

As we got a little older, my mother would drive us to the neighborhood swimming pool, fifteen miles away. We would go at one and return home at four. We really enjoyed the time at the pool; all of us became excellent swimmers, but I know that my mother took us just so she would have a quiet time for her naps. My youngest brother has become a marine biologist, most likely due in part to all the swimming he did as a child. He was diving from the high board at the age of five. My other two brothers and I became very good swimmers, and we were all lifeguards at one time or another during our lives.

My mother's naps were obviously a very important part of my life. For years, our every action was determined by those naps. Even today, thirteen years after her death, whenever my brothers and I get together, one of us will invariably say something that will bring to our minds my mother's naps.

Exercise 14.1

Closely examine "The Nap." Identify the paragraphs as primarily **first, second,** or **third** person.

1. Paragraph 1 is _____ person.

2. Paragraph 2 is _____ person.

3. Paragraph 3 is _____ person.

4. Paragraph 4 is _____ person.

5. Paragraph 5 is _____ person.

6. Paragraph 6 is _____ person.

Check your answers with the Answer Key.

Exercise 14.2

A. Write one paragraph that tells about some event that happened to you. Make your paragraph at least **eight** sentences long and write it in **first person.**
B. Convert your first-person paragraph into **third person.**

Do your work on notebook paper and submit the final draft.

WRITING NARRATION

Writing effective narration is easy; it is simply writing down an event exactly as it happened. Such writing merely requires you to imagine that you are talking aloud to someone about an event. The only difference is that you must write it down rather than tell it aloud.

Every narrative paragraph you write should begin with a strong topic sentence that tells your reader exactly what the paragraph is going to be about. The clearer the opening sentence, the better the chance that your reader will understand exactly what you want to say. The following student-written narrative communicates clearly from the beginning because the topic sentence tells exactly what will be discussed.

THE RACE

My exciting life as a "racer" started the day after I had rebuilt my car's engine. I had been working on it all morning in the shop, and it was finally running up to par. It was on my way home for lunch that the challenge was made. For the last few weeks the guy down the street had been wanting to race, and that day was as good as any. It was rapidly set; we were to meet by the river at 12:45.

Lunch almost never existed; it was gone before it hit the plate. I was too excited to sit, so I began to check my car over. I had done this not more than an hour before, but I was too nervous to remember. When everything imaginable was checked, my brother and I headed out.

Just as I started to pull out of the driveway, my opponent came driving down the street. My brother and I almost died. He had uncapped his headers and changed his back tires to slicks. My mind now began to boggle as he went by with the sweet expression of victory on his face.

Although it seemed forever, it took only a matter of minutes to get to the river. Upon arriving, without saying a word, we lined up and began to burn off to warm up the tires. This disappointed me even more. While I was going up in smoke, thus losing traction, he was getting incredible traction and was launching like a rocket due to the enormous tires. With no further waste of time, we lined up and a passenger from his car got out to act as the starter.

As the starter's hands went up, the needle on my car's tach slowly began to rise. I tried to concentrate, but his car was so loud I had a hard time thinking. Finally, I went deaf to all outside noises and focused on my gauges. I was ready. At the instant the hands fell, out came my foot on the clutch. Although my speedometer jumped to 40 mph, I was barely moving. Out of the corner of my right eye, I watched as he slowly pulled away. As the tach hit redline, I shifted like a madman. The back end of my car swung to the left and then to the right as I fought insanely to straighten it out. Things began to spin and everything went into a dizzy, slow-motion spin. When I finally got stopped, I was out in the middle of a plowed field and my opponent was long gone.

Here a student has effectively told about a humiliating experience of losing a car race. The account is easy to read because the writer honestly tells what it felt like to race against a superior car and driver. Honesty and directness are the most effective tools this narrative writer used. This student-written narrative illustrates what you can do. Anyone can write a narrative about any subject; it is the most natural writing you will ever do.

Choosing a Topic

An important and often distressing part of the writing process is deciding what to write about. People who are learning to write narratives complain that they can't think of anything to write about. You have probably made the same complaint many times. Actually, everyone has something to write about. A man, retired after years as a machinist, recently made the same complaint. But once he realized that his lifetime of skills and experiences could be turned into excellent writing topics, he immediately began writing good papers on a regular basis. Everyone has a similar storehouse of experiences and talents. Of course, if you have never worked, you don't have a job to write about, but you do have many years of other personal experiences to write about. Everyone you ever met and everything that ever happened to you can be the source of good narrative papers. Examine the following list of topics and choose one that you can write about.

1. My first job interview
2. An automobile accident I was in or witnessed
3. My first date
4. The time I learned what fear was
5. A time I was truly embarrassed
6. My most memorable camping experience
7. My experiences at a party
8. Another choice of your own _____

Limiting the Topic

Before writing a narrative paragraph, remember that a paragraph contains only one limited topic. A narrative paragraph is usually five to twelve sentences long, although it may be shorter or longer, and it is about one *particular* incident. A particular incident is not a summer trip to Australia; that would be a long series of incidents. Even the flight to Australia would be too much to write about in a paragraph. In fact, in a single paragraph you could effectively cover just the ordeal of claiming your bags when you arrived at an airport in Australia.

Indeed, most ineffective narrative paragraphs are made weak because the writer attempts to cover too many incidents in too short a space. If you limit your paragraph to a single short event, it will tell the incident in more detail and will be more interesting to read.

Exercise 14.3

Write one paragraph in **first-person narrative**. Make your paragraph at least eight sentences long. Write and revise your paragraph on notebook paper first. Then copy your perfected work in the following space.

_____

_____

_____

_____

_____

_____

_____

_____

_____

_____

_____

_____

_____

_____

_____

Have your work checked by your instructor or a tutor.

Using Chronological Order

Whenever you write a narrative, you must put it in logical order to avoid confusion. It is not enough to simply tell the story; you must be sure that your reader can follow what you are trying to communicate. One way to help your reader follow the story is to use chronological order. **Chronological order** in narrative writing means telling the story one step at a time, beginning with the first event and ending with the last. It is also frequently referred to as "natural time order." Most people who have a story to tell automatically tell it in chronological order. This natural time order is so commonly used in narratives that readers become confused when any event is out of sequence. Notice how the following narrative moves logically from one event to the next.

THE PHOTO TRIP

Nora, Heidi, and Bette went to the Wyoming plateau to do some filming of night animals for a biology project. Upon arriving, they set up their equipment and were waiting in readiness for the night's activities to begin. As the last of the sun's warm rays left them and the coldness set in, the first of the night's activities was starting. They found themselves surrounded by hundreds of bats. At first they found the tough, leathery-looking creatures fascinating, in fact so fascinating that they just sat and watched, not bothering to pick up their cameras. Finally, Nora managed to pick up the movie camera and nudged Bette to pick up her Nikon for still pictures.

Nora had run about two seconds of film by the time Bette finally had her lights adjusted and was ready to zero in on her first target. Just as she was about to click the shutter closed, a bloodcurdling scream split the air. Heidi, who was steadying the tripod, and Bette jumped a foot in the air, upsetting the camera. As Bette's finger clicked the shutter, Heidi's white, terrified face was framed in the viewfinder, and that was to be the best picture taken all night. As Heidi managed to catch the camera, Bette went creeping over to Nora, who was hysterical with fright. Through a garbled type of communication, she learned that a curious bat had become entangled in Nora's long hair. Nora claimed, of course, that the bats were out to kill them by sucking their blood, and that they needed to escape from that awful place as quickly as possible. Bette didn't know if the excitement, the bats, or Nora's fright was responsible, but something triggered their impulse to run. Picking up their cameras and equipment, they ran as fast as possible over the red clay soil. Finally, able to run no more, they collapsed, their fright having been left behind. Suddenly, it was terribly funny, and they sat and laughed until the tears were streaming down their faces.

This narrative is fun to read and easy to follow because the writer tells about each event in natural time order. Another important detail about this true story should be obvious: the story describes a perfectly insignificant event, not an earthshattering, life-and-death struggle. You undoubtedly have experienced dozens of similar situations. When you are searching for topics on which to write narratives, consider the effective paper above, written on such a little incident. Notice also that this writer used third person, creating an interesting effect.

Exercise 14.4

Write another narrative paragraph, similar to the one you did for Exercise 14.3. However, write this one in third person. Be sure to use chronological order in this paragraph.

_____

_____

_____

_____

_____

_____

_____

_____

_____

_____

_____

_____

_____

_____

Have your work checked by your instructor or a tutor.

WRITING DESCRIPTION

Unlike narration, description does not tell a story. Rather, **description** tells what something feels, looks, smells, sounds, or tastes like. Description is commonly used to make a narrative more realistic. Almost every narrative you write will have some description in it. Use description to enhance your narratives. Often the more description you include, the more believable the story. However, there will be times when you will have to write long paragraphs of description only—especially in reports.

Using Details

When writing any description, be complete. Never be too brief when describing because the details you omit may be extremely important. Consider the following injury description from an accident report.

> The wound was approximately two and one-quarter inches long. It was gaping open, showing the skull bone. It was located on the left side of the forehead above the eye. Bleeding easily and profusely, the wound was particularly dangerous because the bleeding was almost impossible to stop.

The paragraph is a good, basic description of the injury. It contains enough detail to be used in a narrative. But for an accident report, it fails to provide enough detail to make the description useful. An insurance company, a doctor, a lawyer, or even a loved one would want to know more about the injury. The following description is far superior because it tells precisely where the wound is located ("above the optic nerve") and how it is shaped. Consider how much more helpful the following paragraph would be.

The two and one-quarter inch wound was on the left side of the injured man's forehead. It was crescent-shaped, beginning directly over the center of the man's left eye, one inch above the eyebrow, approximately forty-five degrees away from the center of the man's forehead. The wound was open with the skin pulled away from the center, and the blood flowed freely without pulsating. At the center of the wound, the whiteness of the skull could be glimpsed when the blood was cleaned away. The wound was apparently above the optic nerve; this was assumed because of its location and because the man's eyesight was apparently unaffected. Although the profuse bleeding was stopped through the use of compresses, bleeding resumed whenever the man rolled over. Each time the bleeding was restarted, it appeared to become more difficult to stop, and only through the application of pressure compresses was the flow controlled.

This second paragraph, because of the detail, is far more useful to anyone involved. Actually, the detail could be extended even more if the situation called for it. A doctor, for instance, would want to know exactly what tissues were involved and if any foreign matter was in the wound. Nevertheless, the paragraph would be adequate for the majority of people who might want to have information about a wound. Notice also that the paragraph does not attempt to describe the accident or what happened to the injured man. Anything other than the actual description of the wound must be placed in previous or following paragraphs.

Wherever possible, appeal to the five senses—sight, sound, smell, taste, and touch—when writing descriptions. In the description of the wound, the sense of **sight** is presented with some very realistic images: the skull, the flowing blood, and the crescent-shaped wound. This clear description helps the reader get an immediate visual picture of the wound. Other paragraphs can appeal to more of the senses in order to help the reader comprehend the object or scene being described. To make a description of an accident more powerful, you might want to include the **sound** of injured people moaning or the **smell** of spilled gasoline and battery acid. When describing food, no description would be complete unless you told the reader how the item **tasted**. Similarly, the sense of **touch** is used extensively in almost every description: of clothing, of fabric in a car's seats, of an injury, of anything a person can feel.

Writing effective description is a matter of deciding beforehand exactly who will read what you write and how much detail the reader will need. A general description in a letter can usually be brief. In many on-the-job situations, however, you will need to furnish your reader with more detail. Those who write technical reports used by purchasers to construct or to assemble items must write very complete descriptions. Most people who write such paragraphs believe that they have not completed the description until the reader can draw a picture of the object. The following descriptive paragraph was written with that completeness in mind.

The cap for the stainless steel vacuum bottle stands apart from most such caps. It was designed to serve two functions—as a cap and as a drinking cup. Its overall diameter is 2 3/4'' at the small end, and 2 15/16'' high. The outer casing on the cap is made of polished stainless steel, which feels perfect-

ly smooth with the exception of the seven fine grip rings which are 1/32"
deep and are 1/64" wide. These grip rings begin 1/8" down from the lip of
the cup and are 1/8" apart. The inside of the cup is lined with a 1/32" egg-
shell colored nylon which serves as an insulator to preserve the heat or cold of
the beverage. The color of this nylon liner is somewhat brownish in places
due to staining from the tea which is drunk out of it. A faint, sweetish honey
odor can be detected; its undoubtedly from the honey used daily as a
sweetener. At the top of this liner, the nylon forms a lip which extends 1/8"
out over the metal to protect the lips of the drinker. Beginning 3/8" down
inside the cup are threads which screw the cap onto the vacuum bottle. The
threads, or thread in this case, make exactly one full circle around the inside
of the cap. One inch below the mouth of the cup, there is a shoulder which
decreases the diameter of the inside of the cup from there to the bottom. At
the very bottom of the cup the nylon liner curves gently to the bottom.

This descriptive paragraph does an effective job of describing a simple cup from
a vacuum bottle easily. Notice that it is a simple cup rather than an elaborate
object. The writer wisely chose to describe only the cup and did not attempt to
describe the bottle in the same paragraph. Had the writer chosen to describe the
bottle too, the description could have been five or six pages long. Every word,
every mark, the thickness and length and width of every part of the object could
be recorded. Remember as you write detailed description that your reader must
be able to clearly envision the object or you have failed. Such elaborate description would be unnecessary for most purposes. A detailed paragraph, such as the
cup description, would be out of place in a letter. You must always ask yourself
how much detail the reader will need before you write a description.

Using a Logical Order

Another concern in writing descriptive paragraphs is order. Order is
achieved by approaching your object in a logical manner. The writer of the
paragraph about the cup described the outside first, going from top to bottom,
and then the inside, again going top to bottom. Normally, a writer attempts to
follow some logical pattern of approach: from top to bottom, from far away to
close, or from outside to inside. Unless you use a logical, consistent order to
describe an item, your reader will be unable to follow the description and your
paragraph will fail, regardless of the care with which you develop it.

Limiting the Description

You should also limit the scope of your description by using a controlling
idea. If you were to describe a dime, you could spend pages doing so; however,
the length of your description could be easily cut in half if you limited it to just
the face of the dime. Such limiting should be carefully done in the purpose
sentence. The controlling idea in the topic sentence of the sample paragraph
limits the writer to a description of the cap of the vacuum bottle, not the entire
bottle with cap.

Exercise 14.5

Write one **descriptive** paragraph (at least five sentences in length) in which you describe a small object in depth. Select any of the following objects. Underline the **limiting word or words** in your topic sentence. Be sure to use a **logical order** as you write your description.

1. a ring   3. a coin   5. a wrench
2. a pencil or pen   4. a comb   6. your choice

_____

_____

_____

_____

_____

_____

_____

_____

_____

_____

_____

_____

_____

_____

_____

_____

_____

_____

_____

_____

_____

Have your work checked by your instructor or a tutor.

COMBINING NARRATION AND DESCRIPTION

Although you will occasionally need to write a paragraph of either pure narration or pure description, you will more commonly combine the two. By combining the two, you can make your writing more realistic and convincing. You should also be aware, though, that writing that combines the two forms is rarely only one paragraph long. Any successful description and narrative combination will be longer. The obvious solution to the danger of excessive length is to carefully limit your topic.

Writing Longer Narration and Description

You will occasionally want to write longer narrative and descriptive papers, perhaps three or four pages long. As with single paragraphs, begin with a strong topic sentence which tells your reader exactly what point you wish to explain. After you have told your reader what you intend to say, begin writing a normal narrative. Your approach should be the same as for shorter papers: each paragraph should describe one specific part of the object or one event in the sequence. When you move from one part of the object or event to the next, you should begin a new paragraph. The following student paper combines narration and description.

THE NIGHT I GOT BAGGED

I have done and have been caught doing some pretty dumb things, but the one that comes to mind most quickly is getting "bagged" for siphoning gas. It all started in late spring on a pleasantly warm Friday evening during my junior year in high school. My father at this time was having back pains and taking a combination pain and sleeping pill. On this particular evening my good friend Jack and I had planned to spend the night cruising around town in his old truck at the expense of someone else's gas. However, my father was at home, making it difficult for me to get out of the house; therefore, when it came time for his usual bedtime snack, I ground up a few of his pills and put them into his sandwich, just to make sure he would sleep soundly. Once he was asleep, I made my break and manned Jack's faded green 1971 Chevy pickup, the typical around-town work truck.

Proceeding with our plan, we headed for a good setup that we had picked out on an earlier date. Our plan called for us to pull around the corner and walk to the intended victim's car with the necessary equipment, consisting of a gas can and a small hose. We were following our plan right to the letter, walking toward this car, when suddenly another car pulled alongside of the intended hit car, which shot our plan right out of the saddle. Turning around, we headed back to Jack's truck. Arriving back at this truck, we spotted a seemingly good setup right across the street. Without thinking, we happily trotted right over, proceeded to put our hose into this car's gas tank, and started filling our can. Everything went well, so well in fact, that we decided to pour this "hot" gas into Jack's truck right there on the spot. This also went off very well, and in spite of my apprehension about doing so, we went back for more. Suddenly, a man in his boxer shorts came out pointing a shotgun in our direction; needless to say, we started to leave in a hurry. We now went into the emergency plan, which called for the person closest to the driver's door to get in, start up the truck, and take off with the passenger getting aboard any way he could. Well, here I was with my hand outstretched for the door handle when that man cut loose with a burst of his shotgun and pellets went flying over my head. I cleared the bed of Jack's truck in one step and ran down the street with Jack right behind me.

When we finally came to a stop, we were looking down the same street we had originally started from. Standing there gasping for breath, we watched this man in his boxer shorts writing down the license number from Jack's old truck. Feeling that the situation was hopeless, we turned ourselves over to this man, hoping that with a few words like, "We're sorry," he would let us go. Fat chance of that. He had already called the law, and within minutes officers began pulling up like a bank robbery was in progress. After going through the usual questioning, off we went for a glorious, fun-filled night in juvenile hall. There I waited for my father, and on the way home I thought he was going to drop me off into a ditch or some hole. Things calmed down, of course, and I am still alive to tell the story. But to this day my dad still does not know why he slept so well while I got out of the house that night.

Exercise 14.6

Write a combination narration and description of some memorable event. Your paper should be at least two paragraphs long. Submit the final copy written in ink or typed. (You may use a computer and print out your final copy.)

PART FOUR

Long Forms:
College Papers and Reports

You will be expected to do some writing on almost every job. It may be only work orders or sales slips, of course. In such a situation, you will be primarily concerned with proper spelling and neatness. In other instances, you will write many memos and business letters on a daily basis. Such writing is considered part of the job, and your ability to explain yourself clearly in writing is a measure of your success as an employee.

In many jobs the writing assignments will become increasingly complex as you become a more experienced and trusted employee. For instance, you will probably write letters to customers only after you become familiar with the company's products or services. No supervisor will ask you to represent the company until you know what you are talking about. When you do begin to write memos and letters, you can expect some initial guidance by a supervisor. This guidance may be provided by a training session in which a number of employees are shown the techniques and styles expected by the company. In other situations, orientation sessions consisting of short descriptive discussions may be personally conducted by your immediate supervisor.

The amount of writing you do on the job will usually parallel your position in the company. As a laborer in a construction company, you will be expected to do little or no writing. If you progress to project engineer, however, you will write reports as a regular part of your job.

As you take on more responsibility in a company, the probability that you will write longer reports also increases. The same is true in college. Your introductory classes may not require long papers, but the more advanced classes certainly will. Just as writing longer reports may be a sign of success on the job, writing longer papers is also part of progressing in your classes. Your class grade will depend primarily on how well you write papers.

15

Getting Your Facts Together

When you have completed this chapter, you will be able to—

1. Identify and incorporate primary resources in papers you write.
2. Identify and incorporate secondary resources in papers you write.
3. Write bibliography cards.
4. Use the card catalog in a library.
5. Use periodical indexes.
6. Use reference books.
7. Use the pamphlet file.
8. Make useful note cards.

When writing a single paragraph, a memo, or a letter, your job as a writer will be to supply only a small amount of information. That information will usually be either well known to you or easy to find. When you are asked to write a report or a college paper, however, you will need a much larger amount of information. Such writing will usually require you to search out ideas, facts, and statistics—sometimes in various locations. Rarely will you be able to write a report or a college paper solely from information you already have.

Primary and Secondary Sources

You will encounter two distinctly different situations that require you to find information for a writing assignment. For example, if you are working for a highway department lab, you might be asked to analyze and report on core samples taken from a proposed highway route. The information in your report would be your firsthand observations of the core sample tests. Such firsthand information is considered a primary source. A **primary source** is any written or spoken account by a person who actually observed or participated in some action.

By contrast, a **secondary source** is a written or spoken account of some action by someone who did *not* directly observe or perform the action. Because they contain secondhand information, secondary sources have been referred to as "hearsay evidence." As a general rule, you will consult a library when you need secondary information. Books and other materials are loaded with facts, statistics, and ideas, much of which is secondary information. Although you might be tempted to think of a library as containing only secondary sources, that is not the case. Every autobiography is a primary source since the book's author tells his or her own personal story. But in spite of these and a few other primary sources, the library is basically a storehouse of secondary sources.

A description of the same action or observation might be primary information in one case but secondary in another. For instance, if you were writing a paper on a new variety of walnut tree *you* had developed, you would describe in detail the tree's development. In that case, you would be the primary source, and no documentation would be required. If instead you spoke personally with the developer of the new variety, you would quote that person as the primary source. If you couldn't speak with the developer personally, you could read what the developer had written about the research and still have a primary source. But if you had to read what *someone else* said about the developer's work, you would be consulting a secondary source.

Any source of accurate information is good. But how do you know when a source is accurate? You can never be absolutely certain. If the person who professes to be an authority is wrong and you use that person as a source of information, your paper or report will be incorrect. Fortunately, that does not occur very often. More commonly, when an error is found in a paper or report, it has come from an incorrect secondary source. If the source you use quoted the primary source incorrectly, you have no way to check the accuracy of the information. Yet you may be faulted for the error. For this reason, secondary sources are *not* as highly regarded as primary sources in report writing.

For college papers, however, secondary sources are frequently the only sources available. Say that you are taking a drama class and have to write about New York's off-Broadway theater. If you live in Miami, you have no choice but to use secondary sources. As a member of the working world, though, you will rarely be writing on anything so remote. You will more likely be writing a report on what is taking place on a job site, in a lab, or in the office. In that case, you will be expected to examine the project you are writing about, to make tests, or to talk with the people involved. When you have consulted these primary sources, you are then prepared to write. Other times you might find it convenient to include both primary and secondary sources in the same paper or report.

Exercise 15.1

In the blank on the left, write **primary** or **secondary** to indicate what each source would be if you used it for a report or paper.

_____ 1. an encyclopedia article

_____ 2. an account of the Battle of Bull Run written in 1986

_____ 3. a lab experiment you did

_____ 4. a magazine article in which a writer describes his adventure in Cuba

_____ 5. a conversation between you and an expert

_____ 6. a video of the president's state of the union address

Check your answers with the Answer Key.

USING PRIMARY SOURCES

Writing reports and college papers that incorporate primary sources is easier than you might think. The key to success when working with primary sources is to properly prepare ahead of time and to use effective interviewing techniques.

Choosing Primary Sources

Once you have decided on a topic, you must identify the people who will most likely give you the needed information. For many reports you will write in connection with your job, the primary sources will be found on the project site. If you were reporting on the progress of one of your company's construction projects, you would make an on-site visit so you could see for yourself what progress had been made. You could be relatively sure that the majority of the personnel found on-site would be the best primary sources. Through discussions and reading, you should find out the names of these people before going to the site. Nothing puts you at a greater disadvantage than going to the project site without knowing the name of the person with whom you must speak to get the desired information.

When you search for people to be primary sources, think seriously about conducting more than one interview. Basing your research on a single source can work well, provided that your choice is accurate, honest, and totally knowledgeable. But by checking with a variety of different sources, you can get answers to questions a single source may not know. Different people may offer a variety of opinions or numerous possible solutions to the same problem. Occasionally, you will find some people who do not wish to be interviewed. When that occurs, you can usually go to someone else with your questions. For some topics, the best sources are often public officials because part of their job is to answer your questions or to provide someone who can.

Preparing the Questions

Before you even approach your interviewee, you must develop a list of questions you would like answered. Don't go up to busy workers and ask them to tell you about their jobs. Good interviews are carefully prepared for ahead of time. Questions should never be worded so they can be answered with a simple **yes** or **no**. Rather, they should allow the primary source to express opinions and offer details. Avoid asking, "Will the job be done on schedule?" or "Will these problems affect the schedule?" These questions would probably get a simple yes or no answer. Better questions would be, "What unexpected problems have you experienced to date?" and "How will these problems affect the schedule?" Always phrase your questions so they encourage the people you interview to respond as the authoritative workers they are.

Asking the Questions

Asking questions without offending is an art. The first thing to remember is that your interview is probably interrupting the normal day's work pattern. You should keep your questions few, brief, and to the point.

In spite of your personal feelings, never approach your resource person as someone obligated to help you. Show that you appreciate the time and effort that person is spending. You will be far more successful if you approach the source as if he or she is the only person in the world who can help you. Assure the person being interviewed of your neutral stand on any controversial issue. In this way, the person will often attempt to provide you with all of the information you need.

Taking Notes

Avoid taking detailed notes while your source is speaking. When you are bent over writing, you force the speaker to talk to the top of your head. This may make your speaker nervous and slow down the speed of the interview. During the interview, you can make notes of some exact facts or statistics that you will need to use later in your report or paper. When the interview is over, find a quiet place to expand on the brief notes you took during the question-and-answer session. You will be surprised how much you can remember if you write your notes immediately. Waiting until the next day to write up the interview, however, will probably produce mediocre results at best.

Many researchers use a tape recorder to avoid the intrusion of writing. But before using it, you must ask your source if the tape recorder is acceptable. Some people refuse to be taped; others become quite distracted and nervous at the sight of a recorder.

When you are combining an on-site interview with your own on-site observations, you should include sketches or diagrams in your notes. You may well need some detail from the sketches or diagrams when you prepare your report or paper at a later time.

Exercise 15.2

   Answer each of the following questions briefly.

   1. Why is a primary source usually better than a secondary source?

   _____

   _____

   2. When would you use a secondary source rather than a primary source?

   _____

   _____

   3. In what type of writing are you most likely to use secondary sources? Why?

   _____

   _____

   4. Why should you avoid taking lengthy notes while interviewing someone? (Give two reasons.)

   _____

   _____

   5. When can you use a tape recorder in an interview?

   _____

   _____

Check your answers with the Answer Key.

USING SECONDARY SOURCES

   Basically, most materials found in a library are secondary sources. These include books of all types: almanacs, dictionaries, encyclopedias, textbooks, or atlases. In addition, most magazines, newspapers, tapes, videos, and videodiscs are also secondary sources. However, the library does contain some primary sources: letters, diaries, photographs, documents, speeches, and clips of events from the twentieth century on electronic resources such as videos or CD-ROM.

   Your main purpose for going to the library is to find information. But unless you know what to do and how to approach research, you can waste an incredible amount of time there. The average library in a large town or on a large campus has many rooms, some containing materials you will not need for a single paper. If you waste your time wandering through areas that contain nothing of use to you, you will become thoroughly frustrated, and the final report or paper may become an unbearable chore.

   The most important thing you can do at this stage of your research is to spend time doing some advance preparation. Your first task in a library is to find out where everything is located. Most libraries have orientation sessions to explain how to use their resources. In addition, many have handout maps to show graphically where specific items can be found. Begin by identifying what is contained in each portion of the facility. Only then can you effectively do your research there.

In your initial survey of the library, note the location of important research tools: the card catalog, indexes, and reference materials. In addition to these traditional devices, many libraries also now contain **electronic research tools** which can be invaluable in helping you locate information quickly and easily. These include bibliographic databases either online or on CD-ROM which may give you access to resources that are located far beyond the walls of the library.

Have a plan of action before you begin searching for information. You do *not* simply walk into the library and begin reading. Two important steps will enable you to use the library without wasting your valuable time: developing a possible source list and selecting appropriate sources.

Step 1—Developing a Possible Source List

Libraries are equipped with devices to help you locate materials rapidly. The card catalog lists all of the books the library owns, and indexes list most magazine articles written on a given subject. As convenient as these aids are, they can also create problems. For instance, these devices list books and magazines that have been checked out or are lost, as well as those that are in the library at the time. If you go from the card catalog or index to the stacks each time you find something you might wish to read, you will soon wear yourself out. The better way is to make a list of possible sources. This is often called a **working bibliography**. Since you normally put the information about the sources on 3 x 5 cards, the cards are called **bibliography cards**.

Bibliography Cards A bibliography card should list all the available information from the catalog or index on a potential source so that you can walk directly to that source. The following items of information should be on each card (if they are available).

1. author's name (last name first)
2. title of article (if in a magazine, newspaper, or book)
3. title of book, magazine, or newspaper
4. editor's name (if there is one)
5. translator's name (if there is one)
6. volume number and date (if an article)
7. place of publication, publisher, and date (if book)
8. pages where it appears (if an article)

All of the information on this list would be helpful at some point in the preparation of every college paper and most reports. You will often be unable to get all the information from a card catalog or an index. Some information will have to come from the actual source itself. How you order the information on your cards is primarily a matter of choice, but there are some standard formats you can use. The following sample bibliography card illustrates the standard format used for a magazine article.

Goodman, Jordan E. "Building
Your Assets on Autopilot."
Money. Vol. 22, February 1993,
pp. 82-83.

The logic of using a bibliography card like this one is that you can easily find the magazine article from the information given on it. Similarly, your bibliography cards for books should allow you to find each book without a struggle. If you use more than one library to do your research, you will need to make a note on your cards to remind you in which library the book can be found. The library can be designated on your card by any abbreviation that you choose. You must also write the call number of the book someplace on the card so you can walk directly to the book when you arrive at the library. The following sample bibliography card illustrates a standard format used for a book.

TX
633
F515

Fisher, M.F.K. The Art of
Eating. New York: Macmillan,
1990.

City Lib.

Exercise 15.3

Write a bibliography card for a book you have in your home.

Write a bibliography card for a magazine article you have in your home.

Have your work checked by your instructor or a tutor.

The number of possible sources you should include in your working bibliography depends on the complexity of your subject. A simple subject may only need two or three sources. For a complex subject, however, you should gather fifteen or more bibliography cards before you begin reading on the topic you have chosen. If you can, get cards from a variety of sources (books, magazines, newspapers, encyclopedias, and pamphlets). Although fifteen potential sources might sound like an exaggerated number, that is actually a minimum number for a thorough paper. When you finally locate the potential sources, you can expect that more than half of them will be unavailable or not closely related to your specific topic. If you cannot find fifteen potential sources, you should check with your instructor.

The Card Catalog   Once you know how to make the bibliography cards, you are ready to begin searching for potential sources. Most library users begin with the card catalog because they are most likely to be somewhat familiar with it already. The **card catalog** is an alphabetical listing of all books in the library. To help you find books fast, each book is listed several times in the file. In fact, most books are listed in three different ways: by **author**, by **title**, and at least once by **subject**.

The following cards illustrate the way author, title, and subject cards appear in a traditional card catalog.

Author Card

QB	Hawking, Stephen W.
981	A brief history of time: from the big bang to
H377	black holes. New York: Bantam Books, 1988.
	x, 198p.; ill; 24 cm.

Title Card

```
                A brief history of time
QB              Hawking, Stephen W.
981                 A brief history of time: from the big bang to
H377            black holes. New York: Bantam Books, 1988.

                x, 198p.; ill; 24 cm.
```

Subject Card

```
                COSMOLOGY
QB              Hawking, Stephen W.
981                 A brief history of time: from the big bang to
H377            black holes. New York: Bantam Books, 1988.

                x, 198p.; ill; 24 cm.
```

In the upper left corner of each card is the **call number**, which tells you where the book will be found on the shelves. The samples illustrate the Library of Congress cataloging system, used by most larger libraries. Smaller libraries may use the Dewey decimal system.

If you examine the three cards closely, you will notice that they are the same except for the first line at the top. The **author** card has the author's name at the top, while the **title** and **subject** cards have the title and subject on top. Although you may do a search by author or title from time to time, it is more likely that you will be searching by subject as you prepare to write your paper.

In many libraries the traditional card catalog has been replaced by an **electronic** or **automated** one. A computer is used to locate possible materials, but the principle is the same: a search by author, title, or subject will provide you with a list of materials available. One advantage to using this automated tool is that it can be speedy. Also, the computer will probably include information about the status of a book (checked out, lost, overdue, or available), possibly making a trip to the stacks unnecessary. The automated card catalog may be networked with other libraries, providing an opportunity for interlibrary loan.

The following illustration shows how a listing for the book by Stephen Hawking might appear in an electronic card catalog. This listing contains the same information about the book, but the information is presented in a different format on the computer screen. Notice that the call number appears in a different location than on the cards and is followed by a notation that the book is stored in the stacks (library shelves) and is available.

Author Listing in Electronic Card Catalog

AUTHOR	Hawking, Stephen W.
TITLE	A brief history of time: from the big bang to black holes.
PUBLICATION	New York: Bantam Books, 1988
DESCRIPTION	x, 198 p.: ill.; 24 cm.
HOLDINGS	QB 981 H377 Stacks AVAILABLE
NOTE	Includes index.
SUBJECT	Cosmology.

As you begin searching by subject, be creative. Look under all headings that are even remotely close to the chosen topic. For example, if you are researching the gooney bird that makes its home on the Midway Islands, you could also look under "albatross," "Midway Islands," "World War II," and "birds," in addition to "gooney." For each book you find listed in the card catalog that sounds helpful, you should make a bibliography card.

Exercise 15.4

Go to the card catalog in the library and do the following.

1. Select an author card for a writer who has the same last name as you. (If no writer has the same name, select the one closest to your last name.) Make a sample bibliography card on that book in the following space.

2. Select a subject card for a book related to your college major and make a bibliography card in the following space.

Have your work checked by your instructor or a tutor.

Periodical Indexes   More helpful than the card catalog for researching many reports and college papers are the **periodical indexes**. They are the most important aid in the library for many writers. An *index* is a list of journal and magazine articles published in a given field or having common characteristics.

The *Readers' Guide to Periodical Literature* lists every article published in 240 of the most popular magazines. These articles are listed by author and by subject. The articles are listed in dated volumes according to when they were published. When you locate the *Readers' Guide*, you should begin by looking up the topic you wish to research, as well as all closely related topics. If you are researching an event, use the volume that contains articles published closest to the date of that event. For some topics you should use only the most recent volumes so that you get the most up-to-date information on the subject.

The first time you use the *Readers' Guide* or any other index, you may find it confusing. In order to use as little space as possible, the editors of the indexes use as many abbreviations as they can. To help you overcome inevitable confusion, every index has a guide at the front of the volume that explains all of the abbreviations. Use these lists of abbreviations. In the following sample, you can see how such abbreviations are used in an entry from the *Readers' Guide.*

RECYCLING (WASTE, ETC.)

> The recycling bottleneck. B. Van Voorst. il *Time*
> *140: 52-4   S 14 '92*

This short entry provides a tremendous amount of information. The **subject heading** (Recycling) is in bold type. The **title** (The recycling bottleneck) is followed by the **author's name** (B. Van Voorst). The "il" is an abbreviation for illustration, meaning the article has illustrations. The name of the **magazine,** *Time,* follows. Longer magazine names are abbreviated; you may need to consult the list of abbreviations. The number before the colon (140) is the **volume** of the magazine; this is followed by the **pages** (52-4) of the article. Finally, S 14 '92 refers to the September 14, 1992 issue of the magazine, the **date** the article appeared. When you make a bibliography card from an index, be sure to include all of the information given.

The *Readers' Guide* is an excellent source of help, but it is not the only or necessarily the best index for every paper or report. If you were working on a report about schools, you might begin your research by looking in the *Education Index.* Not every library has the same indexes because there are dozens of them. If you are not sure which indexes are in your library, ask the librarian. You should consult any index which might relate to your subject.

One of the indexes you will find particularly useful when you are writing on a current topic is the *New York Times Index.* This index lists only the articles which appear in the *New York Times,* one of the most informative newspapers in the world. Because of its large format, many libraries do not keep back issues of this newspaper. Instead, they purchase the paper on **microfilm** (rolls of film about four inches in diameter), which can be stored more easily.

Other newspapers and magazines may also be stored on microfilm in your library. You will need to use a microfilm reader to read the articles. If you need assistance using this machine, be sure to ask a library worker to help you. To conserve storage space, many libraries store periodicals on an even smaller source, **microfiche,** a sheet only slightly larger than a bibliography card.

Many libraries have indexes to newspaper and magazine articles on CD-ROM (compact disc read only memory). Using a computer to access information on the CD, you can search for articles on a given topic as you would with a print index. This technology has many advantages. A great deal of information can be stored on one CD, eliminating the necessity for you to look in many volumes of a print index. Because of the storage capabilities, many of the databases include abstracts of articles. Reading an abstract may help you decide if you really need to locate and read the entire article. If the computer has a printer attached, you can print out a listing of the articles.

Perhaps the greatest advantage of the CD-ROM databases is the flexibility they can provide in searching for information. They allow you to search by subject or word; many also have Boolean search capabilities, which enable you to narrow the search to your specific needs. By using the words "and," "or," and "not," you can connect terms and thus more specifically define your subject. For example, you might be writing a paper on the effect of conservation on the timber industry in recent years. You decide that you do not want to include the controversy over the spotted owl. Then, using a Boolean search, you would have several choices:

> —timber industry **and** conservation (You will find listings for articles that contain both subjects.)
> —timber industry **or** conservation (This will broaden the search considerably to include articles about either the timber industry or conservation.)
> —timber industry **and** conservation **not** spotted owl. (This eliminates references to the spotted owl.)

There are many CD-ROM databases available to libraries. Because some of them are quite expensive, many libraries will only have a few. Among the more common ones are *ERIC, DIALOG OnDISC, Readers' Guide, the Education Index, Info Trac II* (which includes the *New York Times*), and *NewsBank* (an index to a microfiche database of newspaper articles).

The CD-ROM technology allows you to search vast numbers of references quickly. However, each database is slightly different, and you will need to become acquainted with it. Many libraries provide handouts or post charts to introduce the particular system. There may also be instructions on the screen or a tutorial to assist you.

Online Databases Many indexes are now online; that is, they are connected to a database outside the walls of the library and are accessed with a modem. The user decides which database to use, connects with a telecommunications network through the computer, and requests the desired database system. With this type of search, the user can get listings of magazine and newspaper articles as well as other information; abstracts of these materials; or full-text articles. In many cases, the information can be printed out at the library site.

Because this type of search involves the use of a modem and may incur long distance charges for the library, any online searching you do will probably have some sort of time limit. Many of us are accustomed to a leisurely browse through a card catalog or printed index, but with an online search, you must do some advance preparation before the modem connects with the database. It is highly recommended that you follow several preliminary steps to avoid wasting time when you are online:

1. Carefully define your topic.
2. Make a list of key words (and synonyms) associated with your topic or break the topic down into smaller parts.
3. Identify other subjects that overlap your topic.
4. Decide if you should limit your search to a particular time period.
5. Be prepared to connect your search words to make use of the Boolean search technique possible with many databases.

Exercise 15.5

Find the indexes in your library. List the titles of five indexes you might use while doing research on a topic in your field of interest. If your library has electronic indexes, include at least one of them in your list.

1. _____

2. _____

3. _____

4. _____

5. _____

Have your work checked by your instructor or a tutor.

Exercise 15.6

In the blank above each bibliography card that follows, write an index entry exactly as it appears in the index specified. Then convert the information into a bibliography card entry.

1. *Readers' Guide* _____

_____

_____

2. *Any* other index of your choice—Index used: _____

_____

_____

Have your work checked by your instructor or a tutor.

Reference Books   Not all books can be checked out of a library and taken home for use in preparing a report or a college paper. Some books are called **reference books** because they are intended for use only in the library. Not designed to be read from cover to cover, these books are used to locate specific information on a topic. For instance, if you were writing a report on an important American, you might look in *Who's Who in America* for a biographical sketch. You could also look in *Current Biography* for a more detailed account. The most commonly used reference book in most libraries is the encyclopedia. Encyclopedias should be used to locate background information on the topic you are researching. However, they rarely contain sufficient information to be a major source for your paper.

Reference books will be listed in the card catalog and will probably be identified by the letter **R** above the call numbers. As a rule, reference books are found in a special section in a library identified as the Reference Room or Reference Area. Some reference materials are also available on CD-ROM, including certain encyclopedias, atlases, and almanacs.

Exercise 15.7

List four reference books that you could use while preparing a report on a specific topic in your field of interest. If your library has reference works on CD-ROM, include one of these in your list.

1. _____

2. _____

3. _____

4. _____

Have your work checked by your instructor or a tutor.

Pamphlet File (Vertical File)   The pamphlet file, often called the vertical file, can be one of the most valuable sources of help on a current topic. It will most likely be found in the reference area. In this file you will discover booklets, government publications, and newspaper clippings on most current topics relevant to your geographical area. You could expect to find materials on drug abuse, abortion, and alcoholism in all pamphlet files because those issues are important everywhere. But you might also find help in the pamphlet file if you were doing a research project on a nearby dam, on local civil defense plans, or on a nuclear power plant in your area.

Like most reference books, the materials in the pamphlet file may not be checked out; they must be used in the library. Modern technology, however, has been good to researchers. You no longer have to race feverishly through the process of taking notes in a library. Many students make photocopies of an article or a particular page from a book or pamphlet, then take notes at home when they have more time.

As you would with all library sources, you should look under various headings in the pamphlet file, not just under your topic. For instance, if you were doing a paper on some specific topic regarding whales, you would not necessarily find anything listed under "whale." Rather, the listing might be found under "endangered species" or "marine life" or "ecology." Be thorough; consider every possibility.

Exercise 15.8

Find the pamphlet file in your library. Count the number of pamphlets and clippings in the file which give information on each subject listed here.

	Newspaper and Magazine Clippings	Pamphlets
1. Abortion	_____	_____
2. Smoking	_____	_____
3. Welfare	_____	_____
4. Bald eagle	_____	_____

Have your work checked by your instructor or a tutor.

Step 2—Selecting Appropriate Sources

Once you have developed an extensive list of bibliography cards (a minimum of fifteen potential sources), you are ready to locate those sources and determine which will actually be useful to you. At this time, you must narrow your topic to a specific point; in other words, you must focus your attention.

Find the sources a few at a time. If you search for only one at a time, you will spend all of your time running from the stacks to your table.

After you return to your table with the sources, browse through them to see which will be helpful to you. Only some sources will be appropriate. Skim through magazine and journal articles by reading the first sentence of each paragraph and a few paragraphs at random. If the article says nothing that is of relevance to your topic, don't waste your time reading it in depth. Even those books that are appropriate should **not** be read from cover to cover when you are researching a topic. To see if a book is appropriate, use the index in the back of the book to search for information that could be relevant to your report or paper. A book on citrus trees, for instance, might be interesting reading. But if you were doing a report on pruning citrus trees, reading about planting, feeding, watering, and harvesting would be a waste of time. To save time, read only the pages identified in the index as having something to do with pruning.

Step 3—Reading and Taking Notes

When you have finally determined that a particular source will be helpful, you must begin reading it in depth. But reading it is only part of the job. You must also make notes on your reading. You can take notes a number of ways, but one is better than all others. By developing a systematic note-taking procedure, you will waste far less time.

Note Cards   The best note-taking system is to use note cards in conjunction with your bibliography cards. Each time you find that one of your bibliography sources has information on your specific topic, you should begin making note cards on it. Avoid filling a piece of notebook paper with every interesting idea you find in the source. You should make a separate note card for each idea you find in the source with a specific heading at the top of your card. Having separate note cards will help you use the ideas from the source more rapidly. When you are actually writing the report or paper, you can arrange the note cards into groups according to the heading at the top. Then you can order the groups of note cards according to the outline you have developed for your paper. In this manner, you might use three quotes from a particular source in three different places in your paper. As you write, work the quote or fact on top of your stack of note cards into your paper. Then move that card aside after using it; the next note is then at the top of the stack, ready for use in following paragraphs.

To avoid confusion with the bibliography cards and to provide more room for note taking, many writers use a larger card size for notes, such as 3 x 5 cards for the bibliography cards and 4 x 6 or 5 x 8 cards for note taking.

To further save time in note taking, many writers use only the author's name and the page number of the reference at the top of the card rather than copying all of the bibliographic information at the top of every card. The writer then refers to the bibliographic card for the total information. The following cards illustrate this technique.

3 x 5 bibliography card on a magazine article

Fisher, Arthur. "Crisis in Education." *Popular Science.* Vol. 241, August 1992, pp. 58-63+.

4 x 6 note card using direct quote from source

Problem

Fisher, p. 59

"Indeed, the extent of scientific
and mathematical illiteracy
in the United States is
appalling...."

4 x 6 note card using fact from source

Educational aspect

Fisher, p. 60

Fewer than half of recent high
school graduates can cope with
fractions and decimals.

4 x 6 note card using a paraphrase from source

Impact on business

Fisher, p. 60

Poor math skills force businesses
to provide extensive training
to employees, costing billions
of dollars.

You will normally make more note cards than you can possibly use in the writing of the report or paper. It is, however, more convenient to take a few extra notes than to go back to the library when you are writing to find additional information from one of your sources.

Exercise 15.9

Make a bibliography card and three note cards for a book or a magazine article in the library. Choose a specific topic relevant to your major. Make one note card a **direct quote** from the source, one a **paraphrase** from the source, and one a **statistic** or **fact** from the source.

Bibliography card

Note card 1—a direct quote

Note card 2—a paraphrase

Note card 3—a fact

Have your work checked by your instructor or your tutor.

16

Writing College Papers

When you have completed this chapter, you will be able to—

1. Describe the three parts of a college paper.
2. List the differences between the college paper and other types of writing.
3. Choose and narrow a topic.
4. Write a divided thesis statement.
5. Write an umbrella thesis statement.
6. Develop a thesis-topic sentence outline.
7. Write introductory, body, and concluding paragraphs.
8. Write a 750-word college paper which includes library research.

This chapter covers a type of writing found almost exclusively in the college environment: the college paper. Although writing for the job might sound more important to you just now, writing effective college papers will be equally as important—perhaps even more important to you—as long as you are in school. Your ability to write a good formal paper will often determine the grade you receive in a particular course. For this reason alone, you must know how to write the very best paper possible when it is required.

A college paper differs only slightly from other writing you have been doing in this text. For the most part, the differences between the college paper and the other forms of writing grow out of the fact that more formal language is used when writing college papers. College writing is more formal because everyone who reads your paper must be able to get the same message. You do not assume anything about your reader except that the person is intelligent. You would never assume, for instance, that your reader knows a technical term as you might in a memo or business letter, and you would never use an abbreviation that was not defined, unless it was an extremely common one such as UN for United Nations. The basic difference, then, is that the college paper is written to communicate with everyone rather than with a specific individual or group of people.

Because you are assuming a more general audience, the college paper has three other noticeable style differences. The most obvious of these is that college papers usually contain **longer paragraphs** than those used in memos and letters.

While you might use one-sentence paragraphs occasionally in memos or letters, you would rarely, if ever, use anything shorter than a five-sentence paragraph in a college paper. The reason for writing longer paragraphs is that you are unfamiliar with your audience; longer paragraphs allow you to explain yourself fully to anyone who reads your paper.

The second difference found in college writing is that the **sentences** will often be longer and more complex. The sentence variety you have worked to develop in earlier chapters becomes very important in college papers. You should work to develop your ideas using more complex sentences. Although a short simple sentence can be effective in a long paragraph, too many short sentences will destroy the paragraph's effectiveness. Generally, you should try to avoid having more than one simple sentence in a paragraph. Your paper should have more compound than simple sentences and more complex than compound sentences. Not every paragraph will work out this way, of course, but you should work toward variety and longer sentences.

Finally, you will generally use **third person** in college papers. The fact that college papers are written for no one particular person makes third person necessary because it is objective. You will rarely use second person in such papers. Speaking directly to someone you don't know is always awkward, especially so in a college paper.

WHY A COLLEGE PAPER?

You will be required to write many college papers. The basic reasons for writing these papers might occasionally seem unclear; you might be tempted to think of some papers as "busy work." Fortunately, that is rarely the case. College papers actually have two basic purposes: to give you an opportunity to learn new information and to demonstrate what you have learned.

The most common type of college paper you will be required to write is the **essay exam.** The basic purpose of the exam paper is to give you the opportunity to demonstrate your understanding of ideas and facts presented in lectures, discussions, and assigned readings. Because you will normally be required to write this paper in a class period, the required length will often be approximately 500 words. The instructor who assigns one of these papers assumes that you will study your notes and text until you can write on the subject comfortably.

The second type of college paper is the **term paper** or **research paper.** Because of its length, this paper is feared by most students. Frequently over 1,000 words in length, the paper sounds like an impossible task to beginning writers. In fact, the term paper is often easier to write because the time limits of the short essay exam have been removed. The purpose of this paper is different in that it asks you to demonstrate what you have learned outside of class. Because you will be expected to read books, magazines, manuals, and newspapers when preparing this paper, most people call it a research paper. The assigning instructor's assumption is that you will read as much as possible on the subject in preparation for writing the paper. Hopefully, this will increase your understanding of some aspect of the subject matter of the course. You will be graded on how well you explain what you have learned through your research.

Basically, you will write college papers as part of a course requirement. In such instances, all or part of your grade will depend on how well you write these papers. Although these two types of college papers differ in length, both use the same format and writing techniques. When you have completed this chapter, you should be able to write all types of college papers with confidence.

OVERALL STRUCTURE OF A COLLEGE PAPER

Just as there is a standard format for a resume, memo, or letter, there is a standard structure for the college paper. You may sometimes vary this structure, of course, just as you varied the format in letters and memos. When you are writing college papers, however, you are often being graded on how well you follow certain conventions. If you vary the basic structure too much, you might find that your grade suffers. But there is a more practical reason for following the standard structure: your reader expects it of you. If you don't do what the reader expects at a given point in your paper, your reader could become lost and a break in communication will occur.

The commonly accepted basic structure for the college paper is a three-part organization: **introduction, body,** and **conclusion.** Each part should be clearly distinguishable, yet all three parts should work together to make a statement.

The introduction should introduce the subject in the opening sentence. It should then go on to give background information to help the reader understand why the subject is important. The last sentence of the introductory section should be the thesis statement. This sentence states your position on the subject, thereby telling the reader what the paper will be about. (The introduction is usually one paragraph in length unless the paper is exceptionally long.)

The body is the business portion of the paper. It may be a few or many paragraphs in length, depending on the length of the paper. Each body paragraph explains a different part of the overall subject stated in the thesis. The paragraphs in the body portion must begin with clear topic sentences that have an obvious relationship to the thesis. Any of the paragraph strategies studied earlier may be used to develop body paragraphs.

The conclusion sums up what the paper has stated and emphasizes why it is important. This portion begins with a strong summary sentence and ends with an explanation telling why that point should matter to your reader. (Like the introduction, the conclusion is usually one paragraph long.)

The most important requirement for the three parts of a college paper is that they work well together. If they blend together smoothly and work toward communicating your message, your paper will be successful.

A typical paper of 750 words (using five paragraphs) might be diagrammed as follows:

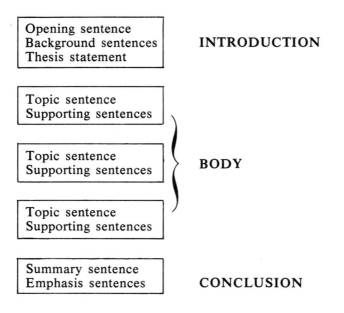

By closely examining this diagram, you can understand how college papers are structured.

Exercise 16.1

1. Give four ways the college paper differs from other types of writing.

(a)_____

(b)_____

(c)_____

(d)_____

2. What are the primary reasons that college papers are assigned?

(a)_____

(b)_____

3. Name two types of college papers.

(a)_____

(b)_____

4. List the three parts of a college paper.

(a) _____

(b) _____

(c) _____

Check your work with the Answer Key.

FINDING A TOPIC AND DEVELOPING A THESIS

When college papers are assigned, usually a subject is also assigned. But you can't just begin writing on the assigned subject. Your instructor will expect you to narrow the subject down to a topic that you can develop in the suggested number of words. This narrowing enables you to write on a subject that the instructor feels is relevant to the course, yet allows you to choose some part of the subject that interests you. The following are typical writing assignments for 750-word papers:

1. Attack or defend the statement that World War II was caused by the excessively harsh terms imposed on Germany at the end of World War I. (A paper for a history class)
2. Analyze the relationship between fruit tree pruning and fruit production. (A paper for a horticulture class)
3. Explain how placing the sea otter on the endangered species list has affected shellfish along the Pacific Coast. (A paper for a marine biology class)
4. Write a cause-and-effect analysis of base failure on asphalt-surfaced highways. (A paper for a civil engineering class)

Any one of these subjects could be written on as it is, if you had enough time and no length limitations. But if you had a 750-word limit, you would need to narrow such topics before writing.

The process of narrowing a subject down to manageable size is simple. Begin the narrowing process by deciding what aspects of the given subject you wish to write on. For instance, the subject given for the sea otter paper would have to be limited. Since many species of shellfish inhabit the same waters as the sea otter, you could not possibly write about how all have been affected by the sea otter's being placed on the endangered species list. You could narrow the subject down to one or two specific species such as the abalone or the crab, or perhaps focus on both. Another way to narrow the topic would be to focus on just one geographic area, such as California's Monterey Bay. The point is to narrow the topic down enough so your paper will not be a meaningless collection of generalities. Only if you carefully focus your paper will you be able to give enough depth to the topic without writing a 50-page paper.

Writing a List of Possible Topics

As you are narrowing the subject, you should develop a list of possible topics, those you suspect might make good topics as you are thinking about how to approach the assigned subject. By listing possible topics, you can consider the subject from a number of different viewpoints. Consider the following list of possible topics for the sea otter paper.

1. effects of sea otter's increased population on abalone
2. growth of sea otter population along Pacific Coast
3. result of decreasing food supply for sea otter population

Depending on your familiarity with them, any of these three topics could be developed into a 750-word paper. Some or all might require further narrowing as you develop the topic into an appropriate thesis, but you could begin writing a thesis statement with any of them.

Writing a Limited Topic

When you decide on a topic from your list of possible topics, you should develop a limited topic. The limited topic is a more specific statement about the possible topic you choose. Suppose that you were assigned a paper in Sociology 1-A on how sports affect participants. The process of narrowing to a usable topic would be as follows:

Subject: effects of sports on participants
Possible topics: 1. high school tennis
                  2. college basketball
                  3. Little League baseball
Limited topics: (Using Little League baseball)
                  1. How Little League baseball hurts pitchers' arms
                  2. How Little League baseball improves father-son relationships
                  3. How Little League baseball teaches three lessons of life

Notice how each of the limited topics examines some aspect of the possible topic, Little League baseball. The limited topics must focus on a small enough part of the total topic to allow you to say everything there is to be said about that specific part in 750 words (the assigned length).

Exercise 16.2

Choose a subject. Then narrow that subject to a list of possible topics. Choose one of the possible topics and write limited topics.

Subjects: 1. alcohol abuse
           2. computers in the home
           3. robotics
           4. religious cults
           5. problems facing the elderly
           6. your own topic

Subject: _____

Possible topics: 1. _____

                   2. _____

                   3. _____

Limited topics: 1. _____

                      _____

                   2. _____

                      _____

                   3. _____

                      _____

Have your work checked by your instructor or a tutor.

Researching Your Topic

When you have narrowed your topic, you are ready to do your research. As you learned in Chapter 15, you should begin by making working bibliography cards, at least 20 of them for a 750-word paper. Your working bibliography should contain material from all areas of the library. For instance, you should find at least the following:

> 10 articles listed in the *Readers' Guide* or other indexes
> 3 books listed in the card catalog
> 3 reference books, such as encyclopedias, almanacs, dictionaries, etc.
> 2 articles or pamphlets from the vertical file
> 2 articles from the *New York Times*

You will probably be unable to develop a working bibliography with exactly the number of cards listed above. You should, however, have at least one from each group listed and a total of 20 cards.

After you have completed your working bibliography, you are ready to read the articles and books, taking notes as you read. The number of note cards you have when you have completed your reading will vary, but you should have at least 30 cards if you have done a thorough job. If you read a good article in a magazine that is four pages long, you should find at least five ideas to list on note cards. Remember, though, put only one idea on each note card. After your notes are prepared, you are ready to begin writing the paper.

Developing a Limited Topic into a Thesis Statement

The limited topic you developed earlier must be narrowed even further by converting it into a thesis statement. The third limited topic of Little League (How Little League baseball teaches three lessons of life) might sound fine;

however, it is not specific enough to serve as a thesis statement. A **thesis statement** is the one sentence that controls the paper: It tells the reader exactly what the point of the paper will be. A thesis statement expresses the main idea of a whole paper, just as a topic sentence expresses the main idea of a paragraph. Notice how one student developed the third limited topic on Little League baseball into a thesis statement.

> Besides learning the actual game of baseball, boys from seven to twelve learn three very important lessons of life in Little League: to respect authority, to work effectively with others, and to practice good sportsmanship.

This thesis is better than the limited topic because it specifies exactly which three lessons of life are to be discussed in the paper. By specifying the exact parts of the topic to be discussed, the writer has controlled the scope of the paper. Such limiting is helpful because it explains ahead of time what the paper will be about.

A thesis will normally be one sentence in length. Occasionally you might write it in two or three sentences if the subject is particularly difficult and the paper excessively long. The best thesis is the one which is the clearest and most direct.

Two types of thesis statements can be used: the **divided thesis** and the **umbrella thesis**. A **divided thesis** clearly states which aspects (or divisions) of the topic will be discussed. The thesis on Little League baseball is a divided thesis. For a short paper of no more than 750 words, a divided thesis is easiest to work with. Such thesis statements make clear from the outset what will be found in each body paragraph of the paper.

The second type of thesis statement is called the **umbrella thesis** or the general thesis. This thesis doesn't specify exactly what aspects of the topic will be discussed in a paper. Rather, the umbrella thesis focuses on the overall point to be made in the paper as in the following:

> Besides learning the actual game of baseball, boys from seven to twelve learn to become better citizens by being exposed to real life situations while playing Little League baseball.

In this thesis, the reader is told that the paper will show how Little League participation helps boys become better citizens. While a more general thesis statement is easier to write, the umbrella is not easy to develop into a college paper. The divided thesis gives you obvious guidelines for writing each body paragraph; these guidelines are absent in the umbrella thesis. The result is that it is easier for the writer to wander off the topic while writing. When you are writing a longer paper, however, the umbrella is more practical simply because a divided thesis statement becomes too long and awkward when it lists five or more divisions.

Exercise 16.3

Choose any two of the limited topics you developed in Exercise 16.2. Develop those limited topics into thesis statements. Write a divided thesis and an umbrella thesis for each topic.

1. (divided) _____   _____

_____

_____

(umbrella) _____

_____

_____

2. (divided) _____

_____

_____

(umbrella) _____

_____

_____

Have your work checked by your instructor or a tutor

WRITING EFFECTIVE TOPIC SENTENCES

Once you have developed a thesis with which you feel comfortable, you can begin developing topic sentences. (If you need a review on writing topic sentences, you should turn back to Chapter 9.) Basically, a topic sentence must be specific enough to control the paragraph that follows it. But when you are developing topic sentences for a college paper, you must be particularly careful that each topic sentence has a direct relationship with the thesis. Write a topic sentence for each body paragraph in the paper. These topic sentences together with your thesis will form a thesis-topic sentence outline. To complete your outline, you should also write a tentative concluding sentence for the whole paper.

A thesis-topic sentence outline for the Little League paper might look like the following:

Thesis: Besides learning the actual game of baseball, children from seven to twelve learn three very important lessons of life in Little League: to respect authority, to work effectively with others, and to practice good sportsmanship.

TS 1:   The first lesson, respect for authority, is taught by the coach and is practiced on and off the playing field.

TS 2:   The second valuable lesson, learning how to work effectively with others, is not only beneficial in baseball but also in everyday activities throughout life.

TS 3:   The most important lesson to be learned is good sportsmanship; this will be needed throughout childhood, adolescence, and adulthood.

CS: Little League is a very essential part of a child's life, not only for the physical activity but also for the values learned.

This would be considered the basic outline for a college paper. From this, a 750-word paper could be developed, provided the body paragraphs were each about 200 words long. If your paragraphs were only 100-125 words long, however, you would need to use a four-part thesis. The parts of the thesis-topic sentence outline represent the major portions of a college paper: the thesis would appear at the end of the introductory section; the topic sentences would appear at the beginning of each body paragraph (three topic sentences would mean three body paragraphs); and the concluding sentence would be the summary which appears at the beginning of the conclusion.

Exercise 16.4

Develop a thesis-topic sentence outline for one of the divided thesis statements you wrote in Exercise 16.3. (Make it appropriate for a 750-word paper.)

Thesis: _____

_____

_____

_____

TS 1: _____

_____

_____

_____

TS 2: _____

_____

_____

_____

TS 3: _____

_____

_____

_____

TS 4: (if needed) _____

_____

_____

_____

CS: _____

_____

_____

_____

Have your work checked by your instructor or a tutor.

WRITING THE INTRODUCTORY PARAGRAPH

Writers rarely use the thesis statement as the very first sentence in a paper. As a general rule, most thesis statements are too difficult to begin the paper with. Your reader would be uncertain *why* you wanted to discuss the subject if you simply began with the thesis. For this reason, the thesis appears at the end of the introductory paragraph. In the sentences before the thesis, you should prepare your reader for the point you want to make. If you are writing a 750-word paper, you should write an introductory paragraph that contains a minimum of five sentences. The first sentence, called an **opening sentence**, must introduce the subject and catch the reader's attention. The following opening sentences illustrate the variety possible for the thesis-topic sentence outline on Little League.

1. Irresponsible children become responsible on the baseball field.
2. To a young child, baseball is as important as a good father.
3. Ever since baseball became a spectator sport, its popularity has risen continually.

Any of these opening sentences could be used, depending on the writer's interests.

After you've written the opening sentence, write the remainder of the introductory paragraph. Three or four sentences of **background** information are usually supplied to tell the reader why the thesis is important enough to write a paper about. For the thesis on Little League baseball, you could give figures on how many adults watch baseball games every year and state how important the sport is to many Americans. You could also write about why it is important for some fathers to have their sons play Little League. One student developed her introductory paragraph as follows:

> Ever since baseball became a spectator sport, its popularity has risen continually. During the baseball season, almost every home has its channel turned to Monday Night Baseball. The knight in shining armor used to be the hero; now it's the baseball player. Baseball is America's favorite pastime, and almost every father wants his son to engage in the sport. No father would mind seeing his son receive a million-dollar contract for being the top pitcher or home-run king. The money involved in baseball is almost unbelievable. But there is more to baseball than money and fame. Besides learning the actual game of baseball, children from seven to twelve learn three very important lessons of life in Little League: to respect authority, to work effectively with others, and to practice good sportsmanship.

The purpose of any introductory paragraph is to involve your reader in the subject to be discussed. An effective introductory paragraph should also move very smoothly from the opening sentence to the background sentences to the thesis. Wherever necessary, you should use transitions to connect your ideas.

Excercise 16.5

Write an introductory paragraph that includes the thesis from the thesis-topic sentence outline you developed in Exercise 16.4. Be sure the opening sentence introduces the thesis and that the background sentences flow smoothly.

_____

_____

_____

_____

_____

_____

_____

_____

_____

_____

_____

_____

_____

_____

_____

_____

_____

_____

_____

Have your work checked by your instructor or a tutor.

WRITING THE BODY PARAGRAPHS

Writing the body paragraphs should be relatively easy once you have developed a thesis-topic sentence outline and written the introductory paragraph. As you write each paragraph, you have only to elaborate on the ideas set forth in the topic sentence. (If you are not certain how to use primary and secondary support effectively, review Chapter 9 briefly.) You must also be sure to select the proper paragraph strategy for each paragraph you write in a college paper.

Using Sources

Since the body paragraphs make up the informational portion of your paper, you must be certain that you can document your facts. For this reason, most instructors refer to all longer papers as research papers and require students to read extensively before writing them. Most college papers are designed to show how much you have learned and should be based on your reading, not on your personal opinions. This does not mean, however, that you should merely copy down the words of other writers. Copying down the words of others does not show that you have learned a thing. The proper approach is to read the ideas of other people and then form your own conclusions. When you include other people's ideas in your paper, you should express their ideas in your own words; that shows learning on your part.

As you convert the words of others into your own words, be careful to avoid copying others' words down and pretending they are yours. Using the words of others as if they were your own is called **plagiarism**, which is a form of stealing. Plagiarism is a serious offense in any writing because it indicates a lack of honesty. If you find a sentence in something you read that says exactly what you wish to say, you can quote it. To quote another writer, copy the sentence or the part of a sentence you wish to use and give credit to that writer by placing the borrowed sentence in quotation marks and identifying the author.

How to Use Note Cards

When you have completed taking notes, you should have at least 30 note cards and a thesis-topic sentence outline. That is all you need to write a truly effective paper. The next step is to arrange your note cards according to where each one will be needed as you write your paper. To do this, look carefully at your thesis-topic sentence outline and sort through your cards, placing each in a stack labeled paragraph number one, two, three, and so on. When you have all of your cards separated into paragraph piles, go through each pile, ordering them according to which will be needed first, second, third, and so on when you actually begin to write.

As you write, you can use any quote, paraphrase, or summary card at any point in your paper except in your thesis and topic sentences. You should always make certain that the thesis and topic sentences in your papers are your words; using quotes or paraphrases in those sentences will make your paper much harder to write because you are then forced to support what someone else has written. The point of doing research is to find information which you can use to support your position as you write your paper.

While you are writing, you must also resist the temptation to use one quote after another. If you use too many quotes or paraphrases, you will weaken your paper. Remember that the basic purpose of such a paper is to show what you have learned while doing your research. You can only show that by converting the ideas you learned into your own words, using a few quotes when you find ideas worded so perfectly that they support your words exactly. Observe the way the author of the following paragraph used a quote.

> The design of the solar heating system is very simple, and the unit is easily constructed. Air or water collects heat by circulating over darkly painted plastic or glass roof panels which are exposed to the sun. This air or water is then transmitted to a storage area for later use. If air is used, the storage system consists of an underground concrete tank filled with rocks which are heated by the air circulating through them. If a water system is used, then the heated water itself is stored in a similar holding tank. Depending on the site of the home and the geographics, the roof panels or collector area usually consists of one-fourth to one-third of the home's floor area. The proper placement of these is of critical importance. "The most efficient collectors face in a southerly direction and are tilted at an angle equal to the location's latitude plus 10 degrees" ("Solar Heating Your House" 6). In the case of a new home, the collectors are built into the roof, and the storage unit may be built underneath the structure. By contrast, if this system is built into an existing home, both units can be built outside and away from the structure, with the collector on the ground and the storage tank nearby.

The quoted sentence was borrowed by the student writer because it perfectly explained the proper placement of the collector. The title of the article after the quotation marks refers the reader to the source of the quote.

You should have noticed something different in the paragraph you just read on solar collectors. You may have been taught to use footnotes whenever you quoted someone's words. That technique of giving credit to someone else is now rarely used. Most schools and businesses have converted over to the new simplified style recommended by the Modern Language Association (MLA). The new MLA style omits all footnotes and bibliographies. The footnote number has been replaced by the last name of the article's author or the article title (if the author's name is not listed). Using such names and titles is called **documenting** your sources.

Exercise 16.6

Write one body paragraph on one of the topic sentences you developed in Exercise 16.4. Use two quotes or paraphrases from your research and properly document the sources. (Examine the sample student paper at the end of this chapter to see how to document your paragraph.)

_____
_____
_____
_____
_____
_____
_____
_____
_____
_____
_____
_____
_____
_____
_____
_____

Have your work checked by your instructor or a tutor.

Writing the Concluding Paragraph

The concluding paragraph must be as carefully written as the rest of the paper. If you consider the purpose of the conclusion, you should have little difficulty writing it. The concluding paragraph begins with a **summary sentence** which sums up what you have explained in the course of the paper. This summing up helps you emphasize the points you have made in the paper. After the summary sentence, the paragraph should go on to explain **why** all of this is important. In other words, after you have summed up your points, explain to your reader why anyone should care about your topic. Consider the following concluding paragraph from the student paper on Little League baseball.

> Little League baseball is a very essential part of each player's life, not only for the physical activity but also for the values learned. All that is learned on the playing field can be put into practice at home, at present and in the future. A young boy is prepared to face the world as he matures by learning to respect authority, to utilize teamwork, and to flow with the ups and downs that accompany life. Learning these values at such a young age is truly inspirational. Along with his parents' lessons, the enthusiastic Little League ball player will always remember the lessons learned from his coach and the other players.

This conclusion works well because it emphasizes the point that was behind the entire essay: that Little League experience is good for children.

Exercise 16.7

Write a concluding paragraph using the concluding sentence from the outline you developed in Exercise 16.4.

_____

_____

_____

_____

_____

_____

_____

_____

_____

_____

_____

_____

_____

_____

_____

_____

_____

_____

_____

_____

_____

_____

_____

Have your work checked by your instructor or a tutor.

HINTS FOR WRITING THE COLLEGE PAPER

By now you have written the three basic parts found in college papers. That should help you see how logically papers of this sort can be written. When you are writing papers as a part of a normal class assignment, the following list of suggestions will help make your writing easier and more effective.

Length When an instructor assigns a paper of a certain number of words—say 750 words—that assignment normally means "not less than 750 words." No instructor expects you to have exactly 750 words. If your paper has slightly fewer words, you probably will not be marked down for it. However, you will find that most instructors mark off when a paper is considerably short. Turning in a 600-word paper when a 750-word paper was assigned is certain to lower your grade. You will find it far safer to write an extra 100 words than to end up short. An instructor will not lower the grade on a paper that is 100 words too long.

Writing Time Give yourself time to write. Don't expect to produce a good paper the night before it's due. In truth, papers are occasionally written in a few minutes the night before they are submitted. Those papers are just as quickly graded by the instructor because of their obvious inferiority. Rarely does such a hastily written paper get a good grade.

The best way to write is to allow a large block of time to develop your outline into a full-length college paper. Avoid writing a few sentences in the morning, a few sentences that evening, another paragraph the next day, and the rest on a third day. Such writing habits often produce a paper that is rough and uneven because you were in a different mood each time you wrote or because you lost your train of thought. A better writing situation is to set aside a large block of time that will allow you to write the entire rough draft in one sitting. For a 750-word paper, this block of time should be about three hours (after you have developed a good thesis-topic sentence outline and done all necessary research).

When you are writing the rough draft, write rapidly, without stopping to correct misspelled words or punctuation errors. After you have completed the rough draft, you should take a break—an hour or even a day—before you begin your revision.

When you are writing an in-class essay exam, you will be unable to revise. You should, therefore, write rapidly but as carefully as possible. The most important point to remember is to get as many facts as possible on paper. A crossed-out word or two will not be held against you.

Revision   As you revise the rough draft the first time, you should correct all punctuation, spelling, and sentence errors. But a good revision requires more. Before you write the final copy of any college paper for grading, you should use the following Checklist to make sure you have considered all aspects of the paper.

COLLEGE PAPER CHECKLIST

1. Proper punctuation in all sentences?
2. Proper spelling throughout?
3. Sentence variety—majority are complex or compound?
4. Strong, clear thesis statement?
5. Topic sentences tied to thesis?
6. Interesting opening sentence?
7. Summary sentence accurately sums up paper?
8. Minimum of five sentences in each paragraph?
9. Uses third person only?
10. Meets minimum length?
11. Accurate documentation?

SAMPLE STUDENT PAPER

A student paper using proper documentation is included on the following pages. You will notice that most of the ideas Susan Sweeny, the author of the paper, borrowed from her sources have been reworded—put into the writer's own words. This technique of rewording is called **paraphrasing.**

You will also notice that this student research paper is fairly long and detailed. Not all papers requiring research will be this long; many will be shorter. The length of any research paper you write will depend on the complexity of the subject and on the length requirements your instructor places on given assignments. Not all papers you write will be research papers, of course, but the following paper clearly shows how to document a paper, as well as the basic structure of a college paper. You will note the author has used a computer in preparing this work. (This paper uses the MLA format.)

On the left facing pages, you will find notes that explain the student paper on the right facing pages. Read this section carefully before writing your paper. Be especially careful as you write your **Works Cited** (what was previously called the Bibliography). The **Works Cited** must be precisely written.

EXPLANATIONS

First Page of Paper

1. Place name and page number in upper right corner, ½ inch below top.
2. Place name block in upper left corner of paper, 1 inch below top of paper.
3. Give your paper a title, but do not underline or put it in quotation marks. The title must be centered on the page.
4. Double space entire paper.
5. Use one-inch margins around the text of your paper—on the top, the bottom, and the sides.
6. Use lead-in to smoothly introduce source of idea or quote used in your paper (see beginning of third paragraph, "German botanist Schemper described...").
7. Place page number and enough information to identify source in parentheses.

Susan Sweeny

English 1A

Mr. R. Mehaffy

17 March 1993

The Rain Forest Dilemma

Every morning millions of people wake up to a cup of coffee. They shower, shave or apply cosmetics, put fruit on their cereal, and drive to work. It may be a beautiful spring morning, not too hot and not too cool, just right to sit on the front porch and read the mail. They may put on their running shoes and go jogging later in the day, or they may just want to relax on their comfortable wicker sofa. Prescription medications make life a little easier for those in need and give some a chance for life they may never have had. Finally, the end of the day might include dessert or a bath, complete with exotic bath oil.

This rather typical day is made possible by a single source which has supplied the ancestor of the coffee bean, the ingredients in the soap, the oils in the cosmetics, and the bananas on the cereal. It gives the medicine in the pills, the rubber on the tires, and the gum on the postage stamp. It provides the wood and wicker for the furniture and even helps to regulate the climate. This single provider is the tropical rain forest! Yet, despite its many benefits, the tropical rain forest is being destroyed at an alarming rate. The importance of the world's rain forests is just now being realized. Rain forests have immeasurable value, not only to the people who live near them but to everyone in the world.

Using the term "rain forest" for the first time in 1898, German botanist Schemper described "a forest that grows in constantly wet conditions." The annual rainfall must exceed 80 inches per year and the rain must also be nonseasonal (Collins 14). It is one of the world's oldest ecosystems, some forests dating back 70 million years to the dinosaur age (Myers 11). Although covering only seven percent of the earth's land area, it holds the largest number of species of plants and animals of any ecosystem, roughly two fifths of the ten million species of plants and animals

Second and Following Pages of Paper

1. Place your last name and the page number in the upper right corner.
2. When no author is given for an article, you must list the article in your lead-in or within the parentheses at the end by its title. Since the title is frequently eight or ten words long, you can abbreviate it to two or three words in order to make it more manageable. The source at the top of the page has been shortened from "Saving Our Tropical Forests" to "Saving Our" simply to make it less wordy.
3. Always underline the title of a book, a magazine, or a newspaper, whether you use it in the text of your paper or in the Works Cited.
4. If you identify your source within your text, only the page number is needed in parentheses. (See first full paragraph on page 2 of Sweeny's paper. The name of the author, Collins, is mentioned in the text of the paper so only the page number is needed.)
5. Observe the documentation in the second full paragraph (Myers 261-62) following the summary of the source. When you summarize information from an author on a given subject, you should tell your reader where the information can be found.

Sweeny 2

on earth! Amazingly, the rain forests exist on relatively poor soil, and they are very fragile ("Saving Our . . ." 48).

Despite covering only a fraction of the earth, the rain forest benefits mankind in many ways. First, it is the home for the native people who live there. They have adapted to a way of life that has changed little over time. As Mark Collins states in his book, The Last Rain Forest, "Surely they have a right to continue living in their traditional lands" (26). This is one important reason for preserving the rain forest, yet it is often overlooked in the light of other more pressing issues.

One such issue is how the forest affects people who live downriver from it. The rain forest receives 75 percent of the earth's rainfall. Catching this heavy rain, it releases the water slowly into the river systems. The massive root system of the forest traps sediment as it flows downriver. The result is that rivers run constant and clear and are purified for drinking as well (Myers 261 -62). Unfortunately, this natural and efficient water resource is not appreciated by the people who benefit the most from it, the people who live downstream.

Yet, rain forests benefit not only the people who live in or near them but also people all over the world. The forest supplies everyday products such as wood for buildings and furniture; rubber for tires, shoes, and other products; oils for toiletries and lubricants; and food sources from candy bars and ice cream to nuts and fruits. As Arnold Newman states in his book, Tropical Rainforest, "Fully 80 percent of what we eat has its origins in the tropics" (35). One amazing fact is that 20 percent of Brazil's diesel fuel comes from a tree called a copa-iba. The oil drained from this tree can be used directly as diesel fuel. University of California chemist Melvin Calvin won the Nobel prize for this discovery, and at this time trees are being propagated for distribution in the United States (Newman 140).

Even in the light of this amazing discovery, perhaps one of the most important products from the rain forest is the medicines. Common medicines such as vincristine to fight cancer and quinine to treat malaria come from rain forest plants. Today, children with leukemia have an 80 percent chance of survival instead of a 20 percent chance thanks to a drug taken from the rain

Explanations Continued

1. To avoid excessive documentation in your paper you can omit the reference at the end of some sentences, provided that no confusion will result. In the fourth sentence of the last paragraph, the words "slash and burn" are quoted but not documented. In this case it is acceptable to wait until the end of the following sentence to give the source since that sentence, too, should be documented.

2. Do not quote excessively. Too many quotes in a paper will weaken your position. Any research paper explains what your research has revealed; therefore, your topic sentences must make a point and the remainder of the supporting sentences in the paragraph must give examples of how that point is true. It is usually better to paraphrase than to quote what an author has said.

3. Topic sentences should not include quotes because they must present your position, not someone else's position.

forest's rosy periwinkle plant (Myers 212; Newman 135). As reported by Mark Collins, "An average of one in four of all purchases from high street chemists (drug stores) contains compounds derived from rain forest species. But scientists believe that we are only scratching the surface." There are thought to be over 1,400 plant species which could have anti-cancer properties, but less than one percent have been tried for medicinal uses (32).

On a global scale, the rain forests serve to regulate climate. The living forest soaks up solar radiation around the equator, which helps to cool the earth. Additionally, the forests are a main storehouse for carbon. One tree has the ability to remove 26 pounds of carbon dioxide each year. It is very easy to see how the removal of large amounts of rain forests can be devastating to our world ("Saving Our . . ." 48). Throughout the years, climate patterns have been established and regulated by the rain forest, to the point of being easily anticipated (Myers 279). We have come to expect certain temperatures at different times of the year. We know approximately how much rain we normally receive and at what times of the year it usually comes. We have also been able to establish a pattern to the water droughts in California. This is all due to the regulating influence of the rain forests.

Despite the many benefits of the rain forests, they are still being destroyed at an alarming rate. It was estimated in 1990 that as much as 55,000 square miles of rain forest were destroyed, an area larger than the state of Florida (Wilson 104). In Sri Lanka, the loss of the rain forest is nearly complete (Sears 75). The main causes for this loss are farming and cattle ranching. Large areas of forest are rapidly cleared by the "slash and burn" method, whereby the area is cut bare and then burned. This method is thought to be responsible for 75 percent of all deforestation (Wilson 104). After the forest is removed, the nutrient-poor topsoil will support crops or grazing vegetation for only a short time. With the forest's protective root system gone, the topsoil is soon washed away, and the land is useless. Farmers and ranchers must then move on and repeat the process (Newman 94-95; Brookwell A1). Unfortunately, the large chunks of deforested land are impossible for the forest to reclaim. When a hole is naturally created by the death of a tree, it is a small hole which the forest can quickly fill in (Verrengla D7). Filmmaker and Venezuelan National

Explanations Continued

1. Occasionally you will want to document what someone has been quoted as having said by the author of an article. Give the name of the person whose words you wish to quote within your text (see the quote by Dr. Jim Miller), and then list the name of the author who used that quote.

2. When using numbers in an essay, write out all numbers nine or below but use numerals for all numbers 10 or above. An exception can be found in the second paragraph. A quote should appear exactly as it does in your source. (See the quote from Quick, "When you think that only 1 to 2 percent...")

Sweeny 4

Congressman Carlos Azpierua states that "Given the erosion-prone quality of the soil, deforestation is practically an irreversible process, the end result of which is total barrenness" (Ellner 631).

Although farming and ranching are the biggest destroyers of the rain forests, other industries play a role as well. Poor logging techniques which harvest acres of trees leave huge tracts of land barren. Mining for gold along rivers with high powered water pumps washes away the thin layer of topsoil, leaving the sterile undersoil exposed and useless (Ellner 631; Brookwell A1). Even the people of these lands contribute to the deforestation by harvesting young saplings for fuel wood. This undermines any attempt at reforestation, but it is hard to make a cold and hungry family understand that the forest is better off left intact (Newman 116).

Should the rain forests become extinct, the losses would be enormous. More than 50 percent of the world's plant genetic material would be lost. This material could aid genetic improvement and cross breeding of plants, enabling them to resist disease and pests without the use of harmful chemicals (Collins 32). As stated previously, the rain forest is responsible for about 25 percent of our present medications. "When you think that only 1 to 2 percent of those plants have been studied as possible sources of pharmaceuticals...the potential loss (of rain forests) is enormous," says Dr. Jim Miller, assistant curator at the Missouri Botanical Gardens (Quick A8). Deforestation also takes its toll on animals. With the removal of their natural habitat, they must find new uninhabited areas. However, the forest can only support so many animals per acre, and the result is very few areas for relocation (Redford 412). At the rate the rain forest is being demolished, the rate of species extinction may already be 50,000 per year (Wilson 104).

Another tragedy of deforestation is that it will eventually harm the people who live in the forests and downstream from them. With the loss of the massive root system of the forest, the sediment, which is normally filtered out, is now carried downstream. The river becomes clogged, stagnant, and polluted. In Venezuela, sediment carried down the river has caused problems with Guir Dam, the nation's main source of hydroelectric power (Ellner 631). The people would also be faced with floods, droughts, and infertile land. There would be the loss of logging; hence, a

Explanations Continued

1. Document all quotes and all paraphrases that include facts and figures, or a writer's unique thoughts on the subject. (See examples of all three of these on the facing page.)
2. Notice the reference to Paul Crutzen in the second paragraph. Because he is quoted in a book by Arnold Newman, you would only list Newman's book in the Works Cited since that is where the reference can be found.

Sweeny 5

loss of jobs in an already depressed economy is inescapable. Lastly, the natives living in the forests would be forced to adapt to a new way of life or become extinct themselves.

The loss of the rain forest would change the climate of the entire world. When rain forests are burned, they release large amounts of carbon dioxide, and it is estimated that the burning is responsible for one-fifth of the present greenhouse gases in our atmosphere (Myers 283; Morrison G14). Carbon dioxide traps heat in the earth's atmosphere, causing temperatures to rise and rainfall patterns to change. There is even the possibility of some melting of the polar ice, which could cause sea levels to rise (Myers 283). Additionally, the burning creates smog. "Carbon monoxide produced by burning vegetation is three times the amount caused by the burning of fossil fuels," reports Pauyl Crutzen, a spokesman for the National Center for Atmospheric Research (Newman 143). It is clear that the rain forests are directly related to the well-being of everyone on this earth.

The facts revealed seem pretty dismal, yet there is hope. Several environmental groups, businesses, and countries are taking steps to help preserve the rain forests. For instance, Japan, one of the world's largest importers of timber, has offered to pay Malaysia to adopt conservation measures (Jones 6). In addition, several pharmaceutical organizations are introducing incentives, such as compensating a country for agreeing to set aside forest for research purposes and involve the people in the search for new plants. The National Cancer Institute will sign a "letter of intent" which "will ensure that the country receives a percentage of any sales" of useful medicines (Worcman 16). The "debt-for-nature swap" is yet another idea; a country can lower its national debt in exchange for protecting its forests (Brookwell A1). An important aspect of these measures is to involve the people of the rain forest in order to show them that they can make more money saving the rain forest and using its natural bounty than they can by destroying it (Jordan A3). Jason Clay, research director of Cultural Survival, reports that if the cost of clearing the land, fence making, and five-year beef production process are taken into account, the profit from harvesting rain forest nuts can go as high as 100 times that of beef (Jordan A3). Perhaps Heidi Hadsell Nascimento and Robert A. Evans have found the key to the problem when they say, "Hope for the

Explanations Continued

1. When a source is documented immediately after a quote (see line 2), the period is omitted after the last word of the quote because a period must be placed after the parentheses.

Sweeny 6

future of the rain forest may rest with those who at first glance seem least concerned about ecology" (1021).

There can be no question that the rain forests greatly benefit mankind. The countless products and services they provide enable us to live longer and more comfortable lives. They are a vast habitat for thousands of species of plants and animals. Without these forests we are doomed to endure climate changes, loss of plant and animal life, and the loss of potential lifesaving medicines. The deforested countries, many of which are economically poor, will lose their biggest marketable asset. The world must learn to harvest the forest's natural bounty without destroying the forest. Cooperation among the consumers, the harvesters, and the countries of the rain forests can ensure the forest's prosperity and all of its benefits for current and future generations.

Works Cited Page Explanations

1. Center the words **Works Cited**.
2. Double space the entire page.
3. Entries are listed in alphabetical order. When no author is listed, arrange the entry according to the title. (Articles such as *A, An,* or *The* are not considered when alphabetizing.)
4. Begin each entry at the left margin, one inch from the edge of the paper. The second and all subsequent lines in an entry are indented five spaces.
5. Page numbers of entire articles in newspapers, magazines, and anthologies are given, but no page numbers are necessary when listing a book by a single author. In some articles, the text will be continued on another page. Indicate such a situation by placing a + after the page number.
6. When a database such as *NewsBank* is used, be sure to include the original location of the article and its location in the database. (See entries six, ten, and fourteen.)
7. Follow the example Works Cited exactly. Every period, comma, underline, and colon must be specifically placed. Notice that article titles in magazines and newspapers are placed in quotation marks while the titles of books, newspapers, and magazines are underlined.
8. For other examples of Works Cited entries, refer back to the earlier discussion of the Works Cited in this chapter.

Works Cited

Brookwell, Joan. "If the Amazon Basin is Destroyed, the Effects Could Be Devastating."
Sacramento Bee 9 Dec. 1990: A1.

Collins, Mark. The Last Rain Forests. New York: Oxford UP, 1990.

Ellner, Steve. "The High Cost of Gold." Commonweal 8 Nov. 1991: 631-32.

Jones, Clayton. "Japan Will Pay Malaysia to Save Tropical Forests." Christian Science
Monitor 28 Nov. 1990: 6.

Jordan, Miriam.   "Candy Bars, Beauty Lotions, May Save the Amazon Rain Forest."
Sacramento Bee 13 Nov. 1989: A3.

Morrison, Patrick T. "As Rain Forests Die, So Do Hopes." Indianapolis Star 2 Mar. 1991.
NEWSBANK INT 64: G14.

Myers, Norman. The Primary Source: Tropical Forests and Our Future. London: Norton,
1985.

Nascimento, Heidi Hadsell, and Robert A. Evans. "Ecologists and Peasants in the Rain
Forest." Christian Century 6 Nov. 1991: 1020-21.

Newman, Arnold. Tropical Rainforest. London: Eddison SE, 1990.

Quick, Julie. "St. Louis Becoming Leader in Study of Rain Forests." St. Louis Business
Journal 20 Apr. 1992. NEWSBANK SCI 16: A7-8.

Redford, K.H. "The Empty Forest." BioScience Jun. 1992: 412-22.

"Saving Our Tropical Forests." Colonial Homes Feb. 1993: 48.

Sears, C. "Jungle Potions." American Health Oct. 1992: 70-75.

Verrengla, Joseph B. "Scientist Burns Rainforests for Study." Rocky Mountain News
6 Dec. 1992. NEWSBANK SCI 40: D7-8.

Wilson, E.O. "Rain Forest Canopy: The High Frontier." National Geographic Dec. 1991:
78-107.

Worcman, Nira. "Prospecting for Drugs." Technology Review Oct. 1992: 16-17.

Exercise 16.8

Write a 750-word library research paper on one of the following topics. (You must include *at least seven* sources in your Works Cited.)

1. drug testing on the job or in professional sports
2. problems faced by young Americans looking for work
3. the need for special training for older job applicants
4. a topic of your choice (get your instructor's approval)

After selecting a topic, follow the steps shown in this chapter for writing the three basic parts of the paper. Do your work on notebook paper. Revise your rough draft, using the Checklist to be sure you have corrected all errors before writing the final copy. Then submit the final copy (written in ink or typewritten) to your instructor.

17

Writing Informal Reports

When you have completed this unit, you will be able to—

1. Combine sentences to achieve variety.
2. Distinguish between passive and active sentences.
3. Develop a formal outline for a report.
4. Develop an informal outline for a report.
5. Develop a topic sentence outline for a report.
6. Identify the various parts of a report.
7. Write a progress report from an outline.
8. Write an external proposal.

Reports come in all sizes. Some, casually written in the form of a memo, are only half a page long. Although often referred to as reports, these are actually considered memos. At the other extreme, formal reports are often hundreds of pages in length. These very long reports, often bound as books before being distributed, are written by professional report writers or by personnel highly trained in writing. Neither of these two types of report writing is covered in this chapter. The extremely short report in memo form is written exactly like the memos you studied earlier. By contrast, the very long, formal report is not included in this chapter because you will almost certainly never be asked to write one unless you have advanced training.

This chapter is concerned with informal reports, which are simply called "reports." Usually longer than half a page, they are designed to convey information to a number of other people. Such reports are almost always filed for future reference.

WHAT IS A REPORT?

A report is not easy to define because it comes in so many different sizes and forms. It cannot be described according to length, for it might be a one-paragraph memo or a 600-page formal report. Further, since it might appear as a memo, a standard form, a letter, a formal report, or an informal report, it cannot be described according to format. But a report, even though difficult to describe by appearance, can be identified by subject matter. A report contains technical information that has been carefully gathered. This information is presented in a concise and objective manner. In addition, the language used to present the information is generally formal and precise.

Reports are always factual and objective. Whatever you include in a report, it must be verifiable. Reports do not contain any guesses. Furthermore, you cannot slant the information to make it support your desired conclusion. Rather, you must remain perfectly objective as you collect information and report the facts to the reader.

Unlike most other types of writing, you should consider the use of diagrams or graphs to help communicate the message. Some technical reports have more diagrams or graphs than written material because visuals often explain the concept or idea better and in less space.

A report is a work-oriented type of writing. Such writing is not commonly required in college classes, although some instructors will require report writing to help you prepare for on-the-job writing assignments. Like any report you write in a college class, your on-the-job report will be a written account of a process, the reasons for doing something, the condition of some object, the progress of a job, or how much your organization would charge to perform a service or to supply materials. In summary, a report can best be defined by its purpose: to communicate technical details to the reader.

Technical Writing

Reports are often simply called technical writing because they use technical language. Almost all reports can be characterized by the use of perfectly clear writing, technical terms, factual information, and dense writing that presents as much information as possible in a short space. By contrast, memos are often highly personal, imprecise and even sloppily written. Technical writing is never sloppy.

Technical writing, as the term implies, is the reporting of technical information, using technical terms and numbers. For instance, in many states a termite report by a state-licensed exterminator company must be filed with the county records office every time a house changes ownership. As you might guess, this involves hundreds of thousands of reports, each using technical terms that are somewhat standard to the industry. Consider the following termite report that was submitted to the purchasers of a single-family dwelling. (The inspector used a format that is frequently used by most extermination company employees.)

DIAGRAM AND EXPLANATION OF FINDINGS

(This report is limited to structure or structures shown on diagram.)

General Description:

<u>Single-story residence--wood frame construction located at 5487 Independence Blvd., Eugene, Oregon.</u>

The interior was furnished and occupied at the time of inspection. Since no authorization had been granted to move furniture, rugs, or carpeting, an inspection of this area was not considered practical and was therefore not included in this report.

1. SUBSTRUCTURE AREA
    A. FINDING: Scrapwood was found in the sub area. (See CD on diagram)
    A. RECOMMENDATION: Remove all cellulose debris large enough to rake.

2. ATTIC
    A. FINDING: Surface fungus was found in portions of the attic shingles. (See F on diagram)
    B. RECOMMENDATION: Scrape off the fungus and treat with a registered fungicide.

3. OTHER
    A. FINDING: Earth contact was found at a fence post attached to the wood siding. (See EC on diagram)
    A. RECOMMENDATION: Install metal flashing between the fence post and the wood siding.

    B. FINDING: Voids in the grout at the hall bath adjacent to the tub is allowing moisture to enter the walls. (See EM on diagram)
    B. RECOMMENDATION: Grout the voids at the tub.

Job Estimate: $263.00

Inspection Fee: $75.00

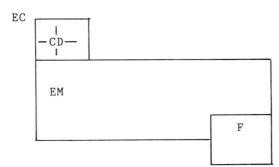

Notice that this termite report describes the findings of the inspector. Technical terminology is used to communicate the information in short, direct sentences. The report, basically an outline, uses a diagram of the house to explain where each problem is to be found. The abbreviations— EC, CD, EM, and F— are carefully defined in the text of the report. This report is typical of many reports written in connection with everyday jobs. Short sentences work well in reports where the information being communicated can be divided into small segments, as in the termite report.

Sentence Variety

Longer informal reports will also use technical language. But instead of all short simple sentences, the sentence lengths and patterns should vary. Using some longer compound and complex sentences is effective in reports, although an excessive number of them can make your writing difficult to follow. To avoid both the choppiness of too many short sentences and the difficulty of too many long sentences, you need to mix the two appropriately.

The following paragraph from an equipment accident report illustrates how rough and uneven a paragraph sounds when it contains an excessive number of short simple sentences.

> One of the company's light-duty pickup trucks was involved in an accident on December 13, 1992. The damaged pickup was equipment number 381. The accident occurred at the job site on 1912 Ocean Avenue. A delivery van sideswiped the company's pickup. The pickup was parked at the time. Damage to the left front fender and the front bumper of the pickup resulted. The company that owns the delivery van admitted responsibility and agreed to pay for repairs. The pickup is currently in the body shop for an estimate.

This paragraph is technically correct, but it would be more effective if some of the simple sentences were combined. Almost every sentence is a simple sentence. Also, the fact that each sentence begins with a subject-verb combination results in a boring writing style. The following revised paragraph illustrates how it could have been made more effective if a greater variety of sentences had been used.

> One of the company's light-duty pickup trucks, equipment number 381, was involved in an accident on December 13, 1992. The accident occurred on the job site at 1912 Ocean Avenue when a delivery van sideswiped the company's pickup. Parked at the time, the pickup suffered damage to the left front fender and the front bumper. The company that owns the delivery van admitted responsibility and agreed to pay for repairs. The pickup is currently in the body shop for an estimate.

This revised paragraph is better than the original because the excessive number of simple sentences has been reduced. Although even more sentences could have been combined quite easily, such combining would not be advisable. More long sentences would have made the resulting paragraph unnecessarily difficult to read. The revised paragraph now contains a good mix of long and short sentences.

Exercise 17.1

Combine simple sentences as necessary to achieve sentence variety and remove the roughness in the following paragraph. You may change or add sentences and ideas if needed.

The durability of the IG5 electrical generating system has been proven in the tropics. This is by far the hardest test of any equipment. The manufacturer used an IG5 unit for two years on the exposed windward side of a Pacific island. The system provided all electricity for a small house. It generated electricity in wet and dry weather. It even provided enough electricity in light wind days. The unit was designed to allow it to be shut down in heavy winds. Damage to the unit could, therefore, be prevented in the event of high winds. The test unit was equipped with an automatic shut-down device. This enabled the generator to protect itself in high winds. These heavy winds occurred on seven percent of the days during the test period. The unit requires only yearly service. That service is relatively inexpensive. It amounts to approximately $135.00. In short, the IG5 has been proven reliable and inexpensive in the harshest conditions.

_____

_____

_____

_____

_____

_____

_____

_____

_____

_____

_____

_____

_____

_____

_____

_____

_____

_____

Have your work checked by your instructor or a tutor.

Active and Passive Voice

Just as too many short sentences will weaken your paragraphs, so too will excessive use of passive voice. In **passive** voice, the subject of a sentence **receives** the action of the verb. In **active** voice, the subject **performs** the action of the verb. Consider the following examples of passive and active voice.

Passive: The *accident* **was caused** by carelessness.
Active: *Carelessness* **caused** the accident.

Passive: The *contract* **was found** to be invalid by the court.
Active: The *court* **found** the contract invalid.

Passive voice sentences tend to be long and wordy. By contrast, sentences using active voice are more powerful and positive.

The use of passive voice is not always incorrect. In fact, there are a number of situations in which passive voice serves a definite purpose. You should use passive voice whenever the object or person who receives the action is more important than the object or person who performs the action. In a paragraph outlining duties of the grounds maintenance staff, for instance, passive voice might be appropriate; it might even be preferable, as shown below.

Passive: The *lawn* **will be fertilized** every six months.
Active: The maintenance *department* **will fertilize** the lawn every six months.

Notice that the passive voice sounds more natural than the active voice in this case. When the identity of the person who is expected to perform the action is perfectly clear, passive voice is more effective. In a manual for maintenance personnel, the passive voice would help the writer avoid boring repetition. The writer will not have to repeat "The maintenance department will . . ." for every instruction given.

Many technical writers use passive voice almost exclusively in their writing because it allows the writer to appear less visible. For instance, when a report presents a committee or department position, it is often better to use passive voice to avoid making the report sound like a personal opinion of the writer.

A supervisor who wishes to avoid sounding pushy might also use the passive voice. Notice the difference in the following sentences. The sentences using active voice sound bossy and demanding. But the passive sentences sound as if they're simply explaining a standard procedure.

Active: You must clean the equipment thoroughly every day.
Passive: The equipment must be cleaned thoroughly every day.

Active: Change the engine oil in the lift truck after every 100 hours of operation.
Passive: The engine oil in the lift truck will be changed after every 100 hours of operation.

Because the subject of the active sentences is either explicit or the understood you, the reader or employee will feel ordered around. By contrast, the passive sentences merely state that the jobs must be carried out, without seeming to be giving direct orders.

Passive voice, in short, does have some valid uses. Unfortunately, the passive sentence is often used incorrectly, thereby weakening the paragraph in which it appears. As a general rule, you can assume that some individual sentences, such as those in directions, can be passive. In a paragraph of formal or technical writing, however, passive sentences rarely work as well as active.

Exercise 17.2

Change all passive sentences to active and all active sentences to passive.

1. A few employees were fired by the boss.

_____

_____

2. The patrolman stopped the speeding bus driver.

_____

_____

3. Your library card must be signed by you before you can check out

books. _____

_____

_____

4. The standard biology experiments were run by the students.

_____

_____

5. Maxine called the meeting to order immediately after lunch.

_____

_____

6. The filters on your furnace must be kept clean.

_____

_____

Have your work checked by your instructor or a tutor.

DEVELOPING THE REPORT

In addition to the technical language and the varied sentences, reports are also unique in other ways. For instance, you should even approach the writing of a report differently than you would an essay for a college class.

Considering the Audience

The most basic consideration before writing a report is identifying who will read it. Your report will communicate only if your reader can understand what you have written. If you use words that the reader cannot understand, you will fail. Similarly, if you don't use technical terms when you are writing for an expert in the field, you may be talking down to your reader. When writing reports, as with all writing, you must properly estimate the level of your reader's knowledge before you begin.

If you are writing for a customer who has a limited knowledge of the subject, the use of technical terms should be limited. A building contractor would be unwise to use undefined terms such as *blocking*, *joists*, *plates*, and *sills* if the reader were a customer who knew nothing about house construction. Similarly, abbreviations must be used with caution. When writing to someone involved in livestock raising, an abbreviation like *AI* might communicate perfectly. Anyone not closely connected to the livestock industry, however, might never guess that *AI* refers to artificial insemination. Identifying your reader at the very beginning will help you avoid communication failure.

Collecting the Data

Regardless of your intended audience, the collection of data is the same. You must search out primary and secondary information in every possible area. To collect data for the termite report, the inspector crawled under the house, walked carefully over the premises, examined the attic, and searched inside the house, always looking for problems. The data collected from such firsthand observation would be primary information. For the most part, you will use such primary information in the on-the-job reports you write.

Occasionally, when firsthand observation is not possible, you will be forced to use other sources. If you were required to do a report on your company's business activities over the past three years, you would be forced to search through the company's files. As you read reports written by others, you would be using secondary sources. Both primary and secondary sources are acceptable for reports, but primary will be much more commonly used.

Organizing the Data

Although there are many reasons for writing reports on the job, the majority of reports written by beginning employees fall into two categories: answering requests for information and writing periodic progress reports. A **request for information** should be easy for you to handle; you merely find the information needed and put it into a report. A **periodic progress report** is any report that must be written at regular intervals. Sometimes the regular interval will be a time interval, such as every thirty days. Other periodic reports will be written at progress intervals, such as when a job is twenty-five, fifty, and seventy-five percent complete.

Once you have collected the data for your report, you will have to organize it into some logical order. You might be tempted to begin writing as soon as you have gathered all material, but you must resist that urge. The only practical method of organizing your information into a useful report is to use an outline. An outline will help you put each fragment of information in the proper place without rewriting the entire report again and again.

A recent study revealed that ninety-five percent of all report writers use outlines. Needless to say, these busy writers would not use outlines if they were a waste of time. They have found that using an outline results in a better report, even though they may spend a great deal of time developing the outline. The time spent outlining is a good investment. When writing a report, you will write faster if you work from an outline than if you attempt to fit the information together without one.

Outlines are very personal things. Some report writers use extremely informal outlines, consisting of only a few words. Other writers use elaborate, detailed outlines that contain pages of complete sentences. Only time and experience can tell you which outline style will work best for you. You should experiment with various outline styles to see which is the most suitable for your needs. However, do not choose the short, informal outline simply because it takes less time to develop. It may require less writing time, but the short outline requires far more time to convert into a full-length report.

Even before beginning to write an outline, many report writers make notes to help them plan the outline. These notes lack any sort of order or formality. They are merely a collection of items to be included in the final report. These notes will contain not only the items you collected on-site or while researching but also your thoughts, observations, and deductions about the data you collected. Such notes are often hastily made on scratch paper. The point of making these notes is to get the ideas down on paper so you won't forget an important point as you write the outline. Also, having a list of notes to be included in the outline will make your outline easier and faster to write. The following notes were written for a week's progress report on a gazebo being installed on a customer's property.

Gazebo Progress

Posts buried in concrete
Rafters
Plate
Sheeting
Roofing 30%
Material used
Estimated progress = 65%

Notice that this list is very brief. Nevertheless, it will help the writer remember what to include in the outline. The following outlines are typical of some used by report writers.

Formal Outlines   The formal outline which is long and complete uses letters and numbers to set off its various parts. The following is a typical formal outline.

Title: Progress of Gazebo Construction at 3218 Park Terrace Road

Purpose: The purpose of the report is to inform customer of the job progress at week's end

I.   Vertical supports installed
   A. 4 x 4 rough cedar stock
   B. Buried three feet deep
      1. Posts treated with asphalt to retard decay
      2. 4" of gravel under vertical supports (for drainage)
      3. Concrete poured around posts to 3" below grade

II.   Plates and rafters installed
   A. 4 x 4 rough cedar stock for plates
      1. Corners mitred
      2. Ends notched
   B. 2 x 8 rough cedar stock for rafters
      1. Attached to centerpiece
         a. Centerpiece manufactured of 6x6 rough cedar
         b. Centerpiece free-floating

III. Sheeting installed
   A. Rough pecky cedar used
   B. Butted against rafters

IV.   Roofing 30% installed
   A. 30# felt paper placed over sheeting
   B. Medium cedar shakes used
      1. Shakes edge-butted against rafters
      2. Extra shakes inserted for antique effect

V.   Estimate job is 65% complete
Estimate job will be completed by end of workday next Wednesday.

This formal outline is designed to help the writer develop a progress report as rapidly as possible. The Roman numerals I, II, III, IV, and V represent separate paragraphs. Notice that each paragraph will discuss a different phase of the construction. The capital letters, here A and B, represent the major steps in each phase of the job. These become primary support sentences in the paragraphs. The numbers below the capital letters — 1, 2, and 3 — represent specific details regarding how that phase was completed. The details in these will be developed into secondary support sentences. Small letters are used to indicate specific examples or additional information about one of the details.

The formal outline is particularly helpful because it is easily developed into a report. To write a report from a formal outline, the writer simply converts the parts of the outline into sentences.

The following report was developed from the preceding outline. Observe that only the body portion of the progress report is actually covered by the outline. This progress report is typical of those written regularly to inform customers, employers, and business associates of the status of a job. Like this one, such reports may present the information in the form of a day-to-day accounting of what occurred. Other progress reports simply explain the status of the job at the close of the reporting period.

Sun Gardens Construction
6841 Spruce Boulevard
Freeport, NY   11520.
September 21, 1993

Betty Hillyard, Manager
Ridgeline Homes
1203 S. Ocean Avenue
Freeport, NY   11520

Dear Ms. Hillyard:

Subject: Gazebo construction at 3218 Park Terrace Road

Abstract. The job is 65% complete. Primary support posts,
plates, rafters, sheeting, and 30% of the roofing have been
installed.

    One of Sun Garden's construction crews began working on your
job site at 3218 Park Terrace Road this week. In keeping with
contract agreements, this progress report presents a written
account of work done to date.
    The vertical support members were installed Monday. Rough
4x4 cedar stock was used for these posts. The bottom three feet
of the posts was treated with asphalt emulsion to retard decay.
The posts were then placed in three-foot-deep holes, which had
gravel in the bottom to assure good drainage. Concrete was then
poured around the posts to a height of three inches below ground
level.
    The plates and rafters were installed on top of the posts on
Tuesday and Wednesday. The plates were constructed of rough 4x4
cedar. To ensure a finished appearance when done, the corners of
the plates were mitred. In addition, the ends were notched to
create an overlap that will increase the strength and rigidity
of the completed gazebo. The 2x8 rough cedar rafters were then
placed on the plate members and attached to a centerpiece
manufactured out of 6x6 rough cedar. The centerpiece was
installed in such a way as to produce a "free-floating"
appearance. The outer ends of the rafters were then cut to allow
a 2-foot roof overhang.
    On Thursday, the sheeting was installed. Rough pecky cedar
1 x 12 stock was used for sheeting. The ends of the sheeting
were butted against the rafters rather than overlapping them.
To provide nailing purchase for the ends of the sheeting, 1 x 2
rough cedar strips were nailed on the sides of the rafters.
    The roofing process was begun on Friday. A layer of 30-
pound felt paper was first placed on the sheeting to provide a
moisture barrier. Over the felt paper, medium weight cedar
shakes were installed. These shakes were also butted against the
rafters. Extra shakes were inserted at random under the

Ms. Betty Hillyard--Page 2

completed shakes to produce an antique effect. At the end of the
work day Friday, approximately 30% of the roofing had been
installed.
        At week's end, the job is approximately 65% complete. If
the weather does not interfere, the crew should complete work
on the gazebo next Wednesday.

                        Sincerely yours,

                        Dwayne Rhoades
                        Construction Foreman

Exercise 17.3

Develop a formal outline for a progress report on any subject. The following are
suggested topics:

1. a class you are taking
2. an assignment from a class
3. a project where you work
4. a project around your home
5. other (have your subject approved by your instructor)

Title: _____

Purpose: _____

_____

_____

I. _____

_____

_____

_____

_____

_____

_____

———————————————————————————————————————

———————————————————————————————————————

———————————————————————————————————————

———————————————————————————————————————

———————————————————————————————————————

———————————————————————————————————————

———————————————————————————————————————

———————————————————————————————————————

———————————————————————————————————————

———————————————————————————————————————

Have your work checked by your instructor or a tutor.

Informal Outlines   Informal outlines are used by writers who are so comfortable with report writing that they need little guidance as they write. Informal outlines ensure that nothing is forgotten and that the various items are in proper order. Because informal outlines are casually written, they vary greatly from writer to writer. Some writers make their outlines in complete sentences, like the following example.

> Title: Progress of gazebo construction at 3218 Park Terrace Road
>
> Purpose: The purpose of this report is to inform the customer of the job progress at week's end.
>
> I.   The vertical support members were installed Monday.
> II.   The plates and rafters were installed on top of the posts on Tuesday and Wednesday.
> III. On Thursday, the sheeting was installed.
> IV. The roofing process was begun on Friday.
> V. At week's end, the job is approximately 65% complete.

This type of informal outline is normally called a **topic sentence outline** because it lists only the topic sentence of each body paragraph. This outline is used by writers who are very familiar with report writing.

Another common type of informal outline is the **phrase outline.** The phrase outline is merely a skeleton and makes sense only to the writer. Consider the following phrase outline.

Title: Progress of gazebo construction at 3218 Park Terrace

Purpose: The purpose of this report is to inform the customer of the job progress at week's end.

I.   vertical support members
     4x4 rough cedar
     treated with asphalt
     concrete over gravel
II.   plates and rafters
      4x4 and 2x8 rough cedar
      mitred and notched
      centerpiece of 6x6 cedar
      2' overhang
III. sheeting
      1x12 pecky cedar
      butted
      1x2 nailing strips
IV.   roofing
      30# felt
      medium shakes 30% installed
V.   job 65% complete

Both types of informal outlines can be equally effective if you are accustomed to report writing. The formal outline, however, will be more helpful to you as a beginning report writer.

Exercise 17.4

Develop a topic sentence outline for the formal outline you prepared in Exercise 17.3

Title: —————————————————————————————

Purpose: ————————————————————————————

————————————————————————————————————

————————————————————————————————————

I. ——————————————————————————————————

————————————————————————————————————

————————————————————————————————————

————————————————————————————————————

_____

_____

_____

_____

_____

_____

_____

_____

_____

_____

_____

_____

_____

_____

Have your work checked by your instructor or a tutor.

The Parts of a Report

Despite the large variety of reports, almost all reports contain common parts. If you can identify these parts and write a typical report, you should be able to adjust your skills to write other types of reports when necessary. To help give you more practice, this section will describe the parts of a typical report and ask you to write a progress report.

Title   Every report must have a **title**. As a rule, the final title is written after the report is completed, but a working title should be developed as you work on your outline. Since the title appears at the beginning of a paper, it must be carefully written, it must be logical, and it must indicate what the reader will find in the report.

Abstract   The **abstract** briefly summarizes what is in a report. It should be no more than a few sentences long. Normally, the abstract is written after the report has been completed. Waiting until you have finished writing the report helps you summarize the report more smoothly. In reports that are shorter than one page, the abstract is often omitted. The purpose of the abstract is to inform a busy reader what to expect in the report so that he or she can decide whether to read the complete report. When reports are circulated in a large company, many employees who receive them may not be affected by the data in a particular report. By reading the abstract, the reader can discover if the report is one that he or she needs to read.

Introduction The **introduction** explains why the report is being written. It should give the background and state the purpose of the report.

Body The **body** is the business portion of your report. Because it is the longest and most important portion, it is the only part of the report included in the outline. The body is made up of one or more paragraphs. Each paragraph should describe a different portion of the total project being discussed.

Conclusion and Recommendations The last portion of a report is the **Conclusion and Recommendations**. First, explain what you think the facts presented in the report have proven—your conclusion. You should end with a listing of recommendations that explain what should be done about the situation described in the report. If you are writing a short one-page informal report, the conclusion and recommendations portion may be omitted.

The parts of a report should be identified in a long report. For instance, if your report is more than two pages long, it is customary to label each portion as **Abstract, Introduction, Body,** or **Conclusion and Recommendations**. Even in shorter reports, the **Abstract**, if you use one, should be labeled. Refer to the gazebo progress report to see how the various parts of a report work.

Exercise 17.5

Label each paragraph in the following report to indicate what section it belongs in: **Abstract, Introduction,** or **Conclusion and Recommendation**.

Date: January 6, 1993
To: Glen L. Overholt, Owner
From: Peter M. Hensey, Foreman
Subject: Replacement trucks

     The recent study you requested of the company's 38 logging trucks clearly indicates that 23 of them should be replaced this year. Service records kept during the past 15 years leave no doubt that Stout trucks hold up better in our operation than those built by Jessup, Hammerton, or Kendrick truck companies.

     This report is the product of an extensive examination of each of the company's logging trucks, the service records dating back to 1976, and the time-lost records of each truck the company has operated since 1976. The purpose of the investigation was twofold: (1) to find out how many trucks were worn out and (2) to find out what make of truck has given the best service in the past.

     The shop inspection team headed by Mr. Morgan spent 297 hours examining the 38 truck fleet. They prepared reports estimating the cost of returning each truck to first-class operating condition, paying particular attention to engine, transmissions, differentials, frame, and cab. Of the 38 trucks, 23 would require repairs in excess of the $4,200.00 figure you gave as indicating replacement was advisable. Of that 23 needing replacement, 6 would require repairs totaling more than $8,000.00.

     Truck foremen Hensey and Anderson conducted an in-depth study of truck serviceability to determine what make of truck has given the best service in our operation over the past 15 years. In terms of repair dollars spent, Stout trucks were our best investment; on the average, they cost $182.00 per year less to maintain than the second cheapest truck. The time-lost records showed that Jessup and Stout had almost exactly the same number of lost operation hours. The average for each was approximately 28 hours per season. Time-lost, of course, has been minimal on the trucks provided by these two companies because of the excellent dealers. Some of the other dealers provided poor service. Some obviously did not care whether or not our trucks were broken down.

     The conclusion that Stout trucks are the best for our operation is inescapable; they are simply cheaper to operate and more dependable. Moreover, after having driven all the trucks mentioned in this report, I can honestly say that Stouts, such as the ones we have, are less tiring for the driver operating them on a day-long basis. My recommendation, based upon this study, is to purchase 23 new Stout logging trucks with 335 HP engines.

Check your answers with the Answer Key.

TYPES OF REPORTS

Many different types of reports exist because every profession presents situations which require reports unique to that business. The progress report presented earlier in this chapter is probably the most common type. Every employee who wants to advance beyond the beginning position in a company can expect to write **progress reports** at some time. These reports are needed to inform people who are unable to visit the job site about the job progress.

The second most common type of report may be the **justification report**. Such a report is used to justify the purchase of new or replacement equipment, or to justify some particular course of action. The report in the previous exercise is an example of a justification report; the foreman, Peter Hensey, uses this type of report to justify the purchase of 23 trucks to replace part of the company's aging truck fleet. The body of the justification report here presents the findings of the inspection team first. It then goes on to a conclusion that includes the overall recommendation that the company purchase the new trucks. You can expect to write such a report any time you want the head of your organization to purchase a major piece of equipment.

You may also be expected to write an **external proposal**, a report that is similar to the justification report. The name external proposal comes from the way this report is used. Such proposals are sent outside of your company to a prospective customer when your company is submitting a bid for supplies or services. After you become familiar with your company's pricing, you may be assigned the task of writing the proposal.

The external proposal should contain five clearly identifiable portions: introduction, list of materials, cost breakdown, time schedule, and conclusion. In longer reports these portions are identified by headings; however, the shorter external proposals you most commonly write will not need them. Consider the differences between the following proposals: Notice that one uses a memo heading while the other uses a letter heading. Also notice that one has a place for signatures at the bottom while the other does not. Neither is absolutely right or wrong, but the one from Akropolis Construction clearly looks more professionally done.

Submitted to: Jay Wentworth, Manager, Frontier Western Co.
Submitted by: Margo Thurman, Northwestern Landscape Artists
Date Submitted: March 30, 1993
Subject: Perimeter Landscape of Parking Lot at 1619 Bixley
          Way, Missoula, MT

Northwestern Landscape Artists proposes to develop plans, install automated sprinklers, and landscape the perimeter of the parking lot at your new store at 1619 Bixley Way at a total cost of $3321.. Landscaping would begin by May 10th, weather permitting, and be completed within 30 days.

We use only the best materials and plants available on our projects, which explains why we are able to give an unconditional 90 day guarantee on our jobs. Should any plants die or sprinklers malfunction, we will replace them immediately without charge during that time period.

Estimated Cost: Materials and Labor

Architectural plans	$300
Obtain city permit	90
Removal of debris	180
Soil preparation	630
Install sprinkler system and timers	910
Plant Photinia shrubs across back	
29 (5-gal size) @ 16.25	471
Plant Carolina Cherry Laurel-side	
22 (5-gal size) @ 15.50	341
Place bark around shrubs	
19 yards @ 21.00	399

Labor & Materials Total $3321

This price is good through April 30, 1993.

If we can get started on May 10th, we will schedule a crew of four until the job is completed to minimize inconvenience to your customers. Assuming the weather cooperates, we could be done in considerably less than 30 days. Our 100% guarantee begins the day our work is completed and continues for 90 days.

We are pleased that you gave us the opportunity to bid this job. We are confident you will find our prices lower than those of our competition and equally certain you will be pleased with our work. We are enthusiastic about the rough plans we have drawn up for your business' parking lot, and we are eager to put one of our crews to work converting those plans into beautiful reality. If we can offer any assistance or advice, please call.

AKROPOLIS CONSTRUCTION

1957 Westwood Drive
Sacramento, CA 95864
(916) 991-4041

PROPOSAL AND/OR AGREEMENT

Stephen Schneider
1203 Ocean Avenue
Daly City, CA 94112

Dear Mr. Schneider:

Subject: New French Drain System

    The proposal is made this 10th day of May 1993 by AKROPOLIS CONSTRUCTION
for the purpose of supplying certain skills, labor, and materials necessary
for the construction of a "French Drain System" at your residence at 1203
Ocean Avenue, Daly City, CA 94112. All work will be performed in accordance
with state laws and regulations, according to the plans and specifications
accompanying this proposal.

    AKROPOLIS CONSTRUCTION will perform the work described in the "SCOPE OF
WORK" section at the above stated address, and shall include all materials,
labor, tools, and supervision necessary to complete the work as described in
the plans and specifications, all of which are incorporated herein and made
part of this proposal for the total sum of $17,797.00.

	SCOPE OF WORK	***COSTS***
1.	Fees, licenses, and permits	$ 350.00
2.	Excavation and trenching	1,800.00
3.	Removal of debris	125.00
4.	Installation of 5/8" gravel: 3 tons @ $250/ton	750.00
5.	Installation of 4" PVC pipes and 6" main section	4,355.00
6.	Installation of dirt screen: 8 rolls @ $30/roll	240.00
7.	Installation of 4" riser sections and drain caps	2,800.00
8.	Soil compacted and refilling of dirt up to grade	1,255.00
9.	Construction and pouring of concrete spillway	3,800.00
10.	Profit of 15%	2,322.00
	Total of Materials, Labor, and Profit =	$17,797.00

EXCLUSIONS

1.   Does not include any new sod or lawn needed to replace that which
might be damaged during construction.

2. All changes in the "Scope of Work" section will result in increases in the total costs.
3. Progress payments will be made according to the payment schedule.
4. All work will be completed within 15 days after work is begun at the job site.

SPECIAL PROVISIONS

This proposal will be void if not expressly accepted in writing within 60 days of the date this document is submitted by the contractor to the owner.

The contractor proposes to furnish all materials and labor to complete the work described herein according to the plans and specifications, and the "SCOPE OF WORK" for the sum of $17,797.00, payable as follows:

PAYMENT SCHEDULE	PERCENT COMPLETE	AMOUNT
1. Upon signing	20%	$ 3,559.40
2. Upon installation of PVC pipes	60%	$10,678.20
3. Upon completion of all work	20%	$ 3,559.40

NOTE! CONTRACTORS ARE REQUIRED BY LAW TO BE LICENSED AND REGULATED BY THE CONTRACTOR'S STATE LICENSE BOARD. ANY QUESTIONS CONCERNING A CONTRACTOR MAY BE REFERRED TO THE REGISTRAR, CONTRACTOR'S STATE LICENSE BOARD, 3132 BRADSHAW ROAD, SACRAMENTO, CALIFORNIA 95826. MAILING ADDRESS: P.O. BOX 26000, SACRAMENTO, CALIFORNIA 95826.

AKROPOLIS CONSTRUCTION
1957 WESTWOOD DRIVE
SACRAMENTO, CA 95864

NO. #358363

This proposal is hereby submitted by the contractor to the owner:

CONTRACTOR   OWNER'S ACCEPTANCE

By:_____   By: _____

Date Submitted: _____   Date Accepted: _____

We thank you for the consideration, and for the opportunity to bid this job. We are confident that we can complete the job promptly and expeditiously to your satisfaction. If we can further assist you in any way, please feel free to contact us at (916) 991-4041.

WRITING THE REPORT

As you develop a report from your outline, you must decide which writing strategy is correct for each paragraph of the material. The gazebo progress report was developed using a series of narrative and descriptive paragraphs. The two body paragraphs in the justification report for truck purchase use different types of writing. The first paragraph begins with narration but shifts to classification. The second paragraph is completely comparison and contrast. Similarly, you will need to choose the best writing strategy for every situation in your own reports.

No one strategy is correct for all report writing. As you decide what you wish to accomplish in a given paragraph, you must also decide how to best present the material. For instance, if you are writing a progress report in which you intend to explain what was done each day, a narrative paragraph would almost certainly be best. If, however, you are going to define a particular term or concept, you would use a definition paragraph. The best procedure to follow in writing effective reports is to plan exactly what paragraph strategy should be used in any situation.

Heading The heading you use at the top of your report will vary. If the report is not going to be read by anyone outside of your organization, you should use a memo heading similar to that used in the truck report. When the report is to be sent to someone outside of your organization, you may use a standard letter format, as shown in the gazebo progress report, or you may use the memo heading.

Putting It All Together Developing the report from your outline might be somewhat time-consuming, but it should not present any special problems. Working from your outline, you should have no trouble putting your ideas on paper. Write rapidly, ignoring for the moment any misspelled words, punctuation errors, or sentence problems. Once you have written the rough draft, you can then go back to revise.

Exercise 17.6

Write a progress report or external proposal on a subject relevant to your job or major. Your report must be at least 350 words long. Write a rough draft of your report and revise it carefully. Prepare the final copy using a computer or a typewriter. Include an abstract and label it clearly.

Answer Key

Exercise 1.1

1. proper—Texas
2. proper—Vietnam War
3. proper—Memorial Day
4. common
5. common
6. proper—Johnson Landscape Company
7. common
8. proper—Honda
9. common
10. proper—New Zealand

Exercise 1.2

Answers will vary; have your work checked.

Exercise 1.3

1. security, guard, incident
2. judge, jury, future, hour
3. promptness, reliability, dedication, promotion
4. summer, California, fire, families, homes
5. man, friends, enemies
6. report, Elizabeth, hours, night
7. business, burden
8. letter, Ben, job
9. telephone
10. committee, Joan, proposal

Exercise 1.4

1. dispatcher
2. people
3. [You]
4. whales
5. agent
6. poles and lines
7. she
8. he
9. they
10. musician

Exercise 1.5

Answers will vary; have your work checked.

Exercise 1.6

1. linking
2. action
3. action
4. action
5. linking
6. linking
7. linking
8. action
9. action
10. action
11. linking
12. linking

Exercise 1.7

1. tree looks	linking
2. Lisa demonstrated	action
3. Carla Fuentes drove	action
4. Mrs. Mayfield offered	action
5. forms are	linking
6. members debated	action
7. complex has	action
8. mail arrives	action
9. problems developed	action
10. briefcase was	linking

Exercise 1 8

Answers will vary; have your work checked.

Exercise 1.9

1. her
2. them
3. they
4. she
5. him
6. it
7. her
8. they
9. he
10. their

Exercise 1.10

Answers will vary; have your work checked.

Exercise 1.11

1. possessive
2. object
3. possessive
4. possessive
5. subject
6. object
7. possessive
8. possessive
9. subject
10. subject
11. possessive
12. possessive

Exercise 1.12

1. C
2. C
3. P
4. P
5. P
6. C
7. C
8. C
9. P
10. C

Exercise 1.13

1. C
2. C
3. P
4. P
5. P
6. C
7. C
8. P
9. P
10. C

Exercise 1.14

Answers will vary; have your work checked.

Exercise 2.1

1. F	5. F	8. F
2. F	6. S	9. S
3. S	7. S	10. F
4. F		

Exercise 2.2

	Subject	Verb
1. <u>truck</u> <u>has</u>	S	S
2. <u>trees</u> <u>have</u> but <u>grow</u>	S	C
3. <u>manager</u> <u>requested</u>	S	S
4. <u>lineman</u> and <u>supervisor</u> <u>solved</u>	C	S
5. <u>they</u> <u>missed</u> and <u>became</u>	S	C
6. <u>John</u> and <u>Les</u> <u>attended</u>	C	S
7. <u>he</u> <u>typed</u> and <u>answered</u>	S	C
8. <u>Don</u> and <u>Sharon</u> <u>wrote</u> and <u>edited</u>	C	C
9. <u>spring</u> <u>broke</u>	S	S
10. <u>Joan</u> <u>cancelled</u> and <u>rescheduled</u>	S	C

Exercises 2.3 and 2.4

Answers will vary; have your work checked.

Exercise 2.5

1. but or yet	6. for
2. and	7. but or yet
3. for	8. or
4. but or yet	9. and
5. or	10. for

Exercise 2.6

1. CD	5. SS	8. SS
2. CD	6. CD	9. CD
3. SS	7. CD	10. SS
4. CD		

Exercise 2.7

Answers will vary; have your work checked.

Exercise 2.8

Answers can vary somewhat.

1. CD (for)	5. NR
2. NR	6. CD (but)
3. CD (but)	7. CD (for)
4. CD (for)	

Exercises 2.9-2.11

Answers will vary; have your work checked.

Exercise 2.12

1. CX	3. CD	5. SS
2. CD	4. CX	

Exercises 2.13 and 2.14

Answers will vary; have your work checked.

Exercise 3.1

1. the first one in years
2. an accounting firm in San Francisco
3. an automated wonder
4. a new state bypass planned for next year
5. the lawyer on our staff
6. hungry grasshoppers and high interest rates
7. a novel about African Americans
8. Gina, Charles, and Steve
9. Vernon Winton
10. an architect; a real estate broker

Exercise 3.2

These are suggested answers only; other answers are possible.
1. Audiences filled the theater each night to see the play by Mamet, a very popular playwright.
2. Many tourists from other countries visit the Grand Canyon, a spectacular natural wonder.
3. Ms. Spaulding, a new employee, wrote a flawless progress report last week.

Exercise 3.3

1. in fact, indeed	5. therefore
2. therefore, thus	6. indeed
3. therefore	7. however
4. moreover, furthermore	

Exercises 3.4 and 3.5

Answers will vary; have your work checked.

Exercise 3.6

The most obvious of all problems that face working students is, of course, the lack of sufficient study time. For instance, if students averaged six hours at work, four hours at school, and the usual eight hours of sleep, there would be only six hours remaining for homework Out of that six hours, however, all necessary functions such as travelling to work and school, preparing and eating meals, and cleaning living quarters and clothes would have to be taken. When the time required for these functions is subtracted from that six hours of study time, very little time remains for actual studying. <u>Indeed,</u> this dilemma of not having enough hours in the day frequently plagues those students who hold jobs<u>; as a result,</u> they often wonder if they can continue to hold up under the strain. Confronted with this problem on a daily basis<u>, however,</u> successful working students eventually learn unique methods of time management. Procrastination and the like are eliminated as new, faster methods of solving problems are developed. <u>Nevertheless,</u> only small amounts of time are available<u>; thus,</u> many students sacrifice the luxury of social interaction and become educational hermits.

Exercise 3.7

Answers will vary; have your work checked.

Exercise 3.8

1. The instructor told the students that their grades would be based on attendance, on homework, on attitude, and on test scores.
   OR
   The instructor told the students that their grades would be based on attendance, homework, attitude, and test scores.
2. Underwater photography means buying good equipment, having patience, and knowing about light refraction.
3. The doctor understood neither the patient nor the disease.
4. Walking through old castles, talking with people, and eating in pubs makes a visit to England a memorable experience.
5. Until the plans are complete, until the bids are in, and until the weather has improved, construction cannot begin.
   OR
   Until the plans are complete, the bids are in, and the weather has improved, construction cannot begin.
6. Maria dislikes being late and attending long meetings.
7. Swimming is not only good exercise but also a clean hobby.
8. By using a helicopter in their logging operation, the Siller Company avoids destroying young trees and creating erosion-causing skid trails.
   OR
   By using a helicopter in their logging operation, the Siller Company avoids the destruction of young trees and the creation of erosion-causing skid trails.

9. The objectives of writing are to be brief, to communicate clearly, and to create sentences that will not offend your reader.
10. Ms. Conrad told me to take the blueprints to the job site and to hurry back.

Exercise 3.9

Answers will vary; have your work checked.

Exercise 3.10

These are suggested answers only; other answers are possible.
1. Receiving a tremendous shock, the electrician fell off the ladder.
2. Rejected by the planning commission, the plan will be resubmitted next week.
3. Knowing the answer to every question the MC asked, Henry Gordon made winning the prize look easy.
4. Ruined by high interest rates and low crop prices, the farmers in the area have abandoned their farms.
5. John, inspired by Mel's example, completed the report in record time.

Exercise 3.11

Answers will vary; have your work checked.

Exercise 3.12

runs	1.	<u>engine stalls</u> but <u>run</u>
C	2.	<u>trees</u> nor <u>tree has</u>
are	3.	<u>is lounge</u> and <u>pharmacy</u>
go	4.	<u>welder</u> and <u>secretary goes</u>
complains	5.	<u>each complain</u>
knows	6.	<u>newsmen</u> or <u>Jackie know</u>
C	7.	<u>heater</u> and <u>conditioners arrive</u>
earns	8.	<u>anyone earn</u>
has	9.	<u>orchestra have played</u>
was	10.	<u>three-fifths were</u>
C	11.	<u>Everyone was</u>
C	12.	<u>pickup was stolen</u>
were	13.	<u>mob was fighting</u>
was	14.	<u>two quarts were</u>
has	15.	<u>Sharon</u> or <u>Linda have taken</u>

Exercise 3.13

Answers will vary; have your work checked.

Exercise 3.14

Various answers are possible; these are suggested answers only.
1. Poisons which were used to kill other birds of prey also killed the eagles.
2. Today, the eagle faces the same problem of survival it faced years ago when the settlers first arrived.
3. Sheepmen hire pilots to shoot eagles out of the sky.

Exercise 3.15

1. its	their
2. he or she has	they
3. she was	they
4. its	their
5. his or her	their
6. they	one

Exercise 4.1

1. The basketball fans were clapping, shouting, and cheering.
2. Carla, John, Ellen, and Ray flew to Denver, attended the seminar, and returned home in one day.
3. Playing in the band, singing in the choir, and writing music take up all Justin's spare time.
4. While driving through Arizona, they ate ribs, they toured a cactus garden, and they visited an Indian reservation.
5. A regular jack-of-all-trades, he built his own house, repaired his own car, and grew his own vegetables.
6. The new delivery van has tinted windows, air conditioning, an automatic transmission, and carpeting.

Exercise 4.2

1. C
2. The foamy, dirty, frigid water poured over the spillway and into the river.
3. They're waiting for a calm, sunny day before they start painting.
4. An eager, courteous salesperson will invariably sell more than one who is pushy or overbearing or threatening.
5. On Jason's desk were three pens, a stack of paper, and a dictionary, but he continued to work at the efficient, new computer.
6. Before April 15, he organized his records, he reviewed his expenditures, and he visited his accountant.

Exercise 4.3

1. We will, therefore, hold another meeting next week.
2. The sales staff did reach their goal, however.
3. Unfortunately, the tournament was cancelled due to rain.
4. Nevertheless, the gardeners continued to overwater.
5. That lawsuit, for instance, was settled out of court.

Exercise 4.4

John, Larry, and Pete had talked about their camping trip for months. In fact, all their friends were tired of hearing about their plans to go swimming, to catch fish, and to take long hikes. The three did not take the time, however, to make a list of what to take or to plan their meals. As a result, they arrived at the campground with a large tent, three sleeping bags, ten cans of vegetables, and a bottle of hot, spicy barbecue sauce. Stakes for the tent, matches, a frying pan, and meat had all been left behind. Fortunately, the men were able to solve the problem when Pete drove to a nearby store for supplies, John made tent stakes out of kindling, and Larry borrowed a frying pan from nearby campers. The trip would have been a great success, but that night it rained and rained and rained. Therefore, the river rose, the tent leaked, and the hiking trails were washed out. The three wet, unhappy campers decided to go home early the next day.

Exercise 4.5

1. C
2. C
3. C
4. C
5. C
6. C

Exercise 4.6

1. They vacationed in Hawaii, the Aloha State.
   OR
   They vacationed in the Aloha State, Hawaii.
2. Kevin and Cory, my nephews, are graduates of the local university.
   OR
   My nephews Kevin and Cory are graduates of the local university.

3. Hanging in baskets in the shade were her favorite flowers, begonias and fuchsia.
   OR
   Hanging in baskets in the shade were begonias and fuchsia, her favorite flowers.
4. The new paint, an unusual shade of green, made the office seem darker.

Exercise 4.7

1. The new supervisor, Janet Henderson, changed their assigned duties.
2. The deadline for the order, April 30, is quickly approaching.
3. C
4. For lunch he ordered trout, his favorite fish.
5. C

Exercise 4.8

1. The ship was heading for the dock, but the fog rolled in.
2. The sailors were eager to go ashore, and their families were waiting impatiently.
3. C
4. Home ownership requires one to paint, to care for a yard, and to make repairs.
5. Therefore, the Silvas put their house up for sale and waited for someone to buy it.
6. C
7. John Hansen, Phillip Andrews, and Susan Alvarez brought prospective buyers to see it.
8. One couple walked into the living room, saw the large backyard, and rushed out the front door.
9. An agent wanted to buy the house herself, but she decided it was too large.
10. Furthermore, she did not like yard work.
11. One agent, Evelyn Morgan, was certain the house would sell quickly.
12. C
13. They liked the house immediately because of its neat, uncluttered appearance.
14. They also appreciated the obvious care the owners gave to the hardwood floors, to the yard, and to the appliances.
15. The Petersons, therefore, decided to buy the house.
16. They were concerned that they would not qualify for a loan, however.
17. John Matthews, the loan officer, told them the loan would be approved.
18. The Silvas, sellers of the house, were as happy as the buyers.
19. C

20. The Petersons now have a new home, and the Silvas live in a townhouse.

Exercise 4.9

1. Preparing for the harvest, the sugar cane workers spent long hours in the fields.
2. For weeks before they burned the fields, the workers did not water the cane.
3. When the leaves had been burned off the stalks, the cane was ready to be harvested.
4. C
5. In town on weekends, the field crews forgot about the dirty jobs in the cane fields.
6. To enjoy life fully, the field crews got up early and stayed up late.
7. True, not all of the workers enjoyed the weekends, but they all were glad to quit on Friday night.
8. Although cane was once harvested with a cane knife, it is harvested today with machinery.
9. Tractors, clamshells, and diesel trucks have replaced the large crews and horse-drawn wagons.
10. Escaping from work in a cane field is still not possible, however.

Exercise 4.10

Answers will vary; have your work checked.

Exercise 4.11

1. The girl, who loved to read, wished she could live in the library.
   or C
2. Patty's cat, running from the dog, was glad to see the tree.
3. Bill Morgan, who has long worked for the district office, has been appointed principal of the high school.
4. C
5. Bob, who was sweeping the walk, cut his hand on a rose bush.
6. In spite of public concern, the slaughter of harp seals continues.
7. Having confidence in the "healers," many people travel to the Philippine Islands to have their ills cured.
8. Because the "healers" have no formal medical schooling, other people insist that allowing them to operate is foolish.
9. Nevertheless, the "healers" do have a remarkable following although they do not advertise their skills.

10. C
11. On the way to the theater, the couple was involved in an accident, but they both escaped injury.
12. As a matter of fact, the accident was more exciting than the movie.
13. The movie, however, was far less expensive than the accident.
14. Bertha Morrison, who loved hang gliding, quit the sport after her friend's injury.
15. C

Exercise 4.12

1. "I will send you a check," said Jane, "as soon as I can."
2. "I hate working in the movie industry," said Skip. "It is too false."
3. C
4. Our new address will be 1284 North K Street, Tacoma, Washington.
5. She was born on July 19, 1946, in Carmel, California.
6. The teacher told the class, "Anyone can take good pictures."
7. C
8. "You must also realize," she said, "that even expert photographers occasionally take bad pictures."

Exercise 4.13

Various answers are possible; these are suggested answers only.
1. Gary fell from the top of the eighty-foot tower, but he survived.
2. Because the wind was very strong, it broke a limb off the tree.
3. The report indicated that older women are the best employees; they seldom miss a day's work.
4. The snow was packed and powdery; therefore, the skiers moved rapidly.
5. At dusk all the people in the campground took binoculars and walked to the meadow; they wanted to see the elk that came out to feed on the grass.
6. Since the beautiful beach is less than a mile from their house, Marian and Jerry swim almost every day.
7. The gopher came up out of the hole without looking; the cat was waiting.
8. The elephant seals are only slightly bothered by humans. They must know that the law protects them.
9. Stacy killed a deer the first day she went hunting; she has never gone hunting since.

10. The shortage of petroleum is threatening our way of life; however, optional power sources can be found.

Exercise 4.14

Answers will vary; have your work checked.

Exercise 4.15

1. Send the letter to James Haskell at 2301 Sixty-fifth Street, Portland, Oregon.
2. C
3. Although Hal's request for supplies was submitted some time ago, he hasn't received anything yet.
4. They were talking about their friends, as they always did, when Jerry walked in.
5. Only three things mattered to him: money, position, and power.
6. California's grain is harvested in May; by contrast, Northern Ireland's grain is harvested in August.
7. Awards for outstanding service were presented to John Bishop, engineer; Phil Gonzales, technician; and Suzanne Friedman, mechanic.
8. You have put too many l's in parallel and not enough s's in misspell.
9. They gave him, wouldn't you know it, a watch for his retirement.
10. The plane was late; it had run into strong headwinds.
11. C
12. After they ate lunch, the surveyors climbed back up the steep, muddy hillside.
13. C
14. Mechanics who join the union must pay monthly union dues of twenty-two dollars.
15. Bill will drop by at noon tomorrow, and he will have a contract with him.
16. C
17. Liz Castro, who usually takes notes, was unable to attend the meeting.
18. Marge McElroy, the company's attorney, just returned from a vacation in the tropics.
19. "You wouldn't believe," she said, "how beautiful the weather was."
20. Yes, I know it's important to arrive on time.
21. At that instant in time, her actions were controlled by just two things: fear and hunger.
22. C
23. The students' cars were parked behind the buses.

Exercise 4.16

1. P	5. C	8. P
2. P	6. C	9. C
3. C	7. P	10. C
4. C		

Exercise 4.17

1. In the course of the party.
   They knew they would get to see all the family members again in the course of the party.
2. Without the help of the Department of Agriculture advisor.
   Without the help of the Department of Agriculture advisor, the farmer would have made an expensive mistake.
3. No matter how much wood is burned.
   They only produce a minimum of heat no matter how much wood is burned.
4. Because of the faulty wiring.
   Because of the faulty wiring, the building caught fire and burned to the ground.
5. Blew leaves and dust into houses and barns everywhere.
   The wind howled across the valley for days, blowing leaves and dust into houses and barns everywhere.
6. Although road crews worked day and night for a week.
   The roads were impassable although road crews worked day and night for a week.
7. The plant polluting the river.
   The plant was polluting the river.
8. Such as pear, apple, peach, prune, and quince.
   The ranch had many fruit trees, such as pear, apple, peach, prune, and quince.
9. In the September issue of the magazine *Machines.*
   In the September issue of the magazine *Machines,* you advertised an interesting machine.
10. John who has worked as a service manager for one of the largest auto dealers in the area.
    John has worked as a service manager for one of the largest auto dealers in the area.

Exercise 5.1

1. Basic reason for using memo is that people forget messages.
2. Three advantages memos have over telephone:
   (1) Memo cuts down on communication mistakes,
   (2) Memo saves time in some instances,
   (3) Memo gives you proof of what was said, and,
   (4) Allows you to put your best foot forward.
3. You should use a confirming memo to make sure the person you call understands what you think you heard.
4. Do not use a memo when (any three of the following):
   (1) You can get information easily in a conversation,
   (2) You have more pressing work to do,
   (3) You wish to criticize someone, or
   (4) You are angry.

Exercise 5.2, 5.3, 5.4, & 5.5

Answers will vary; have your work checked.

Exercise 6.1

1. Possible answers:
   (1) letter more complete
   (2) letter more formal
   (3) letter has more businesslike tone
   (4) Typing more carefully done
2. Memos for use within a company
   Business letters for use between companies
3. Tone is the attitude you express toward your subject and audience. Tone of business letters should be businesslike but natural.
4. The falling rafter hit Bill.
   I took the order.
   The speaker read the message.
   Our company hired a new custodian.
   The last person to go home must unplug the coffee pot.
5. I want you to be satisfied.
   Please submit inventory sheets to me.
   Submit the completed document to me within three days.

Exercise 6.2

1. 2-8 lines
2. 1
3. 2
4. 2
5. 2
6. 2
7. 4

Exercise 6.3

133⁢ Platte Road
St. Louis, MO 63136
May 13, 1993

Busby Stores Incorporated
1742 Pritcher Avenue
Iowa City, IA 52240

Attention: Vice President in Charge of Complaints

Ladies and Gentlemen:

Subject: Inferior service at the St. Louis store

Normally the service ar your St. Louis store is . . .

(Note: The body of the letter does not change.)

. . . I expect nothing more than an assurance that this practice of performing
unnecessary tasks on trusting customer's cars will be stopped immediately.

Sincerely yours,

Martha Albin

Martha Albin

MA: hj
Enclosure: (1) estimate
cc: Manager, St. Louis store

Exercise 6.4

Rockford Public Works
3213 Taft Street
Rockford, IL 61607

Mr. Joseph L. Adams
714 Bedford Lane
Rockford, IL 61111

Exercises 6.5-6.9

Answers will vary; have your work checked.

Exercises 7.1-7.6

Answers will vary; have your work checked.

Exercise 8.1

1. Answers will vary; have your work checked.
2. (1) to avoid overlooked information
   (2) to save time
   (3) to make information objective
   (4) to force reporter to use proper sequence
   (5) to enhance uniformity

Exercise 8.2, 8.3

Answers will vary; have your work cheeked.

Exereise 9.1

Answers will vary; have your work checked.

Exercise 9.2

1. extra money
2. extensive examination
3. prevention of fraud
4. among the middle class
5. depressing novel
6. poor role models presented on everyday television shows
7. health and weight
8. leading risk factor in coronary heart disease
9. financial responsibilities
10. protection and safety

Exercises 9.3, 9.4, 9.5

Answers will vary; have your work checked.

Exercise 9.6

I.	II.	III.
1. TS	1. TS	1. TS
2. PS	2. PS	2. PS
3. SS	3. PS	3. SS
4. SS	4. PS	4. PS
5. PS	5. SS	5. SS
6. SS	6. PS	6. SS
7. PS	7. SS	7. PS
8. SS	8. PS	8. SS
9. SS		9. SS

Exercise 9.7

1.TS		7. SS
2.PS		8. SS
3.SS		9. SS
4.SS		10. SS
5.SS		2 support groups
6.PS		

Exercises 9.8, 9.9

Answers will vary; have you work checked.

Exercise 9.10

1. TS	5. SS	9. PS
2. PS	6. PS	10. SS
3. SS	7. SS	11. SS
4. PS	8. SS	12. CS

Exercise 9.11

Answers will vary; have your work checked.

Exercise 10.1

1. A process is a series of steps that produces a certain result.
2. a) observation process writing explains a process
   b) participation process writing commands the reader to perform a series of tasks
3. Have this item checked; answers will vary.

Exercise 10.2

I. participation process writing
II. observation process writing.

Exercise 10.3-10.7

Answers will vary; have your work checked.

Exercise 10.8

1. the last one
2. 1 and 2
3. 1
4. Anyone who owns a rental, whether an apartment or house
5. participation
6. 2
7. second person

Exercise 10.9

Answers will vary; have your work checked.

Exercise 11.1

Most commonly used as
commercial vehicles
delivery van
diesel bus
dump truck
flatbed truck
heavy-duty pickup
milk truck
fuel tank truck
taxi

Most commonly used as
private vehicles
bicycle
convertible
coupe
four-door sedan
imported economy car
light-duty pickup
sports car

Most commonly used as
emergency vehicles
ambulance
fire truck
motorcycle with two-way radio
squad car
tow truck

Exercise 11.2

THE ACCIDENT

1. skidding sideways after losing control
2. the sound as the two skidding cars collided
3. watching the world spin as the car rolled over after impact
4. the smell of gasoline from the ruptured tank
5. hearing the ambulance attendants talk as they worked
6. the trip to the hospital in an ambulance

LANDSCAPING A YARD

1. trees along the back of property
2. grassy area between fountain and back of yard
3. plants immediately beyond fountain in center of yard
4. ground cover in front of fountain
5. potted plants on patio against house

JOBS IN A BANK

1. owners
2. president
3. credit manager
4. teller supervisor
5. teller
6. assistant teller

Exercises 11.3, 11.4

Answers will vary; have your work checked.

Exercise 11.5

1. elderly persons
2. which are drastically insufficient
3. 2
4. importance

Exercise 11.6-11.8

Answers will vary; have your work checked.

Exercise 12.1-12.3

Answers will vary; have your work checked.

Exercise 12.4

1. 3   2. 2

Exercise 12.5

1. pure contrast
2. block technique
3. two

Exercise 12.6, 12.7

Answers will vary; have your work checked.

Exercise 13.1-13.7

Answers will vary; have your work checked.

Exercise 14.1

1. third   3. third   5. first
2. third   4. first   6. first

Exercise 14.2-14.6

Answers will vary; have your work checked.

Exercise 15.1

1. secondary 3. primary 5. primary
2. secondary 4. primary 6. primary

Exercise 15.2

1. Less chance of error in a primary source
2. when a primary source is too far away

3. college writing
4. a. the interviewee must speak to the top of your head
   b. the interviewee will be interrupted by your writing
5. a. when you have asked permission
   b. when it doesn't distract the interviewee

Exercise 15.3-15.9

Answers will vary; have your work checked.

Exercise 16.1

1. a. only formal language is used in college papers
   b. longer paragraphs are used in college papers
   c. longer. more complex sentences are used in college papers
   d. third person is generally used in college papers
2. a. to demonstrate what you have learned
   b. to learn new information
3. a. essay exam
   b. term or research paper
4. a. introduction
   b. body
   c. conclusion

Exercise 16.2-16.8

Answers will vary; have your work checked.

Exercise 17.1

Answers will vary; have your work checked.

Exercise 17.2 (possible answers)

1. The boss fired a few employees.
2. The speeding bus driver was stopped by the patrolman.
3. You must sign your library card before you can check out books.
4. The students ran the standard biology experiments.
5. The meeting was called to order by Maxine immediately after lunch.
6. You must keep thc filters on your furnace clean.

Exercise 17.3-17.4

Answers will vary; have your work checked.

Exercise 17.5

1. abstract
2. introduction
3. body
4. body
5. conclusion and recommendations

Exercise 17.6

Answers will vary; have your work checked.

Index